SECOND EDITION

NEW PASSWORD 5
A READING AND VOCABULARY TEXT

Lynn Bonesteel

PEARSON
Longman

New Password 5: A Reading and Vocabulary Text

Pearson Education, 10 Bank Street, White Plains, NY 10606

Staff credits: The people who made up the *New Password 5* team, representing editorial, production, design, and manufacturing, are: Pietro Alongi, Rhea Banker, Dave Dickey, Jaime Lieber, Maria Pia Marrella, Amy McCormick, Linda Moser, Carlos Rountree, Jennifer Stem, and Paula Van Ells.

Development editor: Thomas Ormond
Project editor: Helen B. Ambrosio
Text design & composition: ElectraGraphics, Inc.
Cover design: Maria Pia Marrella
Cover photos: istockphoto.com
Illustrations: Susan Tait Porcaro, Wendy Duran

Text credits, photography credits, references, and acknowledgments begin on page x and continue on page 278.

Library of Congress Cataloging-in-Publication Data

Bonesteel, Lynn.
New password 5 : reading and vocabulary text / Lynn Bonesteel.
　　p. cm.
　Includes bibliographical references and index.
　ISBN-13: 978-0-13-701173-5 (with audio cd)
　ISBN-10: 0-13-701173-3 (with audio cd)
　ISBN-13: 978-0-13-701172-8 (without audio cd)
　ISBN-10: 0-13-701172-5 (without audio cd)
1.　English language—Textbooks for foreign speakers. 2.　Reading comprehension—Problems, exercises, etc. 3.　Vocabulary—Problems, exercises, etc.　I. Title. II. Title: New password five.
　PE1128.B624 2009
　428.6'4—dc22
　　　　　　　　　　　　　　　　　2009027218

PEARSON LONGMAN ON THE **WEB**

Pearsonlongman.com offers online resources for teachers and students. Access our Companion Websites, our online catalog, and our local offices around the world.

Visit us at **pearsonlongman.com**.

Printed in the United States of America
ISBN-13: 978-0-13-701172-8　　3 4 5 6 7 8 9 10—V057— 15 14 13 12 11 10
ISBN-13: 978-0-13-701173-5　　2 3 4 5 6 7 8 9 10—V057— 15 14 13 12 11 10

CONTENTS

Scope and Sequence   iv

The Second Edition of the *Password* Series   vi

Overview of *New Password 5*   viii

References, Acknowledgments, and Credits   x

Unit 1: Artistic Innovations   1

Chapter 1 What Is Anime?   2

Chapter 2 The Scientist and the Stradivarius   13

Chapter 3 The History of Rap   25

Unit 1 Wrap-up   39

Unit 2: The Challenges of Youth   45

Chapter 4 Sleepy Teens   46

Chapter 5 Growing Up Gifted   58

Chapter 6 School Bullies   71

Unit 2 Wrap-up   82

Unit 3: Genetics: The Science of Who We Are   89

Chapter 7 The Science of Genetics   90

Chapter 8 Designing the Future   103

Chapter 9 A Terrible Inheritance, a Difficult Decision   116

Unit 3 Wrap-up   127

Units 1–3 Vocabulary Self-Test 1   132

Unit 4: Getting Emotional   135

Chapter 10 Can You Translate an Emotion?   136

Chapter 11 Catching an Emotion   148

Chapter 12 Road Rage   160

Unit 4 Wrap-up   174

Unit 5: Man and Beast   181

Chapter 13 Is Music Universal?   182

Chapter 14 Our Dogs Are Watching Us   195

Chapter 15 The Mind of the Chimpanzee   208

Unit 5 Wrap-up   220

Unit 6: The People Behind the Science   227

Chapter 16 A Woman's Fate   228

Chapter 17 The Father of Vaccination   240

Chapter 18 A Nose for Science   253

Unit 6 Wrap-up   266

Units 4–6 Vocabulary Self-Test 2   272

Vocabulary Self-Tests Answer Key   275

Index to Target Words and Phrases   276

iii

SCOPE AND SEQUENCE

Unit / Chapter / Reading	Reading Skills	Vocabulary Building	Dictionary Skills
UNIT 1: Artistic Innovations			
Chapter 1 **What Is Anime?**	• Understanding topics and main ideas • Understanding cause and effect	• Word families: the suffixes -ity, -al, -ly • Studying collocations: adjectives + prepositions	
Chapter 2 **The Scientist and the Stradivarius**	• Understanding topics and main ideas • Scanning • Understanding inference	• Word families: parts of speech • Studying word grammar: due to, because, so	
Chapter 3 **The History of Rap**	• Scanning • Understanding topics and main ideas	• Word families: the suffixes -ion, -tion, -ance • Studying phrasal verbs: stand by, stand out, call for	
UNIT 1: Wrap-up	• Guessing meaning from context • Understanding inference • Scanning	• Studying phrasal verbs: phrasal verbs with stand • Word families: the suffixes -al, -ance, -er, -ic, -ion, -ist, -ity, -ment, -tion, -ry	• Finding phrasal verbs
UNIT 2: The Challenges of Youth			
Chapter 4 **Sleepy Teens**	• Understanding main ideas, major points, and supporting details	• Word families: parts of speech • Studying word grammar: participial adjectives	
Chapter 5 **Growing Up Gifted**	• Understanding major points • Understanding supporting details • Understanding inference	• Word families: multiple words in word forms • Studying word grammar: prepositions + gerunds	
Chapter 6 **School Bullies**	• Understanding main ideas • Understanding inference	• Word families: using words in word families • Studying collocations: conduct + survey, research, and experiment	
UNIT 2: Wrap-up	• Guessing meaning from context • Understanding main ideas • Understanding inference	• Studying word grammar: compound words • Studying phrasal verbs: phrasal verbs and direct objects • Word families: the suffix -ize	• Finding the correct meaning
UNIT 3: Genetics: The Science of Who We Are			
Chapter 7 **The Science of Genetics**	• Scanning • Summarizing	• Word families: using words in word families • Studying collocations: verbs + prepositions	
Chapter 8 **Designing the Future**	• Understanding inference • Summarizing	• Word families: the suffix -ous • Studying word grammar: adverbs	

Unit / Chapter / Reading	Reading Skills	Vocabulary Building	Dictionary Skills
Chapter 9 **A Terrible Inheritance, a Difficult Decision**	• Interpreting a diagram	• Word families: using words in word families • Studying collocations: medical collocations	
Unit 3: Wrap-up	• Guessing meaning from context • Understanding major points	• Studying word grammar: transitive and intransitive verbs • Word families: the prefixes *un-, in-, dis-, mis-*	• Finding collocations
UNIT 4: Getting Emotional			
Chapter 10 **Can You Translate an Emotion?**	• Understanding inference • Paraphrasing	• Word families: using words in word families • Studying word grammar: transitive verbs and direct objects	
Chapter 11 **Catching an Emotion**	• Understanding major points • Understanding reference words	• Word families: adjectives with *-y* • Studying phrasal verbs: *make up*	
Chapter 12 **Road Rage**	• Understanding inference • Paraphrasing	• Word families: the root *sen* • Studying collocations: driving collocations	
UNIT 4: Wrap-up	• Guessing meaning from context • Understanding inference • Paraphrasing	• Studying collocations: verbs + prepositions • Word families: nouns and verbs with the same spelling	• Finding words in the dictionary
UNIT 5: Man And Beast			
Chapter 13 **Is Music Universal?**	• Understanding main ideas, major points, and supporting details • Summarizing	• Word families: the roots *bio, vis,* and *audi* • Studying collocations: collocations with *system*	
Chapter 14 **Our Dogs Are Watching Us**	• Understanding details • Recognizing tone	• Word families: using different word forms in paraphrase • Studying word grammar: *used to*	
Chapter 15 **The Mind of the Chimpanzee**	• Understanding major points and supporting details • Understanding main ideas • Summarizing	• Word families: using words in word families • Studying word grammar: adjectives that become nouns with *the*	
UNIT 5: Wrap-up	• Guessing meaning from context • Paraphrasing	• Studying collocations: collocations with *bitter* • Word families: the prefix *un-* + verb	• Finding the correct meaning

Unit / Chapter / Reading	Reading Skills	Vocabulary Building	Dictionary Skills
UNIT 6: The People Behind the Science			
Chapter 16 **A Woman's Fate**	• Understanding text organization • Recognizing point of view • Summarizing	• Word families: the prefix *inter-* • Studying phrasal verbs: phrasal verbs with *come*	
Chapter 17 **The Father of Vaccination**	• Understanding reference words • Understanding main points and important details • Summarizing	• Word families: the root *ced*, the prefixes *inter-*, *pre-*, *re-* • Studying collocations: collocations with *mild* and *severe*	
Chapter 18 **A Nose for Science**	• Understanding purpose • Summarizing	• Word families: adjective endings *-ive, -ent, -ary* • Understanding word grammar: reflexive pronouns	
UNIT 6: Wrap-up	• Guessing meaning from context • Understanding inference • Summarizing	• Studying phrasal verbs: phrasal verbs with *turn* • Word families: the root *phys*, the prefixes *uni-* and *agr-*	• Finding idioms

THE SECOND EDITION OF THE *PASSWORD* SERIES

Welcome to *New Password*, the second edition of *Password*, a series designed to help learners of English develop their reading skills and expand their vocabularies. The series offers theme-based units consisting of

- engaging nonfiction reading passages,
- a variety of skill-development activities based on the passages, and
- exercises to help students understand, remember, and use new words.

With this new edition, the *Password* series expands from three levels to five. Each book can be used independently of the others, but when used as a series, the books will help students reach the 2,000-word vocabulary level in English, at which point, research has shown, most learners can begin to read unadapted texts.

The series is based on two central ideas. The first is that the best way for learners to develop their ability to read English is, as you might guess, to practice reading English. To spark and sustain the student's motivation to read, "second language reading instruction must find ways to avoid continually frustrating the reader."[1] Learners need satisfying reading materials at an appropriate level of difficulty, materials that do not make them feel as if they are struggling to decipher a puzzle. The level of difficulty is determined by many factors, but one key factor is the familiarity of the vocabulary. Note that

> There is now a large body of studies indicating that poor readers primarily differ from good readers in context-free word recognition, and not in deficiencies in ability to use context to form predictions.[2]

To be successful, readers must be able to recognize a great many words quickly. So in addition to providing engaging reading matter, the *Password* series carefully controls and recycles the vocabulary.

The second idea underlying the design of the series is that textbooks should teach the vocabulary that will be most useful to learners. Corpus-based research has shown that the 2,000 highest-frequency words in English account for almost 80 percent of the running words in academic texts.[3] These are thus highly valuable

[1]Thom Hudson, *Teaching Second Language Reading* (Oxford, UK: Oxford University Press, 2007) 291.
[2]C. Juel, quoted in *Teaching and Researching Reading*, William Grabe and Fredericka Stoller (Harlow, England: Pearson Education, 2002) 73.
[3]I. S. P. Nation, *Learning Vocabulary in Another Language* (Cambridge, England: Cambridge University Press, 2001) 17.

words for students to learn, and these are the words targeted in the *Password* series.

The chart below shows the number of words that each *New Password* book assumes will be familiar to the learner and the range of the high-frequency vocabulary targeted in the book.

Target word choices are based on analyses of authentic language data in various corpora, including data in the Longman Corpus Network, to determine which words are most frequently used and most likely to be needed by the learner. Also targeted are common collocations and other multiword units, such as phrasal verbs.[4] The target vocabulary is chosen most often for its usefulness across a range of subjects but occasionally for its value in dealing with the topic of one particular chapter. Other factors include the complexity of a word's meanings and uses.

While becoming a good reader in English involves much more than knowing the meanings of words, there is no doubt that vocabulary knowledge is essential. To learn new words, students need to see them repeatedly and in varied contexts. They must become skilled at guessing meaning from context but can do this successfully only when they understand the context. Research by Paul Nation and Liu Na suggests that "for successful guessing [of unknown words] . . . at least 95 percent of the words in the text must be familiar to the reader."[5] For that reason, the vocabulary in the readings has been carefully controlled so that unknown words should constitute no more than 5 percent of the text. The words used in a reading are limited to those high-frequency words that the learner is assumed to know plus the vocabulary targeted in the chapter and target words and phrases recycled from previous chapters. New vocabulary is explained and practiced, encountered again in later chapters, and reviewed in the Unit Wrap-ups and Vocabulary Self-Tests. This emphasis on systematic vocabulary acquisition is a highlight of the *Password* series.

The second edition has expanded the series from three levels to five, increasing the number of reading passages from 76 to 104 and expanding the coverage of high-frequency vocabulary. One completely new book has joined the series, the beginning-level *New Password 1*. *New Password 2, 3, 4,* and *5* have retained the most popular materials from the first edition of the series and added new chapters. The books vary somewhat in organization and content, to meet the diverse needs of beginning- to high-intermediate-level students, but all five feature the popular Unit Wrap-ups and the Vocabulary Self-Tests, and all five will help learners make steady progress in developing their reading, vocabulary, and other English language skills.

Linda Butler, creator of the Password *series*

Highest-frequency words	*New Password 1*	*New Password 2*	*New Password 3*	*New Password 4*	*New Password 5*
2,000					**target words** *absence, acceptable, advantage,...*
1,500				**target words** *appear, attach,...*	**words assumed** *a/an, able, about, active, address, adult, agree, almost, amount, appear, attach,...*
1,200			**target words** *active, amount,...*	**words assumed** *a/an, able, about, active, address, adult, agree, almost, amount,...*	
900		**target words** *able, adult,...*	**words assumed** *a/an, able, about, address, adult, agree, almost,...*		
600	**target words** *agree, almost,...*	**words assumed** *a/an, about, address, agree, almost,...*			
300	**words assumed** *a/an, about, address,...*				

[4]Dilin Liu, "The Most Frequently Used Spoken American English Idioms: A Corpus Analysis and Its Implications," *TESOL Quarterly* 37 (Winter 2003): 671–700.
[5]Nation, 254.

Additional References

Nation, Paul. *Teaching and Learning Vocabulary.* New York: Newbury House, 1990.

Schmitt, Norbert, and Michael McCarthy, eds. *Vocabulary: Description, Acquisition, and Pedagogy.* Cambridge, UK: Cambridge University Press, 1997.

Schmitt, Norbert, and Cheryl Boyd Zimmerman. "Derivative Word Forms: What Do Learners Know?" *TESOL Quarterly* 36 (Summer 2002): 145–171.

OVERVIEW OF *NEW PASSWORD 5*

New Password 5 is intended for students with a vocabulary of about 1,500 words in English, and it teaches over 300 more. From 14 to 20 words and phrases from each nonfiction reading passage are targeted in the exercises for that chapter and recycled in later chapters. Because of the systematic building of vocabulary, as well as the progression of reading skills work, it is best to do the chapters in order.

Most of the target words are among the 2,000 highest-frequency words in English, words that students need to build a solid foundation for their language learning. Other, lower-frequency words are targeted for their usefulness in discussing a particular theme, such as *gene* and *trait* in Unit 3: Genetics: The Science of Who We Are.

Organization of the Book

New Password 5 contains six units, each with three chapters followed by a Wrap-up section. Vocabulary Self-Tests are found after Units 3 and 6. At the end of the book you will find the Vocabulary Self-Tests Answer Key and an index to the target vocabulary.

THE UNITS Each unit is based on a theme and includes three chapters built around readings that deal with real people, places, events, and ideas.

THE CHAPTERS Each chapter is organized as follows:

Getting Ready to Read—The chapter opens with a photo and prereading tasks. Some tasks are for pair or small-group work, others for the full class. *Getting Ready to Read* starts students thinking about the subject of the reading by drawing on what they know, eliciting their opinions, and introducing relevant vocabulary.

Reading—The reading passages progress from about 500 to about 800 words over the course of the book, and they increase in level of reading

difficulty. Students should read each passage the first time without stopping to look up or ask about new words. Tell them the goal for this reading is getting the main ideas and that multiple readings will improve their comprehension and reading fluency. You may wish to have them reread while you read aloud or play the audio, as listening while reading can aid both comprehension and retention and help with pronunciation. The reading is followed by *Comprehension Check*, a brief true/false/? (can't determine the answer from the text) exercise to let students check their general understanding. Go over the *Comprehension Check* statements in class: When a statement is true, ask students how they know it is true; when it is false, have students correct it. By doing so, you send them back into the reading to find support for their answers. Try to avoid spending time explaining vocabulary at this point.

Exploring Vocabulary—Once students have a general understanding of the reading, it is time to focus on new words. This section has two parts:
1. *Thinking about the Vocabulary*.
a. First, students learn and practice a *Guessing Strategy* that develops their ability to guess the meaning of unfamiliar words from context.
b. Next, students look at a list of Target Words and Phrases and circle those that are new to them. Students then return to the reading to see what they can learn about word meanings from context. At first, students may benefit from working on guessing meaning from context as a whole class, with guidance; later you may want them to discuss new word meanings in pairs.
c. In this next step, students shift their focus from meaning to form. They are asked to write each target word or phrase in a word-form chart under the correct heading of *Nouns, Verbs, Adjectives,* or *Other.** (In Chapters 1–3, the word-form chart has been completed for

---

* In the chart, *Nouns* include noun phrases (such as *the wild* and *facial expression*) and noun modifiers (such as *dropout rates*); *Verbs* include phrasal verbs (such as *stand by* and *call for*) and verb phrases (such as *get one's start* and *make sense of*); *Adjectives* include participial adjectives (such as *threatened* and *threatening*); and *Other* includes adverbs, prepositions, etc.

the students. From Chapter 4 on, students complete the charts themselves.) At first, students will probably benefit from identifying the correct word forms as a whole class, with your guidance; later you may want them to complete the chart in pairs.

2. *Using the Target Vocabulary*. This exercise helps students understand the meanings of the target vocabulary as used in the reading. It can be done in class or out, by students working individually or in pairs. When taken as a whole, *Using the Target Vocabulary* is actually a summary of the most important information from the text.

Developing Reading Skills—In this section are tasks that require students to delve back into the reading. They include recognizing and stating topics and main ideas; scanning for details; understanding reference words; recognizing and stating cause and effect; identifying the writer's purpose, tone, and point of view; making inferences; paraphrasing; and summarizing. (See the Scope and Sequence on pages iv–vi for the contents of *Developing Reading Skills* sections.)

Expanding Vocabulary—In this section, students move from understanding the target vocabulary to actively acquiring it. First, they practice using the target words in new contexts. Then, they build on their knowledge of the target vocabulary by learning related items that are in the same word families. Finally, they complete a word grammar, phrasal verb, or word collocation exercise. Grammar exercises include using *due to, because,* and *so*; using transitive and intransitive verbs; the proper use and placement of adverbs; participial adjectives; transitive verbs and direct objects; using *be used to*; adjectives that become nouns with *the*; reflexive pronouns; and gerunds and infinitives. Phrasal verb exercises provide students with practice in using common phrasal verbs. Word collocation exercises focus students' attention on how the target words combine with other words, such as the verb + noun combinations *conduct an experiment* and *perform an operation*. (See the *Vocabulary Building* column of the Scope and Sequence on pages iv–vi for the contents of *Expanding Vocabulary* sections.) After working through these materials, students can turn to their dictionaries for further information.

Putting It All Together—This section includes activities to help students consolidate their understanding of the unit theme, build their fluency, and continue their acquisition of the target vocabulary. In *Discussion*, students are asked to share information and opinions about issues raised in the chapter. In some cases, they are asked to conduct surveys on topics related to the chapter theme. As they talk, they are instructed to use the target vocabulary (including derived forms that were introduced in the chapter). The words that are most likely to be useful to each discussion item are listed with the questions. You may want to specifically assign someone from each group to keep track of how many times the words were used in the discussion. At the end of the discussion, you can ask the class which words or phrases they used the most, and provide additional instruction on any vocabulary they had difficulty using.

The chapter ends with a *Writing* section containing a choice of two topics related to the content of the reading. Students are instructed to use at least five of the target words and phrases in their writing. You can encourage them to choose words or phrases that they need to learn more about. Some of the writing tasks lend themselves to informal writing such as journal entries or letters, while others are more appropriate for formal compositions and short essays.

UNIT WRAP-UPS Each unit ends with a four-part Wrap-up section that provides students with more practice in the reading skills and vocabulary taught in the three chapters. *Reviewing Reading Skills and Vocabulary* includes a 300- to 400-word reading passage related to the unit theme, with 10 to 20 target words and derivations from the unit incorporated into the text. Each passage also contains a few new vocabulary items to give the students practice in guessing meaning from context. The follow-up exercises provide the students with additional practice in the reading skills introduced in the unit.

Expanding Vocabulary contains exercises on word families, phrasal verbs, grammar, and collocations. *Playing with Words* includes a crossword, word search puzzle, or game. *Building Dictionary Skills* contains exercises designed to help students get the most out of their dictionaries, with excerpts from the fourth edition of the *Longman Dictionary of American English*. (See the Scope and Sequence on pages iv–vi for the contents of *Building Dictionary Skills*.)

VOCABULARY SELF-TESTS Two multiple-choice vocabulary self-tests appear in the book, the first covering Units 1–3, the second Units 4–6.

The Teacher's Manual The Teacher's Manual for *New Password 5* contains: the Answer Key for all exercises in the book, six Unit Tests with answers, Quick Oral Review, and sets of prompts you can use for rapid drills of vocabulary studied in each chapter.

ABOUT THE AUTHOR Lynn Bonesteel has been teaching ESL since 1988. She is currently a full-time senior lecturer at the Center for English Language and Orientation Programs at Boston University in Boston, Massachusetts.

REFERENCES, ACKNOWLEDGMENTS, AND CREDITS

REFERENCES

Ackerman, T. "A brave new world of designer babies: Genetic engineering to open Pandora's box of ethical questions." *The Houston Chronicle*, (June 27, 1999): A1. [electronic version].

Ahuja, Anjana. "Socially Superior." Retrieved June 11, 2008 from http://www.timesonline.co.uk/tol/life_and_style/article640746.ece.

Alvarez, L. "Consumers in Europe Resist Gene-Altered Foods." *The New York Times*, (February 11, 2003): A3. [electronic version].

Anderson, W. F. "A cure that may cost us ourselves." *Newsweek*, (January 1, 2000): 74. [electronic version].

Avril, T. "When Science Is Personal." *The Philadelphia Inquirer*, (April 23, 2007): C:01. [electronic version].

Blow, K. "Kurtis Blow Presents: The History of Rap, Vol. 1: The Genesis. (n.d.)." Retrieved January 1, 2003 from http://rap.about.com/gi/dynamic/offsite.htm?site=http%3A%2F%2Frhino.com%2FFeatures%2Fliners%2F72851lin.html.

Bowles, S., C. Jones & E. Poitevent. "An instant of anger . . . a lifetime of regret." *USA Today*, (November 23, 1998): A19. [electronic version].

Burr, C. *The Emperor of Scent: A Story of Perfume, Obsession, and the Last Mystery of the Senses.* New York, NY: Random House, 2002.

Chandler, D. "Ancient note: Music as bridge between species." *The Boston Globe*, (January 5, 2001): A1. [electronic version].

Dayton, T. "Rapper's Delight: The history of hip hop at Yerba Buena Center." *San Francisco Weekly*, Calendar, (May 16, 2001). [electronic version].

"Family Struggles Led to Hunt for Defective Gene." *The Courier Mail*, *Australia*, (April 3, 2007). [electronic version]. Major_U_S__and_World_Publications_TV_and_Rad2008-06-19_07-12.DOC.

Gladwell, M. *Blink: The Power of Thinking Without Thinking*. New York, NY: Little, Brown, and Company, 2005.

Gross, T. "Grandmaster Flash discusses his music and career." *WHYY Fresh Air*, (December 26, 2002). [electronic version].

Harmon, A. "Facing Life With a Lethal Gene." *The New York Times*, (March 18, 2007) [electronic version].

Henig, R. M. "Tempting fates." *Discover*, 5, (May, 1998): 58–64. [electronic version].

Hoag, C. "A Tale of Pain and Hope on Lake Maracaibo." *Business Week*, (May 29, 2000) [electronic version].

Hughley, M. "Godfather of hip-hop DJs." *The Oregonian*, [Arts and Living], (July 5, 2002): 35. [electronic version].

Jackson, J. "Teens: Crazy by Design." *Ottawa Citizen*, (May 17, 2003): G1. [electronic version].

Jayson, S. "Sociability: It's all in your mind." Retrieved June 11, 2008 from http://www.usatoday.com/news/health/2006-09-24-social-intelligence_x.htm.

Ling, K. S. "Pay heed to your emotions." *New Straits Times*, *Malaysia*, (January 13, 2008): Local:2. [electronic version].

McElhenny, J. "Franklin Park Gorilla Escapes, Attacks 2." *Boston Globe*, (September 29, 2003): A1. [electronic version].

Palca, J. "Nancy Wexler discusses her decision not to be tested for Huntington's disease despite her mother's contracting the illness." *Weekend All Things Considered, National Public Radio*, (May 16, 2004) [electronic version].

Patterson, K. "Road Rage: Scientists want to find out what makes a driver go bad." *Calgary Herald*, *Sunday Edition*, (July 7, 2002): A3. [electronic version].

Reader's Digest. "Drugs Get Personal." *Medical Breakthroughs 2001: The Latest Advances in Preventing, Treating, and Curing Nearly 100 Common Diseases*. Pleasantville, NY: Reader's Digest Association, 2002.

(continued on p. 278)

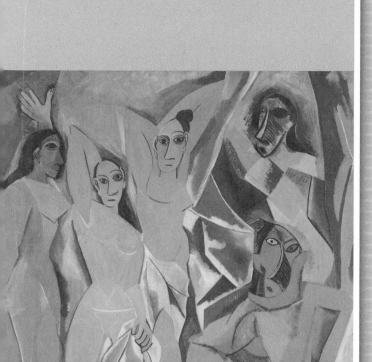

Pablo Picasso.
Les Demoiselles d'Avignon.
1907. Oil on canvas.

ARTISTIC INNOVATIONS

CHAPTER 1

What Is Anime?

*Anime (left) and
Cartoon (right)*

GETTING READY TO READ

 A **Talk with a partner or in a small group.**

1. Did you watch cartoons or read comic books when you were a child? Which ones? Do you ever watch cartoons or read comic books now? Which ones?

2. Compare the picture labeled "Anime" and the picture labeled "Cartoon" above. Check (✓) the words that you think describe the pictures. Explain your answers to your classmates.

	beautiful	creative	intelligent	funny	serious	interesting	simple
Anime	☐	☐	☐	☐	☐	☐	☐
Cartoon	☐	☐	☐	☐	☐	☐	☐

 B **The boldfaced words in the sentences below appear in the reading. Which words are new to you? Circle them. Then, work with a partner. Read the sentences about the reading, and choose the correct answers.**

1. Some of the best, most **talented** artists in Japan work in anime.

   Someone who is *talented*

   a. has a lot of money.   **b.** has a very good natural ability.

2

2. Anime deals with **complex** characters and situations. The stories are usually not simple. A *complex* story

   a. has many parts and is difficult to understand.

   b. usually has a sad ending.

3. In most Hollywood films, it is easy to tell who is good, and who is bad. The **evil** characters do bad things, and the good ones try to stop them. An *evil* character wants to

   a. hurt other people.

   b. meet other people.

4. Both children and adults are **fascinated** by anime, and enjoy watching it together. *Fascinated* means

   a. very surprised.

   b. very interested.

5. Some anime deals with the future and the changes that **technology** might bring to people's lives. Examples of *technology* include

   a. schools, banks, and museums.

   b. computers, digital cameras, and cell phones.

READING

Read the text once without stopping. Don't worry about new words or the numbered words at the bottom of the page. Don't stop to use a dictionary. Just keep reading!

What Is Anime?

1   *Anime* is a special style of Japanese animation.[1] You can immediately see the difference between anime and other cartoons. This is because of the high quality of the artwork and the style, such as characters with large, childlike eyes. In addition, you will see that anime is strongly influenced by Asian, and especially Japanese, religious and cultural traditions. It provides a window into Japanese culture.

2   Anime is closely **related** to Japanese comics called *manga*. Many anime television shows and videos **got their start** as popular manga. Manga is a $3 billion business in Japan. About 60 percent of

---

[1] *animation* = a movie or television program made by photographing pictures or by drawing a series of pictures with a computer

(continued)

all printed materials sold there are manga. And manga and anime are not just for children. They are popular with Japanese of all ages. In fact, a large percentage of manga and anime is made for adults only. Their **popularity** helps explain why the quality of anime is so high—anime and manga are big business. A recent anime film **reportedly** cost $8 million to make, with more than 3,000 animators **involved** in its production. Some of Japan's most **talented** artists and musicians work in manga and anime.

3   But it is not just the quality of the artwork that makes anime so popular. Many anime stories deal with **complex** subjects and characters that change as the stories develop. The "bad guy"[2] of Disney[3] cartoons—completely **evil** and not very believable[4]—is not common in anime. Rather, it is not always clear who the "good guys" and "bad guys" are. Also, death is shown as a natural part of life. Even important characters die sometimes. If your only experience with animation is Disney, you might feel shocked but then **fascinated** when you first watch anime.

4   Some of the most interesting anime deals with modern **technology**. In this type of anime, the differences between machines and people, males and females, and good and evil are not always clear. Anime often looks at the **challenges** of life and culture in a world of **rapid** technological change. The characters in this type of anime deal with deep **moral** questions, such as the possible negative effects of technology on human relationships. This is very different from the simple way that Hollywood films and cartoons usually deal with the same subjects.

5   In Japan, anime appears in three forms: television shows (which often continue for several years), **original** animation video (OAVs, also spelled OVA), and films. The first Japanese anime TV show, *Tetsuawan Atom* ("The Mighty Atom"), started in 1963 and continued for ten years.

6   Anime is becoming popular in countries all over the world. For people who do not speak Japanese, videos are available that have subtitles[5] added or are dubbed.[6] Many people greatly prefer the subtitles, for a number of reasons. Sometimes the dubbing is either too fast or too slow, so what you hear does not match the

---

[2] the *bad guy* = the character in a movie, book, or television show that does bad things and that you are supposed to hate

[3] *Disney* = a U.S. company famous for making cartoons, such as Mickey Mouse, and cartoon movies, such as *The Lion King*

[4] *believable* = easy to believe because it seems possible and real

[5] *subtitles* = words printed at the bottom of a movie screen to translate what is said by the actors in a foreign movie

[6] *dubbed* = a **dubbed** movie or video is one in which the original sound recording is replaced with one in another language

mouth movements. Also, hearing the spoken (and sung) Japanese is part of the cultural experience and **beauty** of anime. Perhaps most importantly, many anime viewers are learning a little Japanese as they watch.

7   Funny, fascinating, intelligent—these are some of the adjectives that describe the best anime. If you share anime with children, you will be sharing with them beautiful art, excitement, and lots of fun. You will also be introducing them to the fascination of Japanese culture.

Comprehension Check

Read these sentences. Circle T (true), F (false), or ? (can't determine the answer from the reading). If you circle F, change the sentence to make it true. You might need to change one or two words, or you might need to rewrite the sentence completely. Check your answers with a classmate. If your answers are different, look back at the reading.

1. Anime and Disney cartoons look very ~~similar~~. *different*   T (F) ?
2. Manga is a special kind of anime.   T   F   ?
3. A lot of anime is made especially for adults.   T   F   ?
4. Anime often deals with very serious subjects.   T   F   ?
5. Important characters never die in anime.   T   F   ?
6. Some anime is specifically made to teach Japanese.   T   F   ?
7. If you don't speak Japanese, you probably won't understand anime.   T   F   ?

EXPLORING VOCABULARY

Thinking about the Target Vocabulary

Guessing Strategy

Learning how to figure out what a new word means is a very important skill. In every chapter of this book, you will learn a strategy to help you guess the meaning of a word from its **context**. The context of a word is the words and sentences before and after it.

These other words help you to guess a word's meaning. For example, look at the context of the word *complex* in the example.

*Many anime stories deal with **complex** subjects and characters that change as the stories develop. The "bad guy" of Disney cartoons—completely evil and not very believable—is not common in anime. Rather, it is not always clear who the "good guys" and "bad guys" are.*

The context tells you that something that is complex changes and is not always clear. Therefore, complex subjects and characters are not simple.

Try It!

Read the sentences, and write a definition of the boldfaced target word.

The **popularity** of anime is growing. Millions of people all over the world are starting to watch it.

Popularity means _____.

 A Look at the target words and phrase. Which ones are new to you? Circle them here and in the reading. Then read "What Is Anime?" again. Look at the context of each new word and phrase. Can you guess the meaning? Use the Guessing Strategy where possible.

Target Words and Phrase

related (paragraph 2)	talented (2)	challenges (4)
got their start (2)	complex (3)	rapid (4)
popularity (2)	evil (3)	moral (4)
reportedly (2)	fascinated (3)	original (5)
involved (2)	technology (4)	beauty (6)

Look at the word-form chart below with the target words and phrase listed as they are used in the reading. Note that verbs are listed in their base form and nouns in their singular form. Verb phrases are listed under Verbs, and noun phrases under Nouns.

Nouns	Verbs	Adjectives	Other
popularity	get one's start	related	reportedly
technology		involved	
challenge		talented	
beauty		complex	
		evil	
		fascinated	
		rapid	
		moral	
		original	

Using the Target Vocabulary

These sentences are about the reading. Complete them with the words and phrase in the box. Circle the words or phrases in the sentences that help you understand the meanings of the target words. Be careful. There are two extra words or phrases.

beauty	evil	moral	rapid
challenges	got their start	original	related
complex	involved	popularity	reportedly

1. Anime is closely _____ to Japanese comic books. They are connected because they have some of the same characters and a similar style of artwork.

2. Many anime television characters first appeared in the pages of popular comic books, and then later on television. They _____ in comic books.

3. Anime is popular with people of all ages in Japan. Because of its _popularity_, anime is big business in Japan.

4. According to newspaper reports, anime films usually cost millions of dollars to make. One recent film _reportedly_ cost $8 million to produce.

5. Many talented Japanese artists and musicians are _involved_ in the making of anime. Over 3,000 artists worked on a recent anime film.

6. The stories in anime are complex, and the characters often have to deal with difficult _complex_ challenges. In anime, the differences between good and evil and right and wrong are often not very clear.

7. Because of technology, life is changing very fast, and many people have difficulty accepting all the changes. Some of the most interesting anime deal with the _challenge_ of living in a world of _rapid_ change.

8. People enjoy watching anime because of its artistic quality and _beauty_.

9. A lot of anime is made first for film and television, and then later appears on video. However, _original_ animation video, or OAV, is made directly for video, not first for film or television.

DEVELOPING READING SKILLS

Understanding Topics and Main Ideas

A reading is about someone or something. That person or thing is the **topic** of the reading. Often, the title of a reading will tell you what the topic is. The **main idea** of a reading is the most important information about the topic. The main idea of a reading is usually written in a full sentence.

Answer these questions.

1. What is the topic of "What Is Anime?" _Japanese animation_

2. What is the main idea of "What Is Anime?"
   a. Anime is a form of Japanese animated film or video that is artistic, fun, and educational.

b. Anime got its start in Japan as manga, or comic books, and is very popular.

c. Anime is better than Disney animation because the characters are more complex.

Understanding Cause and Effect

When you read, it is important to understand the connections between ideas. For example, you must be able to tell the difference between the cause of something and the effect. Often, writers use words like *so*, *because*, and *therefore* to show cause and effect, but sometimes they do not.

Complete these sentences using information from "What Is Anime?"

1. Makers of anime spend a lot of money producing it because _anime is big business in Japan_.

2. Anime is very popular because _of their challenges high artistic quality, funy, fresh. intelligent_

3. When people who watch only Disney cartoons first watch anime they might be shocked because _it is not clear good / an/ people are._

4. People who don't speak Japanese can understand many anime videos because _they have subtitles are dobbed_

5. Many people don't like to watch anime that is dubbed because _what you hear doesn't match the mouth movements._

Using the Target Vocabulary in New Contexts

Complete the sentences with the target words and phrase in the box. Be careful. There are two extra words or phrases.

beauty	got his start	original	related
challenges	involved	popularity	reportedly
evil	moral	rapid	technology

1. The president is _____reportedly_____ traveling to China tomorrow. That's what I read in the newspaper this morning, anyway.

2. She has faced many difficult _____challenges_____, but she has always been successful.

3. Parents have a _____moral_____ responsibility to teach their children right from wrong.

4. The owner of this restaurant _____got his start_____ as a waiter here.

5. Because of the musician's _____popularity_____, he was paid $250,000 to play one show.

6. That is not the _____original_____ painting. It's a copy.

7. Many people think that we are sisters, but we are not _____related_____.

8. We were all _____involved_____ in the discussion, but our boss made the final decision.

9. His English is good, but he still has trouble understanding _____rapid_____ speech.

10. She visits Costa Rica every year because she loves the natural _____beauty_____ of the rain forest.

Word Families

Many words belong to **word families**. When you learn a new word, it is a good idea to learn other words in the same family. Use your dictionary to check the form and meaning of words in the same word family.

The words in the exercise on page 11 belong to the word families of the target words. You will see that they have different endings, or **suffixes**. A suffix is a word part added to the end of a word to make a new word. The new word is often a different part of speech.

- *-ity* is a noun suffix
- *-al* is an adjective suffix
- *-ly* is an adverb suffix

Complete the sentences with the words in the box.

| morally | originality | popularity | rapidly | technological |

1. The most important ___technological___ inventions of the past 100 years include the airplane, the automobile, and the computer.
2. His ___popularity___ as a singer lasted for only a few years. Now, almost no one remembers him.
3. Technology is changing very ___rapidly___ these days. It seems there are new products every day.
4. Stealing is ___morally___ wrong.
5. I love the ___originality___ of your work. It is different from everyone else's.

Studying Collocations

Collocations are words we often put together. **Prepositions** (for example, *in, on, of, to*) often go together with adjectives. Some prepositions can go with certain adjectives, and some cannot. Look at the examples.

> Correct: *He is not **related** to her.*
> Incorrect: *He is not related with her.*

 Read these sentences. Pay attention to the boldfaced words and the prepositions that go with them.

1. My son is __**fascinated** by__ cars. He can tell you the name of almost every car he sees.
2. He didn't decide alone. Many people were __**involved** in__ the decision.
3. Dogs are closely __**related** to__ wolves. A long time ago, there were no dogs, just wolves.
4. She's very __**talented** in__ music. Someday, she would like to be a famous musician.

B Write four sentences about yourself or people that you know. Use the **boldfaced** adjectives + prepositions from Part A.

1. I'm fascinated by guns.

2. When I made decision about marriage, all my family were involved in my wedding process.

3. Bob and mary are related to each other.

4. I'm very talented in plang piano.

PUTTING IT ALL TOGETHER

Discussion

Share your ideas in a small group. As you talk, try to use the vocabulary below. Each time someone uses a target word, put a check (✔) next to it.

beauty	**involve**	**talented**
complex	**original/originality**	

1. The writer of "What Is Anime?" refers to anime as art. However, when many people think of art, they think of famous artists such as Leonardo da Vinci or Pablo Picasso. Do you agree with the writer that anime and other types of animation can be considered art? Why or why not?

2. Have you ever seen an animated film or television show in English? Which one(s)? What have you learned about American culture from watching animated films and television shows?

Writing

Complete one or both of these writing topics. When you write, use at least five of the target words from the chapter. Underline the target words in your paper.

1. Write a paragraph or short essay describing a comic book or cartoon character that you liked when you were a child. Explain why you liked the character.

2. *Comic books and cartoons can be considered art.* Do you agree or disagree with this statement? Write a paragraph or short essay explaining your opinion. Use examples of specific comic books or cartoons.

CHAPTER 2

The Scientist and the Stradivarius

Dr. Joseph Nagyvary with one of his violins

GETTING READY TO READ

 A   **Talk with a partner or in a small group.**

1. Do you play a musical instrument? If so, which one? How long have you been playing? If you don't know how to play a musical instrument, would you like to learn? Which instrument would you choose?

2. The text you are going to read is about a question from the past that someone is trying to answer with modern science. Check (✓) the questions that scientists have been able to answer. Write an X next to those questions that scientists have not yet answered.

    _____ **a.** How were the Egyptian pyramids built?

    _____ **b.** How old is the earth?

    _____ **c.** What killed the dinosaurs?

    _____ **d.** How was our universe formed?

The **boldfaced** words in the paragraph below appear in the reading. Which words are new to you? Circle them. Then, work with a partner. Read this short summary of the reading, and match the words with their definitions. Be careful. There are two extra definitions.

Joseph Nagyvary is a scientist. He has spent many years trying to solve the **mystery** of why the eighteenth-century violins made by Antonio Stradivari sound so much better than other violins. Nagyvary has used his **knowledge** of chemistry to try to understand the **heavenly** Stradivarius sound. He believes that the **chemical** qualities of the materials used to make the violins have an effect on the sound. People who sell Stradivarius violins at very high prices feel **threatened** by Nagyvary's ideas. They do not want the mystery to be solved.

Word	Definition
1. mystery	**a.** information gained through learning or experience
2. knowledge	**b.** worried that something bad will happen to hurt you
3. heavenly	**c.** (coming from) the changes in or qualities of a liquid, solid, or gas
4. chemical	**d.** evil
5. threatened	**e.** something that we don't know much about
	f. fascinated
	g. beautiful or good

READING

Read the text once without stopping.

The Scientist and the Stradivarius

1   When Regina Buenaventura walks onto the stage, all eyes are on her violin. In the fifth row, Joseph Nagyvary closes his eyes and listens. He has spent years in a **laboratory** studying the sound of the most famous instrument of all time. Nagyvary believes that he has finally solved the centuries-old **mystery** behind the **remarkable** sound of the Stradivarius violin.

2　　This young musician holds the result of Nagyvary's scientific efforts under her chin—the Nagyvarius. She begins playing and the violin makes a clear, **brilliant**, **heavenly** sound. Creator Nagyvary opens his eyes. Could this be the magical Stradivarius sound?

3　　For 150 years, violin makers, musicians, and scientists have tried to solve the mystery of the Stradivarius. Antonio Stradivari lived in Cremona, a small northern Italian city. Before his death in 1737, he made over 1,000 violins, violas,[1] cellos,[2] and guitars. Two sons followed him into the business, but they died soon after. The details of how their father and other violin makers from Cremona made their remarkable instruments disappeared with them.

4　　How could an **illiterate** man with no education produce instruments with such a heavenly sound? Did Stradivari and the other violin makers from Cremona have a secret?

5　　Joseph Nagyvary's laboratory in the United States at Texas A&M University is a world away from Cremona. Nagyvary began teaching biochemistry[3] at the university in the late 1960s. About ten years later, he began making violins. Using his **knowledge** of chemistry, Nagyvary believes that he has found the answer to the Stradivarius puzzle.

6　　In 1977, Nagyvary presented the results of his research to the Violin Society of America. He claimed that the high quality of Stradivari's instruments was not **due to** his **artistic** talent. Rather, the remarkable sound was a result of the materials Stradivari used, specifically the **chemical** properties[4] of the wood and varnish.[5] Stradivari himself probably did not understand the importance of these materials. In other words, Stradivari was certainly talented, but he probably owed much of his success to luck.

7　　Nagyvary's **announcement** shocked violin makers and dealers.[6] His **theory** was a direct challenge to the way that violins had been made for years. It also challenged violin makers' **belief** in the importance of their artistic talent.

8　　Nagyvary **stands by** his theory. "The pieces of the puzzle have been around and I have not invented anything new. But I put the pieces, well, together while the others could not. I am the first

---

[1] a *viola* = a wooden musical instrument shaped like a violin but larger and with a lower sound

[2] a *cello* = a large wooden musical instrument, shaped like a violin, that you hold between your knees and play by pulling a bow (= special stick) across wire strings

[3] *biochemistry* = the scientific study of the chemistry of living things

[4] a *property* = a quality that belongs naturally to something

[5] a *varnish* = a clear liquid that is painted onto wood to protect it

[6] a *dealer* = someone who buys and sells a particular product, especially an expensive one

(continued)

chemist of good international standing[7] . . . who, obviously, has a much better understanding of the effects of these natural chemicals."

9   The best **proof** of Nagyvary's theory may be the instruments he makes. By using what he has learned from his research, Nagyvary claims to produce violins with a sound quality very similar to that of a Stradivarius. This is demonstrated in *The Stradivarius Puzzle*, a thirteen-song CD recorded by well-known professional violinist Zina Schiff. On it, Schiff plays both a Nagyvarius and her 1697 Stradivarius, reportedly worth $3,000,000. Schiff says, "I sent *The Stradivarius Puzzle* to a friend of mine who is a conductor[8] and he had no idea . . . He just could not tell . . . The truth is, I would rather be playing on one of Dr. Nagyvary's instruments."

10   So why do violin makers and dealers refuse to even discuss Nagyvary's theory? Schiff believes that it is because the dealers feel **threatened** by the fairly low cost ($3,000 to $22,000) of a Nagyvary violin.

11   Schiff came from a poor family, so she feels very strongly that people who cannot afford Stradivari violins should still be able to have high-quality instruments. According to Schiff, Dr. Nagyvary's violins have made this possible, without having a negative effect on the beauty and value of a Stradivarius.

---

[7] *standing* = someone's position in a system or organization, based on what other people think of him or her

[8] a *conductor* = someone who stands in front of a group of musicians and directs their playing

Comprehension Check

Read these sentences. Circle T (true), F (false), or ? (can't determine the answer from the reading). If you circle F, change the sentence to make it true. You might need to change one or two words, or you might need to rewrite the sentence completely. Check your answers with a classmate. If your answers are different, look back at the reading.

                thinks he knows

1. Dr. Nagyvary ~~is not sure~~ why Stradivari instruments sound so good.   T (F) ?

2. Dr. Nagyvary is both a scientist and a violinist.   T F (?)

3. Dr. Nagyvary is both a university professor and a violin maker.   (T) F ?

4. According to Dr. Nagyvary, the chemicals in the wood and varnish of Stradivari instruments are not very important to the way they sound.   T (F) ?

5. According to Dr. Nagyvary, Stradivari knew why his
   violins had such a remarkable sound.   T F ?

6. Nagyvary violins sound better than Stradivari violins.   T F ?

EXPLORING VOCABULARY

Thinking about the Target Vocabulary

Guessing Strategy

If the unfamiliar word is an adjective (a word that describes a noun),
think about whether it has a positive (good) or negative (bad)
meaning. Look at the example.

*I will never forget the first time that I heard the **remarkable**, clear
sound of a Stradivarius.*

Because the writer describes the sound as clear (a positive quality),
you can guess that the adjective *remarkable* probably has a positive
meaning.

Try It!

Find these target words in the reading. Do they have a positive or a
negative meaning? Write **P** (positive) or **N** (negative).

artistic ____   brilliant ____   illiterate ____

A Look at the target words and phrases on page 18. Which ones are new
to you? Circle them on page 18 and in the reading. Then read "The
Scientist and the Stradivarius" again. Look at the context of each new
word and phrase. Can you guess the meaning? Use the Guessing
Strategy where possible.

Target Words and Phrases

laboratory (1)	knowledge (5)	theory (7)
mystery (1)	due to (6)	belief (7)
remarkable (1)	artistic (6)	stands by (8)
brilliant (2)	chemical (6)	proof (9)
heavenly (2)	announcement (7)	threatened (10)
illiterate (4)		

B Look at the word-form chart below with the target words and phrases listed as they are used in the reading. Note that verbs are listed in their base form and nouns in their singular form. Verb phrases are listed under Verbs, and noun phrases under Nouns.

Nouns	Verbs	Adjectives	Other
laboratory	stand by	remarkable	due to
mystery		brilliant	
knowledge		heavenly	
announcement		illiterate	
theory		artistic	
belief		chemical	
proof		threatened	

USING THE TARGET VOCABULARY

These sentences are about the reading. Complete them with the words and phrases in the box. Circle the words or phrases in the sentences that help you understand the meanings of the target words. Be careful. There are two extra words or phrases.

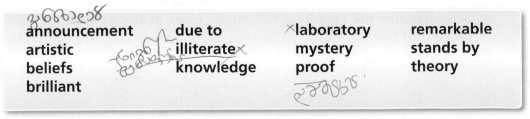

announcement	due to	laboratory	remarkable
artistic	illiterate	mystery	stands by
beliefs	knowledge	proof	theory
brilliant			

1. Dr. Joseph Nagyvary is a scientist who works out of his _laboratory_ at Texas A&M University.

2. Antonio Stradivari could not read or write. He was _illiterate_.

3. Stradivari violins have a very special sound. Dr. Nagyvary has spent many years of his life trying to solve the mystery of why they have such a _brilliant_ sound.

4. Stradivari violins make a sound that is so clear and _remarkable_ that it shines like a light.

5. Dr. Nagyvary believes that the high quality of Stradivari's instruments was not a result of his _artistic_ talent. Rather, Dr. Nagyvary claims that the remarkable sound was _due to_ the materials Stradivari used.

6. Dr. Nagyvary made an _announcement_ about his discoveries during a speech to the Violin Society in 1977.

7. Violin makers and dealers were shocked. Dr. Nagyvary's _theory_ challenged every tradition of violin making.

8. If Dr. Nagyvary is right, then a lot of what violin makers have always believed is wrong. His theory challenges all of their _beliefs_ about what is important in violin making.

9. Many people do not agree with Dr. Nagyvary's theory, but that doesn't bother him. He _stands by_ his theory because he is sure that he is right.

10. One way that Dr. Nagyvary is trying to prove his theory is by making his own violins. Many professional musicians cannot tell the difference between his violins and Stradivari violins. Dr. Nagyvary claims that this is clear _proof_ that his theory is correct.

DEVELOPING READING SKILLS

Understanding Topics and Main Ideas

Answer these questions.

1. What is the topic of "The Scientist and the Stradivarius"? _____
    _____

2. What is the main idea of the reading? (Remember, a main idea must be written in a full sentence.) _____
    _____

Scanning

Sometimes you need to find a piece of information in a reading. To do this, you **scan** the reading. *Scan* means to read rapidly and look for just the information you need.

Read these questions about "The Scientist and the Stradivarius." Scan the reading and write short answers.

1. In addition to violins, what other kinds of instruments did Stradivari make?

    _____guitar____ Cello_____

2. Was Stradivari the only violin maker from Cremona who made instruments with a remarkable sound?

    _____

3. When did Dr. Nagyvary first make a speech about his theory?

    _____1977._____

4. How many and what kind(s) of violins does Zina Schiff play on *The Stradivarius Puzzle*?

    _____

Understanding Inference

Some information cannot be found by scanning. This is because the information is not written directly in the text. Instead, you have to think about what the text says, and then make a logical conclusion, or **inference**.

Answer these questions.

1. According to Dr. Nagyvary, Stradivari never told anyone his secret because
    a. he didn't know he had a   b. he wanted his secret to die
       secret.   with him.

2. Traditionally, violin makers believed that the most important thing in violin making was
    a. their own artistic talent.   b. the materials they used.

3. Stradivari's sons and other violin makers from Cremona made violins using
    a. the same kinds of materials   b. different kinds of materials
       that Stradivari used.   than Stradivari used.

EXPANDING VOCABULARY

Using the Target Vocabulary in New Contexts

Complete the sentences with the target words and phrases in the box. Be careful. There are two extra words or phrases.

announcement	chemical	laboratory	stand by
artistic	due to	proof	theory
belief	illiterate	remarkable	threatened
brilliant			

1. If he's _illiterate_ and can't sign his name, he can just make an X on the signature line.

2. _Due to_ the bad weather, our flight arrived late.

3. You can't be sure that he stole the money. You don't have any _proof_.

4. Everyone thought that he loved his job. We were all shocked by his _announcement_ at the meeting that he was going to quit.

5. Anna got her start working in a research _laboratory_. Then she decided to go to medical school.

6. Due to my father's strong _belief_ in the importance of education, he has decided to give $1 million to help illiterate people learn how to read and write.

7. It doesn't matter what my children do. I feel that I have a moral responsibility to _stand by_ them.

8. My son showed _artistic_ talent at a young age. He painted this beautiful picture when he was only ten years old.

9. A _theory_ is an idea or a set of ideas that explain something about life or the world.

10. This essay is _brilliant_. It is one of the most original essays I have ever read.

11. Look at the _remarkable_ color of those roses. I've never seen such a bright red.

Word Families

As you saw in Chapter 1, a suffix can tell you if a word is a noun, adjective, or adverb. Pay attention to suffixes. They contain a lot of information. However, remember that not all words have suffixes.

 A Study the chart and answer the questions.

Noun (person)	Noun (skill, field, or activity)	Verb	Adjective
announcer	announcement	announce	
artist	artistry		artistic
chemist	chemistry		chemical

1. Which two suffixes show that a word refers to a person? __er__ ,

   _____

2. Which two suffixes show that a word refers to a skill, field, or activity? __ent__ , __y__

3. Which two suffixes show that a word is an adjective? _____,

   _____

4. Which word in the chart does not have a suffix? _____

B Complete the sentences with words from the chart. Be careful; you will not use all the words.

1. Who told you? Did he __announce__ it, or did his boss?

2. The radio __announcer__ lost his job because he made too many mistakes when he was reporting the news.

3. She is a famous __artist__. The museum just bought some of her paintings.

4. That __chemical__ company develops products that are used in making new drugs.

5. He studied __chemistry__ in college, and now he works for a company that develops new drugs.

6. To be a good designer, you need both technical skill and __artistry__.

Studying Word Grammar

There are many words and phrases that describe why something happens. Look at the sentences from the reading.

- *He claimed that the high quality of Stradivari's instruments was not **due to** his artistic talent.*
- *Schiff believes that it's **because** the dealers are threatened by the fairly low cost ($3,000 to $22,000) of a Nagyvary violin.*
- *Schiff came from a poor family, **so** she feels very strongly that people who cannot afford Stradivari violins should still be able to have high-quality instruments.*

Due to, because, and *so* all explain why something happens. However, the grammar that follows each one is different. *Due to* is followed by a noun or a noun phrase. *Because* is followed by a full clause (subject + verb). *So* is also followed by a full clause, but it introduces an effect, or result, rather than a cause. Also there is always a comma in front of *so*.

A Complete these sentences with *due to, because,* or *so.*

1. She is successful _____because_____ she has worked hard.
2. Her success is _____due to_____ her hard work.
3. She has worked hard, _____so_____ she is successful.
4. _____due to_____ a family emergency, Frank will not be in this afternoon.

B Write three sentences about your life. Use *due to, because,* and *so.*

1. I didn't do my best for exam, so I had lower scores.
2. Due to my so
3. _____

PUTTING IT ALL TOGETHER

Discussion

Share your ideas in a small group. As you talk, try to use the vocabulary below the question. Each time someone uses a target word or phrase, put a check (✔) next to it.

1. What are some of the ways that artists such as painters, musicians, and dancers use technology in their work?

   artistic/artistry   brilliant   due to   knowledge   remarkable

2. Imagine that you are a group of scientists and musicians, and you have to interview Dr. Nagyvary. Your goal is to find out more about his theory and how and why he developed it. Make a list of the questions you will ask him.

announce/announcement	**chemical**	**proof**
artistic/artistry	**due to**	**remarkable**
belief	**knowledge**	**theory**
brilliant	**laboratory**	**threatened**

Writing

Complete one or both of these writing topics. When you write, use at least five of the target words from the chapter. Underline the target words in your paper.

1. Write a paragraph or short essay describing a mystery that you would like to see scientists solve. Imagine how science could be used to solve the mystery.

2. Imagine that you are Dr. Nagyvary, and write a letter to a newspaper defending your theory. Use the questions that you and your group wrote for question 2 in the Discussion section above as a guide.

CHAPTER 3

The History of Rap

DJ Grand Master Flash

GETTING READY TO READ

  Talk with a partner or in a small group.

1. What kind of music do you like? What kind of music don't you like? Who is your favorite musician or singer?

2. Do you like to sing? Have you ever sung or done some other type of performance (for example, acting or dancing) in front of people? If so, tell your partner about it.

3. Look at the chapter title and the photo. Write three questions that you think the reading will answer.

   a. <u>When did rap music first become popular?</u>

   b. _____

   c. _____

   d. _____

B   The **boldfaced** words below appear in the reading. Which words are new to you? Circle them. Then, work with a partner. Read the definitions of the words, and complete the sentences next to each picture with the words.

equipment = the special tools, machines, etc., that you need for a particular activity or type of work
spinning = turning around and around very quickly
scratched = made a thin mark on a hard surface with something sharp or rough
performer = an actor, musician, dancer, etc., whom people watch

1. She is a _perfermer_.

turntable

2. There is a _spinning_ record on the turntable.

3. The DJ just _scratched_ the record.

4. The DJ has a lot of musical _equipment_.

READING

Read the text once without stopping.

The History of Rap

1   Rap is a spoken form of musical **expression**. It involves words spoken in **rhyme** with a recorded or **live** rhythm section.[1] Many people use the terms "hip hop" and "rap" to mean the same thing. In fact, hip hop is the culture that modern rap **grew out of**. Hip hop is a culture with its own language, clothing styles, music, and ways of thinking, and it is constantly growing and changing. It includes

---

[1] a *rhythm section* = the part of a band that provides a strong beat using drums and other similar instruments

several different art forms, including visual art,[2] dance, and music. Rap is just one part of hip-hop culture.

2   Although there is a lot of disagreement about exactly where and how rap began, most people agree that it got its start in the mostly African-American[3] neighborhoods of the Bronx in New York City in the 1960s. At that time, large outdoor street parties called *block parties* were becoming popular. Young people who could not afford expensive musical instruments or **equipment** took simple turntables[4] and microphones[5] out onto the streets. But instead of just playing the music, they moved the **spinning**, or turning, records with their hands. At the same time, they **scratched** them with the needles of the turntables. The changes in the sound of the music became known as *cutting* or *scratching*. The young people who played the music were called *disc jockeys*. These disc jockeys, or *DJs*, used their turntables as instruments to create a new musical form.

3   Other **performers** working with the DJ **interacted** with the crowd by talking louder than the music, often in rhyme. These performers were called *emcees*, or *MCs*, and their interaction with the crowd became known as *rapping*. Later, the MCs became known as *rappers*. Interaction between the performers and the crowd is an important **characteristic** of rap.

4   Among the many people who **contributed** to the development of rap, artist Grandmaster Flash **stands out**. The **techniques** he invented have become an important part of hip-hop culture. Flash was one of the first DJs to begin using a turntable as a musical instrument, rather than just a piece of equipment that played records. First, he would find a short section of a song that he liked. This was called the *break*. Then he would use two copies of the same record and two turntables to invent creative ways to play the break over and over without stopping.

5   In the 1970s and 1980s rap's popularity grew, and the rhymes became more complex and **clever** as the performers **competed** with each other. The music that they rapped to included recordings of famous African-American musicians and breaks from popular disco[6] and rock music of the time. Many rappers also performed with live musicians.

---

[2] *visual art* = art such as painting that you look at

[3] an *African-American* = a Black American of African ancestry

[4] a *turntable* = the round flat surface on a record player that you put records on

[5] a *microphone* = a piece of equipment that you hold in front of your mouth when you are singing, giving a speech, etc., in order to make your voice sound louder

[6] *disco music* = a type of dance music with a strong repeating beat that was popular in the 1970s

(continued)

6   Today, hip-hop culture is popular all over the world, and young people everywhere listen to rap. There are many reasons for rap's popularity. It offers young people the chance to express themselves freely. It is an art form that can be performed without a lot of money, training, or equipment. Rapping involves verbal[7] skills that many people already have or can develop. You can rap slowly, or you can rap fast. All of this allows rappers with very different **personalities** to express themselves.

7   This does not mean that rapping is easy, however. It **calls for** a quick mind, an ability to use language well, originality, and an excellent sense of rhythm.[8] It presents the performer with many challenges, but only two rules: rhyme to the beat of the music, and be original.

---

[7] *verbal* = spoken, rather than written

[8] *rhythm* = a regular repeated pattern of sounds or music

Comprehension Check

Read these sentences. Circle T (true), F (false), or ? (can't determine the answer from the reading). If you circle F, change the sentence to make it true. You might need to change one or two words, or you might need to rewrite the sentence completely. Check your answers with a classmate. If your answers are different, look back at the reading.

1. Hip hop is a ~~kind of music~~ culture.   T (F) ?
2. Many people confuse rap and hip hop.   T   F   ?
3. Rap got its start in Africa. N . Y   T   F   ?
4. The first rappers didn't have a lot of money.   T   F   ?
5. Rappers do not perform to live music.   T   F   ?
6. To be a good rapper, you need to be able to sing well.   T   F   ?

EXPLORING VOCABULARY

Thinking about the Target Vocabulary

Guessing Strategy

The signal word *or* can help you guess the meaning of unfamiliar words. Look at the examples.

> But instead of just playing the music, they moved the **spinning**, or turning, records with their hands.

> Young people could not afford expensive musical instruments or **equipment**.

In the first sentence, *or* shows that what follows it—*turning*—means the same thing as *spinning*. In the second sentence, *or* shows that the word that follows it—*equipment*—is different in meaning from *musical instruments*. To determine what meaning the word *or* signals, look carefully at the punctuation. If there are commas around *or* and the word(s) following it, the meaning is similar. If there are no commas, the meaning is different.

Try It!

Read the sentences, and write a definition of the boldfaced target words.

1. Rappers can perform to **live** or recorded music.
   Live means _hem or different ways._

2. One of raps' **characteristics**, or special qualities, is that the performers speak to the beat of the music.
   Characteristic means _special qualities_.

 Look at the target words and phrases on page 30. Which ones are new to you? Circle them on page 30 and in the reading. Then read "The History of Rap" again. Look at the context of each new word and phrase. Can you guess the meaning? Use the Guessing Strategy where possible.

Target Words and Phrases

expression (1)	scratched (2)	techniques (4)
rhyme (1)	performers (3)	clever (5)
live (1)	interacted (3)	competed (5)
grew out of (1)	characteristic (3)	personalities (6)
equipment (2)	contributed (4)	calls for (7)
spinning (2)	stands out (4)	

B Look at the word-form chart below with the target words and phrases listed as they are used in the reading. Note that verbs are listed in their base form and nouns in their singular form. Verb phrases are listed under Verbs, and noun phrases under Nouns.

Nouns	Verbs	Adjectives	Other
expression	grow out of	live	
rhyme	scratch	spinning	
equipment	interact	clever	
performer	contribute		
characteristic	stand out		
technique	compete		
personality	call for		

Using the Target Vocabulary

These sentences are about the reading. Circle the meaning of each boldfaced word or phrase. Then circle the words or phrases in the sentences that help you understand the meanings of the target words.

1. Rap is a special type of musical **expression**. Rap performers show their personalities through their music. *Expression* means
   a. something you say, write, or do that shows what you feel.
   b. an instrument that you play with great feeling.
   c. something that is becoming very popular.

2. Rap involves words spoken in **rhyme**, like in some poems. *Rhyme* means
   a. a very loud or very soft voice.
   b. two words ending in the same sound, like "hit" and "sit."
   c. a slow, soft, musical sound like "shhhh."

3. Hip-hop culture existed before rap, so we can say that rap **grew out of** hip-hop culture. *Grew out of* means
    a. had an effect on.
    b. developed from.
    c. created.

4. Rap artists **interact** with the crowd. The crowd shouts things out, and the performers answer them in rhyme. *Interact* means
    a. argue.
    b. communicate.
    c. sing.

5. In fact, crowd and performer interaction is one of the **characteristics** of rap. *Characteristics* means
    a. important problems.
    b. fastest parts.
    c. special qualities.

6. Grandmaster Flash **contributed** a lot to the development of rap. *Contributed* means
    a. sang.
    b. gave.
    c. spent.

7. Grandmaster Flash wasn't the only person who was involved in rap's development, but his work **stands out**. It was very important to rap's popularity. *Stands out* means
    a. is clearly better.
    b. is much harder.
    c. is a lot faster.

8. Flash invented a **technique** that involved using two turntables as musical instruments. *Technique* means
    a. special way of dancing.
    b. machine to make music.
    c. special skill that needs to be learned.

9. Rappers are good at using language, so their rhymes are often very **clever**. *Clever* means
   a. fast and difficult to understand.
   b. unusual and interesting.
   c. loud and funny.

10. Rap artists **compete** with each other to make the best rhymes. *Compete* means
    a. try to be stronger than someone else.
    b. try to be better than someone else.
    c. try to be kinder than someone else.

11. Every rapper has a different way of performing. That's because each rapper has his or her own special **personality** and way of expressing himself or herself. *Personality* means
    a. person who helps them in their work.
    b. people who like their way of performing.
    c. character and way of behaving.

12. Rapping is not easy. It **calls for** many different skills. *Calls for* means
    a. teaches.
    b. achieves.
    c. needs.

13. Sometimes rappers perform to **live** music, and sometimes they perform to recorded music. *Live* means
    a. performed with many singers or musicians.
    b. performed for people who are watching.
    c. performed in a new or different way.

DEVELOPING READING SKILLS

Scanning

A **Where is the information about these topics in "The History of Rap"? Scan the reading, and write the paragraph number (1–7).**

_3_ **a.** MCs and rappers

_1_ **b.** how rap and hip hop are related

_5_ **c.** the development of rap in the 1970s and 1980s

_6_ **d.** why rap is popular

_4_ **e.** Grandmaster Flash's contributions to rap

_2_ **f.** how rap got its start

_7_ **g.** the challenges of rap

B **Write a sentence or two about each of the seven topics from paragraphs 1–7. Use information from the reading, but do not copy. Use your own words.**

Paragraph 1: <u>Hip hop is a culture that includes several different art forms. One of the art forms is rap.</u>

Paragraph 2: There is a lot of disagreement about where and how rap began.

Paragraph 3: Emcees are performers, they work with DJ.

Paragraph 4: Grandmaster was one of the first who began to contribute develop. of rap.

Paragraph 5: In 1970-80s rap's became more popular.

Paragraph 6: Hip-hop is popular all over the world.

Paragraph 7: Rapping is very difficult reqs. lot of quality.

Understanding Topics and Main Ideas

Answer this question.

What is the main idea of "The History of Rap"? Write a full sentence.

_____

EXPANDING VOCABULARY

Using the Target Vocabulary in New Contexts

Complete the sentences with the target words and phrases in the box. Be careful. There are two extra words or phrases.

calls for	contributes	live	spinning
characteristics	expression	performers	stands out
clever	grew out of	personality	technique
competing	interact	rhyme	

1. I love his _characteristics_. He's so clever, funny, and kind.
2. We need somebody really special for this job. The job _____ someone who is artistic, smart, and ready to work hard.
3. Police officers who work in big cities have to _interact_ with all different kinds of people every day.
4. He is one of the most brilliant students I've ever had. He really _stands out_
5. That artist uses a special _technique_ to make his colors look very bright.
6. What a _clever_ idea! You have a great imagination.
7. Stories for very young children are often written in _rhyme_. Little children like them because they sound like songs.
8. The two brothers are always _competing_ for their parents' attention. It's really sad.
9. She _____ about $1,000 a year to a children's hospital.

10. She plays the piano with wonderful _____. She hasn't been playing for a long time, but she knows how to communicate her feelings through her playing.

11. One of the most important _____ of a musical performer is talent.

12. It is much more exciting to go to a _____ live _____ performance than to watch it on TV.

13. His desire to become an artist _____ his fascination with color as a child.

Word Families

In Chapters 1 and 2, you learned that the suffixes *-ity*, *-ry*, and *-ment* show that a word is a noun, and the suffixes *-er* and *-ist* show that a word is not only a noun but also a person. Other common suffixes for nouns are *-ion*, *-tion*, and *-ance*. Often, these suffixes are added to verbs to change them to nouns.

A Add the correct suffix to make the noun form. Use your dictionary to check your answers.

Verb Form	Noun Form
express	expression
perform	
interact	interaction
compete	competition
contribute	contribution
fascinate	fascination

B Complete the sentences with the nouns from Part A.

1. He's usually a great actor, but his _performin_ in that movie was not very good.

2. Our team won the _competition_.

3. I think that babies should have _contribution_ with a lot of different kinds of people, not just their mothers or fathers.

4. Your _interaction_ to the work of the team was very important. Thank you!

5. She wrote him a poem as an _exp r_____ of her love.

6. I don't understand your _fasci nation_ with cars. What is so interesting about them?

Studying Phrasal Verbs

Stand out and **call for** are **phrasal verbs**. Phrasal verbs have two or more parts: a verb (such as *stand* or *call*) and one or more particles (such as *out* or *for*). The meaning of a phrasal verb is different from the meaning of just the verb alone. In Chapter 2, you learned the phrasal verb *stand by.*

Rewrite the underlined part of these sentences using the phrasal verbs *stand by, stand out,* **and** *call for.* **You may need to change the form of the verb to fit the sentence.**

1. Many of the musicians have some talent, but only two of them <u>are really remarkable</u>. _____

_____stands out_____

2. If you really believe in something, you should <u>defend</u> it. _____

_____stand by_____

3. That job <u>requires</u> someone who is very strong. _____

_____call for_____

PUTTING IT ALL TOGETHER

Discussion

Work in a small group.

1. Ask each other these questions about music. Have one person write down everyone's responses. Decide who enjoys music most and who enjoys it least. Tell the class a few of the most interesting things you found out about each other.

   a. How many CDs do you buy a year?

     1. 0–5   **3.** 16–25

     2. 6–15   **4.** more than 25

b. How much time on average do you spend listening to music every day?

    1. none or almost none   **3.** 30 minutes

    2. about 15 minutes   **4.** an hour or more

c. How many CDs (or cassettes or records) do you own?

    1. fewer than 10   **3.** 31–50

    2. 11–30   **4.** more than 50

d. How many concerts do you go to a year?

    1. none   **3.** 3–5

    2. 1 or 2   **4.** 6 or more

e. How do you usually listen to music?

    1. on my computer   **3.** on an iPod

    2. on the radio   **4.** on a CD player

f. Check (✓) all of the statements that are true for you.

    _____ I listen to music while I study or work.

    _____ I listen to music when I feel sad.

    _____ I listen to music when I feel happy.

    _____ I like to dance when I listen to music.

    _____ I listen to music when I want to relax.

    _____ Listening to music helps me fall asleep.

g. How often do you get music off the Internet?

    1. never   **3.** sometimes

    2. rarely   **4.** often

2. The reading describes rap in a very positive way. However, although rap is very popular in many parts of the world, there are some people who really don't like it. In fact, older people often do not like music that is popular with younger people. Why do you think this is true? Discuss your ideas. Try to use the vocabulary below the question in your discussion. Each time someone uses a target word, put a check (✓) next to it.

characteristic   **interact/interaction**

compete/competition   **live**

contribute/contribution   **performer/perform/performance**

express/expression   **personality**

Writing

Complete one or both of these writing topics. When you write, use at least five of the target words from the chapter. Underline the target words in your paper.

1. Choose a type of music that you like, and do some research on it (either at the library or on the Internet). Then, write an essay about it. Your essay should include the following information:

   - A description of the music (for instance, the instruments used)
   - The history of this type of music (where, when, and how it got its start)
   - Well-known performers of this type of music
   - Why you like it

2. Imagine that you have the opportunity to interview a famous performer (living or dead). Make a list of at least ten questions that you would like to ask during the interview.

REVIEWING READING SKILLS AND VOCABULARY

Read the text. Do not use a dictionary.

1   Among the many talented artists of the twentieth century, Spanish painter Pablo Ruiz Picasso stands out. Due to his brilliant talent and originality, he is considered by many to be the most important artist of his time.

2   Picasso was born in 1881 in Málaga, Spain. His father was an art teacher, and he knew very early that his son Pablo was remarkably talented. At the age of fourteen, Picasso entered the Academy of Fine Arts in Barcelona, Spain. In one day, he completed the entrance test that traditionally took students a month to finish.

3   From 1900 to 1904, Picasso lived in both Spain and France. During that time, he worked in a completely original style, which became known as his Blue Period. The name came from Picasso's use of only the color blue in his paintings of the time. In 1904, Picasso moved to France, where he began working in a variety of modern artistic styles.

4   One of Picasso's many contributions to the history of art was the invention of the artistic technique of collage—using materials such as letters, cloth, or pieces of newspaper to make a piece of art. He was also involved in the development of cubism—a new style of modern art in which people and things are painted using shapes such as triangles and squares. In fact, many people consider Picasso's 1907 painting *Les Demoiselles d'Avignon* the first cubist painting.

5   Picasso's popularity today might make one forget that throughout his lifetime, he challenged Western European artistic traditions. Picasso died in 1973, but the beauty, complexity, and originality of his artistry live on in the many works he left behind.

Comprehension Check

Read these sentences. Circle T (true), F (false), or ? (can't determine the answer from the reading). If you circle F, change the sentence to make it true.

1. Picasso had a great influence on modern art.   T   F   ?
2. Picasso's father taught him how to paint.   T   F   ?
3. *Les Demoiselles d'Avignon* was painted during
   Picasso's Blue Period.   T   F   ?
4. Picasso was not the only painter to contribute to
   the development of cubism.   T   F   ?
5. Picasso did most of his work in a traditional style.   T   F   ?

Guessing Meaning from Context

Answer this question.

What is the meaning of *Academy* in paragraph 2?

_____

Understanding Inference

Check (✔) the sentences that you can infer from the text. Remember, an inference is not written directly in the text. You have to think about what the text says, and make a logical conclusion.

_____ 1. Picasso began to paint before the age of fourteen.

_____ 2. In his lifetime as a painter, Picasso used the color blue more
         than any other color.

_____ 3. Collage is a technique that is still used by artists today.

_____ 4. Picasso was not a popular artist when he was alive.

_____ 5. Picasso knew how to paint in a traditional style.

Scanning

Scan the reading to find the information to complete the sentences.

1. Pablo Picasso is considered one of the greatest painters of modern
   times because

_____

_____ .

2. The years from 1900 to 1904 were called Picasso's Blue Period because

_____

_____.

3. *Les Demoiselles d'Avignon* is a very important painting because

_____

_____.

4. Picasso's contributions to art did not end with his death because

_____

_____.

EXPANDING VOCABULARY

Studying Phrasal Verbs

As you learned in Chapter 3, a **phrasal verb** has a verb and one or more particles. *Stand by* and *stand out* are phrasal verbs. It is often difficult to figure out the *exact* meaning of a phrasal verb, but you can get a *general idea* of the meaning by thinking about the meaning of the verb and the particle(s). The context will help you gain a more complete understanding of the meaning.

 A **Read these sentences. Match the phrasal verbs to their definitions.**

1. Why are you just **standing around**? Don't you have any work to do?

2. His name is Philip J. Johnson. The "*J*" **stands for** his middle name, Jackson, which was his grandfather's name.

3. I don't understand why you let him treat you so badly. Why don't you **stand up for** yourself?

4. He's my boss. I don't like the way he treats me, but if I **stand up to** him, I might lose my job.

Phrasal Verb	Definition
1. stand around	**a.** support or defend a person or idea that is being attacked
2. stand for	**b.** refuse to accept bad or unfair treatment from a person or organization
3. stand up for	**c.** stand somewhere and not do anything
4. stand up to	**d.** represent a word, name, or idea, especially in a short form

B On a piece of paper, write your own sentences with the phrasal verbs from Part A.

Word Families

As you learned in Chapters 1–3, different word forms have different suffixes.

A Put each suffix in the box into the correct category in the chart.

-al	-er	-ion	-ity	-ry
-ance	-ic	-ist	-ment	-tion

Noun (person)	Noun (not a person)	Adjective

B Complete these sentences with the words in the box. All of the words are related to target words from the unit.

complexity	involvement	relevance	technical	theorist

1. He got into trouble because of his _complex_ in criminal activity.

2. How is that point connected to what we are discussing? What is its _____ to the topic?

3. The _____ of that chemistry problem makes it very difficult to solve.

4. When you study computers, you must learn the _____ language that people who work with computers use.

5. She studies how different cultures are related, and then writes about her ideas. She is a cultural _____.

PLAYING WITH WORDS

Complete the puzzle with words you studied in Chapters 1–3.

Across

2. talk to other people, work together with them, etc.

6. something you say, write, do, or make that shows what you think or feel

10. very, very bad

11. facts, information, papers, etc., that prove that something is true

12. connected in some way

13. something that is difficult, especially in a way that is interesting

14. a quality that things, places, or people have that makes them attractive to look at

Down

1. the place where scientists or researchers do their work

3. produced first (for example, a movie); not copied or based on anything else

4. the feeling that something is definitely true or definitely exists

5. something important that someone says

7. make a thin mark on a hard surface with something sharp or rough

8. according to what people say or report

9. very fast

BUILDING DICTIONARY SKILLS

Finding Phrasal Verbs

Phrasal verbs do not have their own entries in most dictionaries. They are part of the entry for the verb. Usually, the phrasal verbs are listed at the end of all the definitions for the verb.

Look at the dictionary entry for phrasal verbs with *call*.

> **call¹** /kɔl/ *v* **1** TELEPHONE [I,T] to telephone someone: *I called about six o'clock.* | *He said he'd call me tomorrow* . . . **9** CALL IT A DAY *spoken* said when you want to stop working, either because you are tired or because you have done enough: *Come on, guys, let's call it a day.*   **call** (sb) **back** *phr v* to telephone someone again, or to telephone someone who tried to telephone you earlier: *Okay, I'll call back around three.* | *Can I call you back later?*   **call for** sth *phr v* **1** to ask publicly for something to be done: *Parents are calling for a return to basics in education.* **2** to need or deserve a particular type of behavior or treatment: *a situation that calls for immediate action* **3** to say that a particular type of weather is likely to happen: *The forecast calls for more rain.*   **call in** *phr v* **1** **call** sb ↔ **in** to ask or order someone to come and help you with a difficult situation: *The governor called in the National Guard to deal with the riots.*   **2** to telephone the place where you work, especially to report something: *Jan called in sick this morning.* **3** to telephone a radio or television show to give your opinion or ask a question   **call** sb/sth ↔ **off** *phr v* **1** to decide that a planned event will not happen or will not continue: *The game had to be called off due to bad weather.* **2** to order a dog or person to stop attacking someone: *Call off your dog!* **call on** *phr v* **1** to formally ask someone to do something: *The UN has called on both sides to observe the cease fire.* **2** to visit someone for a short time: *a salesman calling on customers*   **call out** *phr v* **1 call** (sth ↔) **out** to say something loudly: *"Phone for you," Rosie called out.* **2 call** sb/sth ↔ **out** to ask or order someone to come help you in a difficult situation: *The Army has been called out to help fight the fires.* **call up** *phr v* **1 call** (sb ↔) **up** to telephone someone: *Dave called me up to tell me about it.* **2 call** sth ↔ **up** IT to make information appear on a computer screen

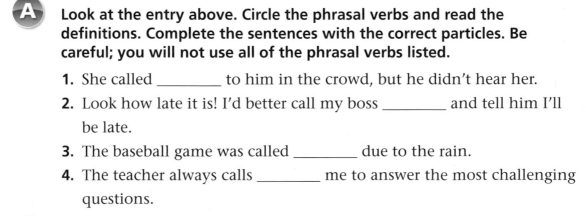

A **Look at the entry above. Circle the phrasal verbs and read the definitions. Complete the sentences with the correct particles. Be careful; you will not use all of the phrasal verbs listed.**

1. She called _____ to him in the crowd, but he didn't hear her.

2. Look how late it is! I'd better call my boss _____ and tell him I'll be late.

3. The baseball game was called _____ due to the rain.

4. The teacher always calls _____ me to answer the most challenging questions.

B **Write your own sentences with the phrasal verbs from Part A.**

2

THE CHALLENGES OF YOUTH

CHAPTER 4

Sleepy Teens

Why is this teenager so sleepy?

GETTING READY TO READ

 Complete the activity below. Then, talk with a partner or in a small group about the results.

Walk around the class, and ask your classmates about their sleeping habits. Try to find at least one person for each category. Write their names in the chart. Ask your classmates if they are happy with their sleep habits. If not, what would they like to change?

Gets enough sleep	Doesn't get enough sleep	Falls asleep during class	Sleeps less than 6 hours a night	Sleeps more than 8 hours a night	Likes to take naps	Usually goes to bed before 12:00

B The **boldfaced** words and phrases below appear in the reading. Which words are new to you? Circle them. Then, work with a partner. Read the definitions of the words, and complete the sentences next to each picture with the words.

> **experiment** = a scientific test done to find out how something or someone will react in a particular situation, or to find out if a theory is true
>
> **patterns** = regularly repeated arrangement of shapes, lines, or colors on a surface
>
> **in tears** = crying
>
> **depressed** = feeling very unhappy

1. The researchers in the sleep laboratory are doing an _experiment_. They want to find out if teenagers' brains are active when they are sleeping.

2. They are checking the brain wave _patterns_ of the people who are sleeping.

3. Like many other teenagers, this girl is _depressed_. Sleep researchers think that it might be because she is not getting enough sleep.

4. This boy tried to go to bed at 8:30. He is _in tears_ because he is upset that he can't fall asleep.

READING

Read the text once without stopping.

Sleepy Teens

1   When school superintendent[1] Russell Dever enters the local coffee shop at around 7:20 A.M., it is crowded with students. "The line is out the door because our high school kids are getting coffee," he said.

2   And they are not standing in line for the decaf[2]—they need the caffeine[3] to stay awake in class. Talk to American high school students and you hear the **complaints** about how late they **stay up**, how little they sleep—and how early they must be in class.

3   These days, there is increasing **concern** in schools across the United States about students who are not completely awake in morning classes. School **officials** in some states have even changed start times so teenagers can sleep later.

4   According to sleep **expert** Mary Carskadon, the fact that many teenagers work long hours outside of school and have computers and televisions in their bedrooms contributes to a serious **lack** of sleep. But, she said, the problem is also due to biology.[4] As the bodies of teenagers develop, their brains also change. These changes make teens more **likely** than adults to have trouble sleeping at night.

5   Teenagers need **at least** eight to nine hours of sleep a night, but the average teen gets a lot less. Carskadon's study, completed in the fall of 2001 with researcher Amy Wolfson, showed that nearly 30 percent of students in the tenth grade slept less than six hours on school nights. Less than 15 percent got more than eight hours of sleep each night. Eighth-graders averaged eight hours of sleep a night, although that age group, she said, needs at least nine hours a night.

6   Even more remarkable are the results of a 1997–1998 school year study. In that study, 12 out of 24 U.S. high school students who

---

[1] a *school superintendent* = someone who is responsible for all of the schools in a particular area of the United States

[2] *decaf* = short form of the phrase *decaffeinated coffee*, coffee that has had the caffeine removed

[3] *caffeine* = the chemical substance in coffee, tea, and some other drinks that makes people feel more active

[4] *biology* = the scientific study of living things

were part of an **experiment** at a sleep laboratory had brain wave **patterns** similar to those of someone with narcolepsy, a serious condition that affects sleep. "What's going on is that at 8:30 in the morning these kids . . . would normally be in school sitting in a classroom, but . . . their brain is still in the middle of the night," said Carskadon.

7   Parent Dawn Dow says her son just cannot go to bed before 10 P.M. "Last year he was trying to put himself to bed at 8:30 and was coming in at 9:30 and 10 **in tears** saying, 'I just can't go to sleep.' It is not a case of children wanting to be up late. . . . It is a change in his chemistry."

8   So would letting teenagers wake up later make a difference? Kyla Wahlstrom of the University of Minnesota in the United States studies the effects of changing school start times. She has looked at students in Edina and Minneapolis, two cities in Minnesota, where public school officials have moved high school starting times past 8:30 A.M. In Minneapolis, the middle school begins at 9:30 A.M. She said the later starting times have **reduced** student **absences**. They have also lowered **dropout** rates by 8 percent over four years. In addition, she said, teachers report that students are not sleeping at their desks during the first two hours of class anymore. She said 92 percent of parents from Edina reported that their teenagers are easier to live with. The students reported that they were feeling less **depressed** and were getting better grades.

9   Big changes in school start times may not be possible in some areas. However, Wahlstrom said her research shows that even small changes can contribute to a solution to this serious problem.

Notes

Mary Carskadon is professor of psychiatry[5] and human behavior at Brown University in Providence, Rhode Island, U.S.A., and director of sleep and chronobiology[6] at Bradley Hospital in East Providence, Rhode Island, U.S.A.

Amy Wolfson is a researcher at the College of the Holy Cross in Worcester, Massachusetts, U.S.A.

Kyla Wahlstrom is associate director[7] of the Center for Applied Research and Educational Improvement at the University of Minnesota, U.S.A.

---

[5] *psychiatry* = the study and treatment of mental illness

[6] *chronobiology* = the study of the effects of time on living things

[7] an *associate director* = someone who assists the director

Comprehension Check

Read these sentences. Circle T (true), F (false), or ? (can't determine the answer from the reading). If you circle F, change the sentence to make it true. Check your answers with a classmate. If your answers are different, look back at the reading.

1. Most teenagers sleep more than they should.   T   F   ?

2. There are scientific reasons that explain why teenagers have difficulty sleeping at night.   T   F   ?

3. The brains of teenagers are the same as the brains of adults.   T   F   ?

4. Teenagers can do their best schoolwork in the early morning.   T   F   ?

5. It's easier for adults to fall asleep at night than teenagers.   T   F   ?

6. Some schools start their classes later so that teenage students can get more sleep in the morning.   T   F   ?

7. Many parents do not want high school officials to change school start times.   T   F   ?

EXPLORING VOCABULARY

Thinking about the Target Vocabulary

Guessing Strategy

Often, writers don't want to repeat a word, so they use a **synonym**. Synonyms are words that have similar meanings. If you don't know a word, look at the sentences nearby to see if there is a synonym. Look at the example.

*Some students who don't get enough sleep get **depressed**. And because they feel so unhappy, they can't concentrate on their schoolwork.*

Based on the context, you can guess that the words *depressed* and *unhappy* are similar in meaning.

Try It!

Circle the word in the second sentence that is a synonym for the boldfaced target word.

She said the later starting times have **reduced** student absences.

They have also lowered dropout rates by 8 percent over four years.

A Look at the target words and phrases. Which ones are new to you? Circle them here and in the reading. Then read "Sleepy Teens" again. Look at the context of each new word and phrase. Can you guess the meaning? Use the Guessing Strategy where possible.

Target Words and Phrases

complaints (2)	expert (4)	experiment (6)	absences (8)
stay up (2)	lack (4)	patterns (6)	dropout (8)
concern (3)	likely (4)	in tears (7)	depressed (8)
officials (3)	at least (5)	reduced (8)	

B Complete the word-form chart with the target words and phrases as they are used in the reading. Write the base form of verbs and the singular form of nouns.

Nouns	Verbs	Adjectives	Other
complaint	complain	likely	
exper.	stay up		
officials	reduced		
	concern.		

Using the Target Vocabulary

These sentences are **about the reading**. Complete them with the words and phrases in the box. Circle the words or phrases in the sentences that help you understand the meanings of the target words. Be careful. There are two extra words or phrases.

absences	concern	in tears	official	reduced
at least	dropout	lack	patterns	stay up
complaint	experts	likely		

1. Russell Dever is a school _official_. He is responsible for several schools.

2. High school students _stay up_ late at night, so they have trouble waking up early to go to school.

3. A common _complaint_ from young people is that they don't get enough sleep. They are unhappy that school begins so early.

4. Some parents and school officials are worried that many high school students are too tired to learn. Because of their _concern_, some school officials have decided to change the time when high school classes start.

5. Researchers who study sleep patterns say that teenagers get much less sleep than they really need. According to these _experts_, there are many reasons for this serious _lack_ of sleep.

6. The main reason that teenagers are more _likely_ to have trouble sleeping than adults is that their bodies are changing.

7. Most teenagers need _at least_ eight hours of sleep a night. In fact, it's even better if they get nine or ten hours.

8. When teenagers don't get enough sleep, they are more likely to miss class. In one school where start times were changed from 8:30 A.M. to 9:30 A.M., there are now fewer _absences_. The later start times seem to have _reduced_ the number of students who don't go to class because they can't wake up in the morning.

9. The later start times have also lowered the _dropout_ rate. This means that fewer students are quitting school.

DEVELOPING READING SKILLS

Understanding Main Ideas, Major Points, and Supporting Details

A reading generally has one **main idea**, with several **major points** to support it. Those major points are supported by **supporting details**. For example, in "Sleepy Teens" there is one main idea, three major points to support it, and many supporting details to illustrate the major points.

Answer these questions.

1. What is the main idea of "Sleepy Teens"?
   a. Some schools in the United States are experimenting with later school start times because experts say that teenagers will be happier and do better in school if they get more sleep.
   b. Many teenagers have difficulty falling asleep at night because of the biological changes in their brains and because they have televisions and computers in their rooms.
   c. Most American teenagers are depressed because they do not get enough sleep.

2. Match the major points and their supporting details. Be careful. Some of the major points have more than one supporting detail.

Major Points

_b_ 1. There are many reasons that teenagers have trouble sleeping at night.

_a_ 2. Research shows that many teenagers do not get enough sleep.

_e_ 3. Schools that are experimenting with later start times are happy with the results.

Supporting Details

a. Thirty percent of students in the tenth grade sleep less than six hours on school nights.

b. Many teenagers work long hours outside of school.

c. There are biological changes in the brains of teenagers that make it difficult for them to fall asleep at night.

d. In one school that changed its start time from 8:30 to 9:30 A.M., the number of student absences has gone down.

e. The students feel less depressed and get better grades when they get enough sleep.

EXPANDING VOCABULARY

Using the Target Vocabulary in New Contexts

Complete the sentences with the target words and phrases in the box. Be careful. There are two extra words or phrases.

absences	depressed	expert	official
at least	dropout	lack	reduce
complaint	experiments	likely	stay up
concern			

1. She has written more than ten books on education. She is an _____ on the subject.

2. I don't remember exactly how much money I have in the bank, but I know it's _____ $500. I might have more. I'll have to call the bank to check.

3. I'm going to take a nap so that I can _____ late to watch that TV special.

4. Take your umbrella. The weather report said that rain is _____ later this afternoon.

5. The service in that restaurant was terrible. I'm going to write a letter of _____ to the manager.

6. Thank you for your _____, but I'm fine. Don't worry about me.

7. If you want to lose weight, you must _____ the amount of food that you eat.

8. They are concerned about their son's complete _____ of interest in his studies. He doesn't seem to be interested in any subject.

9. You have too many _____. You need to make sure you attend all of the rest of the classes, or you will have to repeat the course.

10. My town has a serious _____ problem. Students are leaving high school early and can't find jobs.

11. He works for the government. He is the _____ who is responsible for public safety.

Word Families

Look at the target words in the box. Then, in the paragraph below, circle the words that are related to these target words, and complete the chart with the words you circled.

absence	concern	dropout	official
complaint	depressed	experiment	reduced

It's 7:20 A.M., and teenagers are standing in line on the sidewalk in front of the local coffee shop. They (complain) that school starts too early in the morning, so they have to drink coffee to stay awake in class. They also complain of being depressed. Some students are absent because they can't wake up, and students who are absent a lot are more likely to drop out of school. This concerns many parents and school officials, so some schools are experimenting with a change in school start times. They hope that if teens can sleep a little later in the morning, they will be able to pay better attention in class. They also hope that the later start times will result in a reduction in the number of students who miss class. And some teens are reporting that their depression has disappeared since they started getting more sleep. If the experiment works, the schools will probably make the change official.

Nouns	Verbs	Adjectives
absence official reduction depression experiment	complain ~~absent~~ concerns experimenting drop out	depressed absent official

Studying Word Grammar

Some adjectives are formed by adding *-ing* or *-ed* to the end of a verb. These adjectives are called **participial adjectives**. Look at the examples.

Verb	Participial Adjective (*-ing* form)	Participial Adjective (*-ed* form)
Expresses an action	Describes a person or thing that **causes** a feeling or reaction	Describes a person who **experiences** a feeling or reaction
*The story **depresses** John.*	*It is a **depressing** story.*	*John felt **depressed** after reading the story.*

A Complete the sentences with the *-ing* or *-ed* form of the **boldfaced** verbs.

1. Your theory **fascinates** me. I think it is _fascinating_.
2. Science **fascinates** my daughter. She is _fascinated_ by everything related to science.
3. That teacher likes to **challenge** her students. The homework she gives is usually _challenging_.
4. I like my teachers to **challenge** me. I learn more when I feel _challenged_.
5. If you **threaten** a wild animal, it might attack you. When wild animals feel _threatened_, they often react with violence.
6. It is against the law to **threaten** someone with words or actions. I am going to report his _threatening_ behavior to the police.

B Working with a partner, answer the questions. Make sure you use the correct form of the **boldfaced** words.

1. What is the most **fascinating** movie that you have ever seen? Explain why you felt so **fascinated** by it.
2. If a friend feels **depressed**, what can you do to make him or her feel better?
3. What is the most **challenging** thing that you have ever done?
4. Do you like easy classes, or do you prefer to feel **challenged**? Why?
5. What are some of the things people do when they feel **threatened**?

PUTTING IT ALL TOGETHER

Discussion

Share your ideas in a small group. As you talk, try to use the vocabulary below. Each time someone uses a target word or phrase, put a check (✔) next to it.

absence	lack
at least	likely
complaint	official
concern/concerned	reduce/reduction
depressed/depressing/depression	stay up
dropout/drop out	

1. Talk about problems that specifically affect teenagers. Give your opinion about the causes of the problems, and as a group come up with some possible solutions.

2. Not everyone agrees that changing school start times is such a good idea. As a group, come up with as many reasons as you can why schools should **not** change their start times.

Writing

Complete one or both of these writing topics. When you write, use at least five of the target words from the chapter. Underline the target words in your paper.

1. Imagine that you are the parent of a teenage girl in the Edina school system, and you do not agree with the change in the school start times. Write a letter about your concerns to an official at your daughter's high school.

2. Choose a problem that affects teenagers, and write an essay explaining the problems, the causes, and some possible solutions. Be sure to support your major points with details.

CHAPTER 5

Growing Up Gifted

Chess prodigy Pascal Charbonneau in 2003

GETTING READY TO READ

 A **Talk with a partner or in a small group.**

1. Do you have a special skill or talent (for example in sports, music, painting, mathematics, science)? What is it? At what age did you become aware that you had talent?

2. If you could choose to be talented in one thing, what would you choose? Why?

3. A *child prodigy* is someone who shows remarkable talent in a particular subject at a very young age. Put a check (✓) next to the phrases that you believe would describe most child prodigies. Compare your answers, and discuss any differences.

✓ know a lot about many different things	✓ have a large vocabulary
____ want to be perfect	____ love school
____ are happy	✓ are original thinkers
____ are self-confident	

The **boldfaced** words and phrases in the sentences below appear in the reading. Which words are new to you? Circle them. Then, work with a partner. Read the sentences about the reading, and choose the correct answers.

1. Pascal Charbonneau is an extremely talented chess player who has won many games. He is only a teenager, but he has already **achieved** more than most players twice his age. Someone who has *achieved* a lot has

   a. succeeded after trying hard.

   b. made a lot of money.

   c. played very well.

2. In general, very talented young people like Pascal **tend to** enjoy learning about different things. Usually, they are interested in many subjects, not only the one in which they have talent. If you *tend to* do something, you

   a. take care of it.

   b. are involved in it.

   c. are likely to do it.

3. It is not easy to **survive** in the world of professional chess. Only the strongest players do well and earn enough money to live on. *Survive* means

   a. be successful enough to continue doing something.

   b. have fun and want to continue doing something.

   c. decide to stop doing something.

4. Although he is very talented at chess, Pascal doesn't feel different from his **peers**. He thinks that he's just an average teenager. Your *peers* are

   a. your parents.

   b. your teachers.

   c. other people your age.

Read the text once without stopping.

Growing Up Gifted

1   Canadian teen chess[1] player Pascal Charbonneau has all the qualities of a child prodigy. He is smart, knows a lot about a variety of subjects, has **achieved** a lot at a young age, and is confident in his abilities. But Charbonneau does not like to be called a prodigy. "Winning a **championship** at this age is considered special, but I don't like thinking of myself as someone who is very different from other people," he said.

2   Like many eighteen-year-olds, Charbonneau is trying to decide where to go to college. School has always been easy for him, as it is for most **gifted** students. Many gifted students choose to finish school early to avoid getting bored, but Charbonneau decided to cruise through[2] his classes so he could **concentrate on** chess and some of his other interests, such as sports and French **literature**.

3   In general, gifted students **tend to** have an insatiable appetite[3] for information. They are also **perfectionists**. In addition, most are independent and **sensitive** to **injustice**. Other characteristics include specific ability in one area along with the ability to concentrate on it for a long time, excellent reading ability, a large vocabulary, originality, rapid mastery[4] of new skills, and an ability to see connections between ideas.

4   Having these characteristics can be challenging, even depressing, said Charbonneau. He is **critical** of even his best performances. "I'm rarely ever happy with what I do."

5   Charbonneau knows that the **pressure** on him will soon begin to grow, as every young chess player tries to become the next champion. That pressure has destroyed a lot of talented young people. For example, many young musical prodigies have walked away from their careers after discovering they will not become the star[5] of their dreams, says Francois Gagne. Gagne is an expert on

---

[1] *chess* = a game for two players who move their playing pieces across a special board to try to get their opponent's King

[2] *cruise through* = do something well with very little effort

[3] *have an insatiable appetite* = want more and more of something

[4] *mastery* = complete understanding or great skill

[5] a *star* = a famous and successful performer in entertainment

gifted children at the University of Quebec at Montreal, Canada. "When you are a prodigy, your goal is to become an international master musician," he said. "If you cannot become someone at the very top,[6] you are not interested in becoming a musician in an orchestra."[7]

6   World-famous violinist Itzhak Perlman has seen many talented young musicians simply **burn out**. "Rarely do you see people **survive**, and that's the goal, to survive your gift," he once told the *New York Times*.

7   Between 2 and 5 percent of young people are gifted, two to three years beyond their **peers**. But extremely gifted prodigies—the Beethovens and Mozarts—are much less common, perhaps one in a million, said Gagne. Here are some facts about several well-known child prodigies:

- Probably the most famous child prodigy of all, Wolfgang Amadeus Mozart (1756–1791) began writing music before he was five. By age six, he had written a remarkable amount of music and performed throughout Europe.

- Some of Ludwig van Beethoven's (1770–1827) music was **published** when he was only twelve. **Despite** losing his hearing as an adult, he continued to write music until his death.

- It is often said that the great scientist Albert Einstein (1879–1955) failed at school. In fact, he did well and could be described as a prodigy. Einstein was always a high achiever, although his best work was done when he was in his twenties.

---

[6] *at the very top* = successful and famous

[7] an *orchestra* = a large group of musicians playing many kinds of instruments

Comprehension Check

Read these sentences. Circle T (true), F (false), or ? (can't determine the answer from the reading). If you circle F, change the sentence to make it true. Check your answers with a classmate. If your answers are different, look back at the reading.

1. Pascal Charbonneau enjoys the attention he gets for being a child prodigy.   T (F) ?

2. Most child prodigies like to spend all of their time on just one subject.   T F ?

3. Gifted students often finish school earlier than their peers.   (T) F ?

4. Gifted children usually have the ability to study or practice one subject for a long time, until they become almost perfect at it.

 T F ?

5. Most gifted children have parents who put a lot of pressure on them to succeed.

T F ?

6. Most musical prodigies become famous musicians.

T F ?

EXPLORING VOCABULARY

Thinking about the Target Vocabulary

Guessing Strategy

You learned in Chapter 2 that one way to guess the meaning of an adjective is to determine whether it has a positive or negative meaning. In fact, the same strategy can be used with any part of speech—adjective, noun, verb, or adverb. Look at the example.

*He's smart, has **achieved** a lot at a young age, and is confident in his abilities.*

Because the words *smart* and *confident* have positive meanings, you should be able to guess that the verb *achieve* has a positive meaning too.

Try It!

Find these target words or phrases in the reading. Do they have a positive or a negative meaning? Write P (positive) or N (negative).

burn out _N_   championship _P_   critical _N_

 A Look at the target words and phrases on page 63. Which ones are new to you? Circle them on page 63 and in the reading. Then read "Growing Up Gifted" again. Look at the context of each new word and phrase. Can you guess the meaning? Use the Guessing Strategy where possible.

Target Words and Phrases		
achieved (1)	perfectionists (3)	burn out (6)
championship (1)	sensitive (3)	survive (6)
gifted (2)	injustice (3)	peers (7)
concentrate on (2)	critical (4)	published (7)
literature (2)	pressure (5)	despite (7)
tend to (3)		

B Complete the word-form chart with the target words and phrases as they are used in the reading. Write the base form of verbs and the singular form of nouns.

Nouns	Verbs	Adjectives	Other
	achieve		

Using the Target Vocabulary

These sentences are **about the reading**. Complete them with the words and phrases in the box. Circle the words or phrases in the sentences that help you understand the meanings of the target words. Be careful. There are two extra words or phrases.

achieved	critical	literature	published
burn out	despite	perfectionists	sensitive
championships	gifted	pressure	survive
concentrate on	injustice		

1. __Gifted__ children have special talents, and usually learn things at an earlier age than their peers.

2. Gifted children can usually __concentrate on__ one subject for a long period of time, without getting bored.

3. Most gifted children are interested in many different subjects. For example, Pascal Charbonneau has won many chess _Champion_, but he also likes to read French _literature_ and play sports.

4. Another characteristic of gifted children is that they understand other people; they are _sensitive_ to the feelings of others.

5. Gifted children do not like it when other people are treated unfairly. They do not like to see _injustice_.

6. Prodigies are rarely satisfied with their performance. They are _critical_ of themselves, even when they perform brilliantly.

7. Prodigies don't like to make even a very small mistake. They are _perfectionists_.

8. The lives of musical prodigies are not easy. Everyone expects them to perform brilliantly all of the time. Some prodigies cannot deal with the constant _pressure_ and decide to quit performing.

9. Because of the pressure on them, many gifted young musicians get so tired that they stop performing. They _burn out_.

10. Beethoven was one of the most famous musical prodigies. He wrote and _published_ music at a very young age.

11. _Despite_ their talent, many prodigies never become famous.

DEVELOPING READING SKILLS

Understanding Major Points

Answer these questions in your own words. Do not copy from the reading.

1. Why might it be depressing to be gifted?

   _____

2. Why don't many young musical prodigies end up having a career in music?

   _____

3. The reading says that one of the characteristics of gifted children is a tendency to be sensitive to injustice. The reading does not say why this is true, but we can imagine the reasons. Why do you think gifted children might be more sensitive to injustice than other people?

_____

Understanding Supporting Details

Answer these questions.

1. In order to be considered gifted, how much more advanced than their peers do children have to be?

_____

2. What percentage of the general population is gifted?

_____

Understanding Inference

An **inference** is more than just a guess. You should always have a good reason for making an inference, and you should be careful that your inference does not go too far beyond what is written in the text. Look at the sentence.

Einstein was always a high achiever, although his best work was done when he was in his 20s.

It would _not_ be correct to infer from this sentence that Einstein did good work **only** when he was in his 20s. That inference goes too far beyond what is written.

Read these sentences from "Growing Up Gifted." Then, read the two sentences that follow. Put a check (✔) next to the sentence in each set that is a reasonable inference based on the sentences from the reading. The numbers in parentheses are the paragraphs that the sentences come from.

1. Having these characteristics can be challenging, even depressing, said Charbonneau. He is critical of even his best performances. "I'm rarely ever happy with what I do." (4)

_____ Many child prodigies perform poorly because they are too critical of themselves.

_____ Child prodigies are often unhappy because they can't be perfect.

2. Charbonneau knows that the pressure on him will soon begin to grow, as every young chess player tries to become the next champion. (5)

_✓_ Charbonneau was the winner of the last chess championship.

_____ Charbonneau will be the next chess champion.

3. World-famous violinist Itzhak Perlman has seen many talented young musicians simply burn out. "Rarely do you see people survive, and that's the goal, to survive your gift," he once told the _New York Times_. (6)

_✓_ Many gifted young musicians do not have successful careers, despite having remarkable talent.

_____ Many young musicians are not quite talented enough to achieve their goals.

EXPANDING VOCABULARY

Using the Target Vocabulary in New Contexts

Complete the sentences with the target words and phrases in the box. Be careful. There are two extra words or phrases.

burn out	despite	peer	published
championship	gifted	perfectionist	sensitive
concentrate on	injustice	pressure	tended to
critical	literature		

1. He is the oldest player to ever win an international tennis _championship_

2. I'm concerned that you are working too hard. I know you enjoy your job now, but if you aren't careful, you'll _burn out_ by the time you're thirty!

3. She's a gifted mystery writer. She's already written at least three books. Her first book was _published_ ten years ago.

4. Be careful how you talk to him. He's very _sensitive_. Yesterday, he was in tears because of something a kid said to him.

5. I hate it when teachers treat their male and female students differently. The _injustice_ really makes me angry.

6. _despite_ the complete lack of proof that he was involved in the crime, he was arrested and put in jail.

7. In English _literature_, William Shakespeare stands out as one of the most brilliant writers.

8. I'm a _perfectionist_. I am never satisfied unless I do something exactly right.

9. Stop playing around on the computer and _concentrated_ your homework! It's almost time for bed.

10. After 100 performances in just three months, she got very sick and had to go in the hospital. The doctors said that the _pressure_ of performing live seven nights a week was too much for her.

11. My daughter has been placed in a program for _gifted_ children. Her teachers think that the challenge of interacting with other talented children will be good for her.

12. He's very sensitive. He doesn't like it when his teachers are even just a little _critical_ of his work.

Word Families

When you learn a new word, you can build your vocabulary by learning forms of the words that are in the same family. Sometimes within the same word family, there is more than one word for a word form. Usually, the two words have related, but different, meanings. Look at these sentences.

*You shouldn't **criticize** him. He is doing the best he can.*

*Would you please read my essay and **critique** it?*

The verbs *criticize* and *critique* are in the same word family. They have related, but different, meanings. *Criticize* means "to judge someone or something severely." *Critique* means "to evaluate the positive and negative aspects of someone or something."

Study the chart. Then, complete the sentences with words from the chart. If there are two words listed for one word form, look up the words in the dictionary. Be careful; you will not use all the words.

Noun (person)	Noun (thing)	Verb	Adjective
	achievement	achieve	
	concentration	concentrate	
critic	criticism, critique	criticize, critique	critical
publisher	publication	publish, publicize	
	tendency	tend	
	pressure	pressure, pressurize	
perfectionist	perfection	perfect	perfect
champion	championship		

1. He received an award for remarkable _achievement_ in the arts.
2. Just like her mother, she has a _tendency_ to get depressed.
3. He is a _publisher_ of children's books.
4. There was a party to celebrate the _publication_ of her most recent book.
5. The new theory is fascinating, but experts are likely to _criticize_ the way the researchers did their experiments.
6. I'm tired of all the complaints and _criticism_. I'm just trying to do the best job I can.
7. Thank you for your _critique_ of my performance in the competition. It was very helpful to me.
8. Please watch my performance and _criticize_ it. Don't be afraid to be honest!
9. I did badly on the test because my _achievem_ was poor.
10. Please don't _____ him. You know how sensitive he is.
11. She beat all of her competitors. She is the new _____.
12. He's a good soccer player, but he wants to be better. He wants to _____ his skills.
13. The film _critic_ didn't like the movie at all, but I loved it.
14. It doesn't matter how hard you try. You will never achieve _pressure_.
15. His test score was _perfect_. He got every answer right.

Studying Word Grammar

Prepositions can be followed by nouns or pronouns. Since **gerunds** (base form of verb + -*ing*) act as nouns, they can follow prepositions, too. Look at the sentence from the reading.

*"If you cannot become someone at the very top, you are not interested **in becoming** a musician in an orchestra."*

A **Complete the sentences with the -*ing* form of the verbs below.**

achieve   burn out   criticize   pressure   publish

1. Great news! There are two companies interested in _publishing_ your new book. You're going to have a career as a writer!

2. He's decided to take a long vacation. He's been working so hard lately that he's afraid of _criticizing_.

3. Instead of _burning out_ everyone else's work, why don't you concentrate on improving your own?

4. I don't believe in _pressuring_ children to do things that they aren't ready for. If we push them too much when they are young, they'll burn out.

5. Despite _achieving_ more than anyone else in his class, he was not selected to participate in the end-of-year performance.

B **Complete the sentences with information about yourself. Use a gerund after the preposition.**

1. I like to be left alone when I'm concentrating on _____.

2. I don't believe in _____.

3. Instead of _____, I _____.

4. Despite _____, I _____.

PUTTING IT ALL TOGETHER

Discussion

Share your ideas in a small group. As you talk, try to use the vocabulary below. Each time someone uses a target word or phrase, put a check (✔) next to it.

achieve/achievement	peer
burn out	perfectionist/perfect/perfection
champion/championship	pressure
concentrate on	sensitive
critic/critical/criticize/criticism	survive
gifted	tend to
just/unjust	

1. Sometimes, school officials take the best students out of regular classes and put them in classes with other gifted children. Make a list of the advantages and disadvantages of separating the gifted students from the other students. Consider how this might affect not only the gifted students but also the other students.

2. When you were a child, did your parents ever pressure you to develop a talent or skill, or to achieve something difficult? If so, explain what happened. Was it a positive or a negative experience? If you have children, will you pressure them in the same way? Why or why not?

Writing

Complete one or both of these writing topics. When you write, use at least five of the target words from the chapter. Underline the target words in your paper.

1. Write an essay in support of or against separating gifted and other students in different classes.

2. Choose a famous person who was a child prodigy. Do some research either at the library or on the Internet. Then, write an essay about the person. Your essay should include the following information:

   • Date and place of birth

   • Age that the prodigy's talent was discovered

   • How the prodigy's talent was discovered

   • Major achievements

   • Current situation (for someone who is still living)

   • Any other interesting information that you discover

CHAPTER 6

School Bullies

Bullying: What can be done?

GETTING READY TO READ

 A   **Talk with a partner or in a small group.**

1. A **bully** is someone who uses his or her strength or power to frighten or hurt someone who is weaker. A **victim** is someone who has been attacked or treated very badly. Were there any bullies in your school? Describe them for your group. What did they look like? Who were their victims? What did they do to their victims?

2. Put a check (✓) next to the words that you think describe most bullies. Compare your answers with those of your group members.

  _✓_ popular   ____ female

  _✓_ male   ____ competitive

  ____ sensitive   _✓_ given a lot of freedom by parents

  ____ confident   _✓_ depressed

3. Put a check (✓) next to the words that you think describe most victims of bullies. Compare your answers to those of your group members.

___ thin   ✓ male   ___ depressed
✓ sensitive   ✓ intelligent   ✓ from poor families
___ confident   ✓ female

B The **boldfaced** words and phrases in the paragraph below appear in the reading. Which words or phrases are new to you? Circle them. Then, work with a partner. Read this paragraph introducing the topic of the reading, and match the words with their definitions. Be careful. There is one extra definition.

Go into any school, and you will probably find at least one school bully. The school bully usually chooses a weaker classmate as a victim. Bullies **pick on** their victims in many different ways. Their **aggression** involves words, actions, or both. Some bullies use just words to frighten their victims, but others also attack their victims **physically**. Most victims do not **stand up for** themselves, even when they are attacked repeatedly.

Word		Definition
_b_	**1.** pick on	**a.** defend
_c_	**2.** aggression	**b.** treat someone in a way that is not kind
_d_	**3.** physically	**c.** angry or threatening behavior or feelings that often result in fighting
_a_	**4.** stand up for	**d.** by using the body rather than the mind or feelings
		e. cry

READING

Read the text once without stopping.

School Bullies[1]

1   A middle school student is regularly beaten and threatened by his classmates. A 14-year-old boy dies after being pushed down the school stairs by a classmate. Parents send their 3-year-old children to special classes in self-defense so that they will not become

---
[1] a *bully* = someone who uses his or her strength or power to frighten or hurt someone who is weaker

victims when they begin school. These shocking stories are all real examples of an ugly side of school life: bullying.

2   Dan Olweus, a professor of psychology[2] at Bergen University in Norway, has spent twenty years studying **aggression** in schools. Dr. Olweus **examined** the results of a **survey** of 150,000 Norwegian[3] students. The **data** showed that 15 percent were either bullies or victims. His research is interesting because it challenges what people tend to believe about bullying.

3   First, bullies do not always **pick on** the **overweight** kid wearing glasses. Second, bullies are often popular, and they do not become bullies due to low **self-esteem**. Third, the size of the school, class size, and the **economic** and social **background** of the students do not make much difference in the amount of bullying. Fourth, bullying does not tend to take place as students are going to and from school. Fifth, bullying is not related to competition among students. Finally, more boys than girls are involved in bullying, and many girls are bullied by boys.

4   What do the victims of bullying have in common? Dr. Olweus's research shows that "the typical victim tends to be more **anxious** and less secure than his classmates and usually has a negative **attitude** towards violence."

5   In surveys, parents of male victims report that the boys were cautious[4] and sensitive at an early age. They probably had difficulty **standing up for** themselves, and therefore were disliked by their peers. These characteristics, combined with the fact that many of the boys were **physically** weak, contributed to their becoming victims of bullying.

6   The typical bully, on the other hand, is neither anxious nor insecure, and has a strong need for power and dominance.[5] "Too little love and care in childhood and too much **freedom** are conditions that strongly contribute to the development of bullies," says Dr. Olweus. In other studies that he has **conducted**, Dr. Olweus has found that about 60 percent of boys who were bullies between the ages of 11 and 15 had been involved in criminal activity by the time they were 24. Dr. Olweus's research has also shown that bullying victims are much more likely to be depressed than children who have not been bullied.

---

[2] *psychology* = the study of the mind and how it works

[3] *Norwegian* = coming from Norway

[4] *cautious* = careful to stay away from danger or risks

[5] *dominance* = the fact of being more powerful, more important, or more noticeable than other people

(continued)

7   **On the basis of** his research, Dr. Olweus has designed a program that has reduced bullying by 50 percent in forty-two Norwegian schools. It is now used by schools all over the world. The program, which is described in Olweus's book, *Bullying at School—What We Know and What We Can Do* (Oxford: Blackwell Publishing, 1993), starts with an anonymous questionnaire.[6] Next, there is a school conference day to discuss the answers to the questionnaire. Then there are meetings with both parents and teachers involved.

8   At school, teachers and other adults pay close attention to children's behavior. Adults are always present—not only during class time, but also between classes and at lunch. In class, students and their teachers write rules against bullying and have regular meetings to discuss the subject. Immediate action is taken if anyone thinks that a child is being bullied, and victims are protected. Bullies and victims are spoken to separately. In serious cases, school officials **contact** the parents.

9   Dr. Olweus strongly believes that bullies can be beaten. However, schools must take responsibility for developing programs like his to deal with this serious problem.

[6] an *anonymous questionnaire* = a written set of questions given to a large number of people who answer without giving their names

Comprehension Check

Read these sentences. Circle T (true), F (false), or ? (can't determine the answer from the reading). If you circle F, change the sentence to make it true. Check your answers with a classmate. If your answers are different, look back at the reading.

1. Dr. Olweus's research explains the causes of bullying and ways to deal with the problem.   T F ?
2. Bullies do not have many friends.   T F ?
3. Bullies do not have a lot of self-esteem.   T F ?
4. Victims of bullying usually do not like violence and do not fight back against bullies.   T F ?
5. Most bullies did not get enough love when they were children.   T F ?
6. Most criminals were bullies when they were children.   T F ?
7. According to Dr. Olweus, it is the responsibility of parents, not schools, to deal with the problem of bullying.   T F ?

EXPLORING VOCABULARY

Thinking about the Target Vocabulary

Guessing Strategy

By thinking about the logical relationship between the subject and the object of a verb, you can often guess the meaning of the verb. Look at the example.

*Bullies often **pick on** children who are smaller and weaker than they are.*

The object of the target phrasal verb *pick on* is *children who are smaller and weaker than they are*. The subject is *bullies*. Bullies often treat smaller, weaker children badly. Thus, you can guess that to pick on someone means to treat someone in a bad way.

Try It!

Read the sentences, and write a definition of the boldfaced target word.

Dr. Olweus **examined** the results of a study of 150,000 students. He learned that 15 percent of the students were either victims or bullies.

Examine means _____.

 A **Look at the target words and phrases. Which ones are new to you? Circle them here and in the reading. Then read "School Bullies" again. Look at the context of each new word and phrase. Can you guess the meaning? Use the Guessing Strategy where possible.**

Target Words and Phrases

victims (1)	overweight (3)	standing up for (5)
aggression (2)	self-esteem (3)	physically (5)
examined (2)	economic (3)	freedom (6)
survey (2)	background (3)	conducted (6)
data (2)	anxious (4)	on the basis of (7)
pick on (3)	attitude (4)	contact (8)

B Complete the word-form chart with the words and phrases as they are used in the reading. Write the base form of verbs and the singular form of nouns.

Nouns	Verbs	Adjectives	Other
victim			

Using the Target Vocabulary

These sentences are **about the reading**. Complete them with the words and phrases in the box. Circle the words or phrases in the sentences that help you understand the meanings of the target words. Be careful. There are two extra words or phrases.

aggression	conducted	examines	picked on
anxious	contact	freedom	self-esteem
attitude	data	on the basis of	survey
background	economic	overweight	

1. Dr. Olweus has led many studies on the causes of bullying. He has _____ a lot of research on the topic.

2. For more than twenty years, Dr. Olweus has been collecting information from bullies and victims. He then _____ that information to find patterns to explain why some students become bullies, while others become victims.

3. Dr. Olweus has collected information about bullies from countries all over the world. He then studies the _____ to understand school aggression.

4. In one large study of 150,000 students in Norway, 15 percent of the students who answered a _____ on bullying reported that they were either victims or bullies.

5. Bullying happens in both rich and poor schools. The _____ situation of the school's town has no effect on the amount of bullying.

6. The economic and social _____ of a bully are often exactly the same as that of his victim.

7. Physically weak children are often victims of bullies. However, _____ children are not any more likely to be picked on than thin children.

8. Victims have a tendency to worry a lot. They are often very _____.

9. Bullies are often very self-confident. They have high _____.

10. Typically, victims do not like violence. Their _____, or feeling, toward it is negative.

11. Bullies' parents do not pay enough attention to their children when they are small. Often, their children have the _____ to do whatever they want to do.

12. In schools that follow Dr. Olweus's program, school officials _____ both sets of parents when their children are involved in bullying. They ask them to come into school to talk about the problem.

13. Dr. Olweus's program is so effective because it is the result of years of careful research. He designed the program _____ research.

DEVELOPING READING SKILLS

Understanding Main Ideas

Answer the question.

What is "School Bullies" about? On a piece of paper, write one or two sentences that give the main idea.

Understanding Inference

A **misconception** is an idea that is wrong or untrue but that people believe because they do not understand it correctly. If you can identify the misconception in a text, you can use inference to figure out the truth about the idea.

Read paragraph 3 on page 73 again and label the following statements T (for true) or M (for misconception).

__M__ **1.** Most victims are overweight and wear glasses.

____ **2.** Bullies are popular with their peers.

____ **3.** Bullies are insecure.

____ **4.** There is more bullying in big schools with large classes than in small schools with small classes.

____ **5.** The amount of bullying in rich schools is about the same as the amount of bullying in poorer schools.

____ **6.** Most bullying happens when students are arriving at or leaving school.

____ **7.** Bullying often starts when students are competing against each other.

____ **8.** Boys do not usually bully girls.

EXPANDING VOCABULARY

Using the Target Vocabulary in New Contexts

Complete the sentences with the target words and phrases in the box. Be careful. There are two extra words or phrases.

anxious	contact	freedom	self-esteem
attitude	data	on the basis of	stand up for
background	economic	overweight	survey
conduct	examine	physically	

1. My daughter really doesn't like to read. Her _____ towards her literature class is terrible.

2. When we finish the experiment, we will _____ the results and then write up a report.

3. I believe in _____ and justice for all people.

4. Tim and Mark are brothers, but they don't look at all alike. Tim is tall and thin, while Mark is short and a little bit _____.

5. My husband lost his job _____ just one customer complaint. I think that is very unjust.

6. Despite the town's serious _____ problems, the people voted to buy new computers for the schools.

7. I can't concentrate on my work because I'm so _____ about my math test.

8. We don't have enough _____ on the causes of depression. We need to conduct more research.

9. The school is trying to find out why there are so many absences among students in the third grade. They have asked the parents of all third graders to complete a _____.

10. People with a strong educational _____ often have a higher social position than people with less education.

11. If you have any questions, _____ our office immediately.

12. My son never thinks he does anything right. His teachers say that he doesn't have much _____.

13. To test their theories, scientists often _____ experiments.

Word Families

 Complete the chart with the correct forms of the words. Check your answers in your dictionary. There may be more than one word for some word forms.

Noun (thing)	Verb	Adjective
aggression		
		anxious
		economic
	examine	
survey		
freedom		

Working with a partner, answer the questions. Make sure you use the correct forms of the boldfaced words.

1. What should parents do if they have an **aggressive** child?
2. What kinds of health problems can **anxiety** cause?
3. How is the **economy** of your country?
4. If you had to **economize**, what things would you stop spending money on?
5. How often do you go to the doctor for a physical **examination**?
6. If researchers want to find out about bullies, whom should they **survey**?
7. Do you think that scientists who use animals in research should **free** the animals when they finish using them in experiments? Why or why not?
8. When is your next English **exam**?

Studying Collocations

Certain nouns are used with certain verbs. Look at the sentence.

> Dr. Olweus **conducted a survey** on school bullies.

The noun *survey* is often used with the verb *conduct*. Other nouns that are often used with *conduct* are *research* and *experiment*. When *conduct* is used with these nouns, it means "do," and it follows this pattern:

conduct (= do)	a survey research an experiment	on	object (what or who the survey, experiment, or research is about)

Working with a partner, answer the questions. Make sure you use the correct form of the boldfaced words.

1. Do you think that it's morally wrong for scientists to **conduct experiments on** laboratory animals? Why or why not?
2. If you could **conduct a survey on** the lives of gifted children, what questions would you ask?
3. What are some of the things that doctors and scientists are **conducting research on** today?

PUTTING IT ALL TOGETHER

Discussion

Work in a small group.

Design a survey with at least five questions, and use at least five target words from this chapter. When you have finished writing your survey, have your teacher check it. Then, conduct the survey on the other members of your class, or peers from other classes. Finally, present your results to the class in a group presentation.

Choose one of the following survey topics:

school bullies   **teenagers**   **special talents**

Writing

Complete one or both of these writing topics. When you write, use at least five of the target words from the chapter. Underline the target words in your paper.

1. Write a report on your group survey project. Your report should include
   - The topic
   - What you were trying to find out
   - Who participated
   - How many people participated
   - The results
   - Interesting patterns in the results
   - What you think about the results

2. Write a story about a school bully. It can be a true story, or you can use your imagination. Try to make the story "come alive" for your reader. Tell the story from one of the following points of view:
   - The bully
   - The bully's friend
   - The bully's parents
   - The victim
   - The victim's friend
   - The victim's parents
   - A teacher

Wrap-up

REVIEWING READING SKILLS AND VOCABULARY

Read the text. Do not use a dictionary.

1   After conducting much research, scientists now have definite proof of what parents have known for centuries: Teenagers are different from everyone else. And the differences go much deeper than simple behavior. In fact, the brains of teenagers are very different from those of children or adults.

2   Until recently, scientists believed that the human brain was fully developed by the age of three. According to this theory, the teen behaviors that most concern parents—risk-taking, a lack of sensitivity to how their actions affect both themselves and others, increased aggression, reduced concentration, a negative attitude— were thought to be due to bad parenting or changes in body chemistry. However, new technology has allowed researchers to examine the healthy brain at work, and what they have discovered might surprise you. Not only does the brain continue to grow past the age of three, but the brain of a teenager is larger than that of an adult.

3   As teen brains are flooded with chemicals during adolescence,[1] the brain grows. However, at the same time, the cells of the brain that are used more compete with those that are used less. Only the cells[2] and the connections between the cells that are used the most will survive the competition. Those that are used less begin to die off until the brain reaches what will be its adult size.

4   The way that teens spend their time influences which connections remain, and which disappear. On the basis of this knowledge, experts advise parents to be sensitive to how their teenagers spend their time. What teens do today will affect their brains for the rest of their lives.

---

[1] *adolescence* = the period of time, from about 13 to 17 years of age, when a young person is developing into an adult

[2] a *cell* = the smallest part of an animal or plant that can exist on its own

Comprehension Check

Read these sentences. Circle T (true), F (false), or ? (can't determine the answer from the reading). If you circle F, change the sentence to make it true.

1. Scientists now know that the human brain continues to develop for years after we are born. T F ?

2. The brain of a three-year-old is larger than the brain of a teenager. T F ?

3. People with big brains are smarter than people with smaller brains. T F ?

4. If a teenager uses a particular part of the brain too much, the brain cells in that area will die off. T F ?

5. Teen behavior has an important effect on the physical development of the brain. T F ?

Guessing Meaning from Context

Answer this question.

What is the meaning of *flooded with* in the first line of paragraph 3?

_____

Understanding Main Ideas

Answer this question.

What is the main idea of the reading?

_____

_____

Understanding Inference

Read these sentences from the text. Then, read the two sentences that follow. Put a check (✔) next to the sentence in each set that is a reasonable inference based on the sentences from the reading. The numbers in parentheses are the paragraphs that the sentences come from.

1. Scientists now have definite proof of what parents have known for centuries: Teenagers are different from everyone else. (1)

   _____ Until recently, scientists did not know exactly why teenagers behave the way that they do.

   _____ A long time ago, parents proved that teenagers are different from everyone else.

2. Until recently, scientists believed that the human brain was fully developed by the age of three. (2)

   _____ There is new scientific information to suggest that the human brain continues to grow past the age of three.

   _____ Scientists used to believe that humans are more intelligent at the age of three than at any other time in their lives.

3. On the basis of this knowledge, experts advise parents to be sensitive to how their teenagers spend their time. What teens do today will affect their brains for the rest of their lives. (4)

   _____ Experts think that if parents are more sensitive to what teenagers need, teenagers will behave better.

   _____ Experts think that parents should help their teenagers to develop healthy patterns of behavior.

EXPANDING VOCABULARY

Studying Word Grammar

Some words are actually a combination of two words. They are called **compound words**. *Dropout* is an example of a compound word. Some compound words have a special type of punctuation called a *hyphen* (-) that combines the two words together into one word. *Self-esteem* is an example of a compound word containing a hyphen.

Read the following sentences, and write definitions of the boldfaced words.

1. She is an excellent student, but she is never satisfied with her grades. She is an **overachiever**.

   Overachievers are people who <u>put a lot of pressure on</u> <u>themselves to perform well, and are very unhappy if they don't</u> <u>achieve everything they want to.</u>

2. He's very clever, but he is lazy. He could be successful if he tried a little harder. He is an **underachiever**.

   Underachievers are people who _____

   _____

3. Artists try to communicate their ideas and feelings through their art. **Self-expression** is very important to them.

   Self-expression is the act of _____

   _____

Studying Phrasal Verbs

Some phrasal verbs are followed by a direct object (a person or thing). Other phrasal verbs have no object. For example, the phrasal verb *stand up for* must have an object, but the phrasal verb *stand out* never takes an object.

Read these sentences, and pay attention to whether the boldfaced phrasal verb takes an object or doesn't take an object. Write O (object) or NO (no object).

1. _____ He went to college, but he **dropped out** after just one year.

2. _____ Stop **picking on** your little brother.

3. _____ How late did you **stay up** last night?

On a piece of paper, write answers to these questions. Use the boldfaced phrasal verbs in your answers.

1. What are some of the reasons that teenagers **drop out** of high school?

2. Has anyone ever **picked on** you? Who?

3. How late do you usually **stay up**?

Word Families

The suffix *-ize* shows that a word is a verb. Here are some verbs that end in *-ize*. (The words in parentheses are target words that are in the same word family.)

criticize (critical)   **pressurize (pressure)**   **victimize (victim)**
economize (economic)   **publicize (publish)**

Complete these sentences with the verbs.

1. Don't let that bully _____ you! Protect yourself!

2. My husband lost his job, so we really have to _____.

3. I don't like to _____ my problems. I prefer to keep them private.

4. You shouldn't _____ your teacher. She is only trying to help you.

5. Before engineers figured out how to _____ the inside of airplanes, flying at very high altitudes was not possible.

PLAYING WITH WORDS

There are 12 target words from Unit 2 in this puzzle. The words go across (→) and down (↓). Find the words and circle them. Then use them to complete the sentences on page 87.

1. He was a high-school dropout. He does not have a strong educational _attitude_.
2. The researcher's _____ prove that his theory is correct.
3. Children whose parents are depressed are more _likely_ to become depressed themselves.
4. Some people think that the rise in physical _aggression_ in the schools is due to the violence that children see on television.
5. Why do you have so many _absences_? Have you been sick?
6. She's a _perfectionist_. She always wants to do everything exactly right. She hates making mistakes.
7. He did poorly on the test due to his _____ of knowledge.
8. If you don't study, you will never _pa_____ at that university.
9. I would like to find curtains that match the _patterns_ on the sofa.
10. He is a government _official_, so he cannot be too critical of the government.
11. They went to the beach _despite_ the bad weather.
12. She has won several piano competitions. She is very _gifted_.

BUILDING DICTIONARY SKILLS

Finding the Correct Meaning

Many words have more than one meaning. Look at the dictionary entries below. Read each sentence and write the number of the meaning.

> **sur·vive** /sɚˈvaɪv/ v [I,T] **1** to continue to live after an accident, illness, etc.: *Only one person survived the crash.* **2** to continue to live normally or exist in spite of difficulties: *Few small businesses survived the recession.* | *How do you manage to **survive on** such a low salary?* | *It's been a tough few months, but **I'll survive**.* **3** to continue to exist after a long time: *Only a few Greek Plays have survived.*

1. **a.** _____ Only three people **survived** the airplane crash.
   b. _____ There is a lot of competition in the food business these days. It isn't easy for new restaurants to **survive**.

> **pres·sure¹** /ˈprɛʃɚ/ *n*   **1** [U] an attempt to make someone do something by using influence, arguments, threats, etc.: *Kay's family is **putting pressure** on her to get married.* | *The company is **under pressure** to reduce costs.* | *The president faces **pressure from** militants in his own party.* **2** [C,U] the conditions of your work, family, or way of living that makes you anxious, and cause problems: *I've been **under** a lot of **pressure** at work lately.* | *There is a lot of **pressure on** children these days.* | *the **pressures of** modern life*   **3** [C,U] the force that a gas or liquid has when it is pushed and held inside a container: *The air pressure in the tires might be low.*   **4** [U] the force produced by pressing on someone or something: *the **pressure of** his hand on her shoulder*

2. **a.** ____ She's having a hard time. The **pressure** of work, school, and family is too much for her.

   b. ____ There is a lot of **pressure** on him to accept the job.

   c. ____ Did you check the tire **pressure**? Do we need to add air?

> **back·ground** /ˈbækɡraʊnd/ *n*   **1** [C] someone's education, family, and experience: *kids from very different **ethnic/religious/cultural backgrounds*** | *Steve **has a background in** computer engineering.* | *The position would suit someone **with a background** in real estate.*   **2** [C usually singular] the area that is behind the main things that you are looking at, especially in a picture or photograph: *Palm trees swayed **in the background**.*   **3 in the background** someone who keeps or stays in the background, tries not to be noticed: *The president's wife preferred to stay in the background.*   **4** [singular] sounds that are in the background are not the main ones that you can hear: *I could hear cars honking **in the background**.*

3. **a.** ____ We didn't give her the job because she doesn't have the educational **background** we are looking for.

   b. ____ When I was talking to my friend on the phone, I could hear her son crying in the **background**.

   c. ____ What's that in the **background**? Is it a person, or a tree?

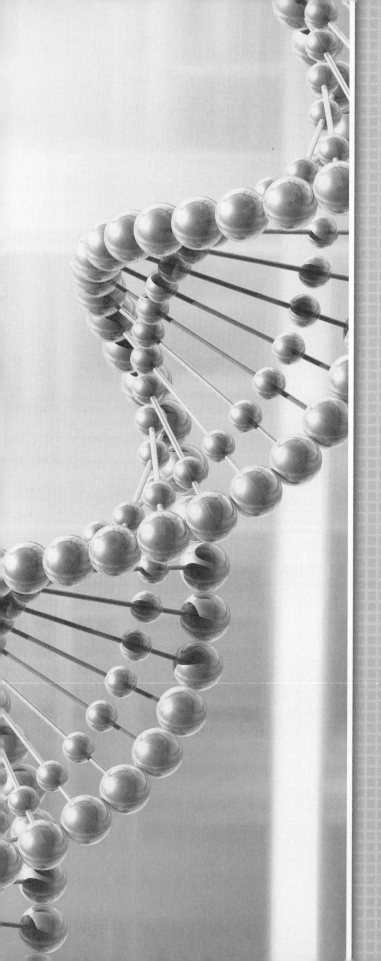

GENETICS: THE SCIENCE OF WHO WE ARE

CHAPTER 7

The Science of Genetics

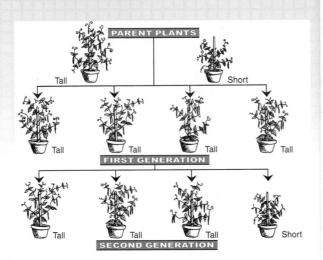

Gregor Mendel and his pea plant experiment

GETTING READY TO READ

 A **Talk with a partner or in a small group.**

1. Complete the chart with the names of family members who are similar to you in appearance or character. Then share your answers.

How I Am Similar to People in My Family	
Characteristic	**Family Member's Name and Relationship**
Face (for example, eyes, nose, mouth)	
Body size and shape (for example, height, weight)	
Character (for example, shy, funny)	
Other?	

2. Look at the chapter title and the illustrations. Make a list of questions you think "The Science of Genetics" might answer.

a. <u>What is a gene?</u>

b. _____

c. _____

d. _____

B The **boldfaced** words and phrases in the sentences below appear in the reading. Which words or phrases are new to you? Circle them. Then, work with a partner. Read the sentences about the reading, and choose the correct answers.

1. We get many **traits** from our parents. Eye color and height are two examples. *Traits* are

   a. gifts.   **b.** qualities.   **c.** interests.

2. If someone has a genetic **disease**, it means that his or her genes are not working correctly, so they have health problems. *Disease* means

   a. sickness.   **b.** trouble.   **c.** fever.

3. Doctors can **prevent** some types of sicknesses by changing the person's genes. When they are successful, people don't get these sicknesses. *Prevent* means

   a. begin doing something.   **b.** stop something before it happens.   **c.** fix completely.

4. In the future, scientists will try to **get rid of** genes that cause sickness. This would be the best solution because people would never worry about these sicknesses again. *Get rid of* means to cause something to

   a. become smaller.   **b.** get better.   **c.** disappear.

5. Children look like their parents because they **inherit** genes from them. *Inherit* means

   a. receive.   **b.** require.   **c.** get money.

READING

Read the text once without stopping.

The Science of Genetics

1   Who are we? Where did we come from? How are we related to each other and to other living things? The written record of the search for the answers to these questions goes back at least 2,500 years. At that time, Pythagoras, the famous Greek mathematician,[1] believed that children got all of their physical **traits** from their fathers. Later, Aristotle, the Greek philosopher,[2] **realized** that children **inherit** characteristics from both of their parents. However, he incorrectly believed that a child was the direct product of the mixing of the mother's and father's blood.

2   Modern genetics, the science that helps us to understand how and why we get traits from our parents, was not born until the nineteenth century. The father of modern genetics was Gregor Mendel, an Austrian scientist. Through eight years of experiments on pea[3] plants, Mendel proved that characteristics from the "mother" plant and characteristics from the "father" plant are not mixed together when the two plants cross-pollinate[4] and produce the next **generation** of plants. Rather, the characteristics that are dominant (stronger) will **come out** in the first generation. The characteristics that are recessive (weaker) will only appear in the second generation.

3   For example, if you take a very short pea plant and cross-pollinate it with a very tall pea plant, you might expect the new pea plant to be of average height. But in fact, the first generation of plants will all be very tall, because that characteristic is dominant. Short plants will not appear until the second generation, because that characteristic is recessive.

4   The theories that Mendel developed using plants were later applied to all living things, including human beings. Future research that would explain how parents pass traits on[5] to their children through their **genes** grew out of Mendel's work.

---

[1] a *mathematician* = someone who studies or teaches mathematics

[2] a *philosopher* = someone who teaches about life and what it means, and how we should live

[3] a *pea* = a small round green seed that is cooked and eaten as a vegetable

[4] *cross-pollinate* = transfer pollen (a powder produced by plants) from one plant to another

[5] *pass traits on* = give someone or something a particular trait

5   What is a gene? Explained very simply, a gene is a set of **instructions** that you get from your parents before you are born. Your genes are similar to an instruction book for a computer. When you open the book, you see a list of all of the parts of the computer. Then, you see instructions telling you how to make the computer work. Your genes, like the instruction book, contain a complete list of all of the parts that make a human being. They also contain instructions on how to put the parts together to make one special **individual**—you.

6   Today, scientists are learning more and more about genes and their effect on what we look like, how we behave, how smart we are, and what kinds of sicknesses we have or are likely to get in the future. They are using this information in two exciting areas: *genetic engineering* and *genetic testing*.

7   Through genetic engineering, scientists change how genes work, or put new genes into **cells** to **replace** genes that are missing or not working correctly. Because all living things (not only humans) have genes, scientists also use genetic engineering to produce plants and animals that are healthy, grow rapidly, or are useful to us in some other way.

8   When doctors do genetic testing, they take DNA[6] from a person (or other living thing) and examine it carefully. One important use of genetic testing is to discover if someone has or might get a genetic **illness**. If the person already has the **disease**, doctors might be able to use genetic engineering to **cure** it. If the testing shows that the person does not have the disease, but might get it at some point in the future, doctors might be able to use genetic engineering to **prevent** it. The treatment involves taking out the gene that causes the disease, and injecting[7] the patient with healthy genes.

9   Sometimes, genetic testing and genetic engineering can be used to **determine** a child's **gender**. In the future, genetic engineering might be used to allow parents to choose **desirable** traits or **get rid of** undesirable ones before their child is even born.

---

[6] *DNA* = deoxyribonucleic acid, an acid that carries genetic information in a cell

[7] *inject* = put a liquid, especially a drug, into the body by using a special needle

Comprehension Check

Read these sentences. Circle T (true), F (false), or ? (can't determine the answer from the reading). If you circle F, change the sentence to make it true. Check your answers with a classmate. If your answers are different, look back at the reading.

1. Around 2,500 years ago people already knew that children get their traits from both their mother and their father.   T   F   ?

2. The study of how and why certain traits are passed from one generation to the next is called *genetics*.   T   F   ?

3. People look different from one another because they have different genes.   T   F   ?

4. Our genes do not have an effect on our behavior.   T   F   ?

5. Genetic engineering is used only on animals.   T   F   ?

6. In some cases, doctors use genetic testing to find out if someone is sick, or to find out if they might get sick in the future.   T   F   ?

7. In the future, parents will be able to use genetic engineering to change a child's gender before the child is born.   T   F   ?

EXPLORING VOCABULARY

Thinking about the Target Vocabulary

Guessing Strategy

When writers use technical terms, you might not need to guess their meaning because those terms are often defined directly in the reading itself. Look at the example.

*Rather, the characteristics that are **dominant (stronger)** will come out in the first generation. The characteristics that are **recessive (weaker)** will only appear in the second generation.*

Pay attention to words in parentheses. They often contain definitions of the words that come before them.

Try It!

Read the sentence and answer the question.

Many scientists are doing research in gene therapy (treatment using the part of a cell that carries inherited traits).

What is **gene therapy**? _____

A Look at the target words and phrases. Which ones are new to you? Circle them here and in the reading. Then read "The Science of Genetics" again. Look at the context of each new word and phrase. Can you guess the meaning? Use the Guessing Strategy where possible.

Target Words and Phrases

traits (1)	genes (4)	illness (8)	gender (9)
realized (1)	instructions (5)	disease (8)	desirable (9)
inherit (1)	individual (5)	cure (8)	get rid of (9)
generation (2)	cells (7)	prevent (8)	
come out (2)	replace (7)	determine (9)	

B Complete the word-form chart with the target words and phrases as they are used in the reading. Write the base form of verbs and the singular form of nouns.

Nouns	Verbs	Adjectives	Other
trait	inherit	individual	
other	come out		
genes	replace		
instruct	determine		
cells	get rid of		
illness	prevent		
disse	determine		
gender	cure		

Using the Target Vocabulary

These sentences are **about the reading**. Complete them with the words and phrases in the box. Circle the words or phrases in the sentences that help you understand the meanings of the target words. Be careful. There are two extra words or phrases.

cell	determine	illnesses	realize
come out	gender	individual	replace
cure	generation	instructions	traits
desirable	genes	prevent	

1. A long time ago, people didn't know why children tended to look like their parents. They didn't _____ that traits are passed from one _____ to the next.

2. Today, we know that our _____ contain all of the information that is necessary to make a human being. They contain a list of detailed _____ on how to "build" a human being.

3. One _____ is different from another because each person has his or her own genes.

4. The science of genetics (the study of how traits are passed from one generation to another) has shown that some traits will appear in the first generation. Other weaker traits will not _____ until the following generation.

5. Through genetic engineering (changing or replacing genes), doctors are trying to help people with genetic _____ get better. They are trying to _____ them.

6. In one technique, scientists remove a gene that is not working correctly from a _____ (the smallest part of a person or other living thing). Then they _____ it with a healthy gene.

7. It is also possible for scientists to use genetic testing to determine a child's _____ (sex).

8. Genetic testing can be used to _____ (find out) whether a child is likely to develop a genetic illness.

9. In the future, parents might be able to make sure that their children are born with _____ traits such as intelligence or beauty.

DEVELOPING READING SKILLS

Scanning

Where is the information about these topics in "The Science of Genetics"? Scan the reading, and write the paragraph number (1–9).

____ **a.** The birth of modern genetics

____ **b.** The definition of a gene

____ **c.** Possible future uses of genetic engineering and genetic testing

__1__ **d.** Some past ideas about how humans get their traits

____ **e.** How genetic engineering can be used with animals and plants

____ **f.** What scientists are learning about genes

____ **g.** What happens when you cross a small pea plant with a tall one

____ **h.** How later scientists used Mendel's research

____ **i.** How genetic testing and genetic engineering are used today in humans

Summarizing

When you **summarize** a text, you should include the main idea and the major points about the main idea. Your summary should include details only if they help you explain the major points. Always write a summary in your own words. Do not copy from the text.

Write a sentence about each of the nine topics from the Scanning exercise above. Use information from the reading, but do not copy. Include only the most important information. Together, the nine sentences should summarize the reading.

Paragraph 1: _In the past, there were many different theories about_
why children look and act like their parents.

Paragraph 2: _____
_____
_____

Paragraph 3: _____
_____
_____

Paragraph 4: _____
_____
_____

Paragraph 5: _____

_____

_____

Paragraph 6: _____

_____

_____

Paragraph 7: _____

_____

_____

Paragraph 8: _____

_____

_____

Paragraph 9: _____

_____

_____

EXPANDING VOCABULARY

Using the Target Vocabulary in New Contexts

Complete the sentences with the target words and phrases in the box. Be careful. There are two extra words or phrases.

came out	determines	got rid of	instructions
cells	genders	illness	realize
cured	generations	individual	replace
desirable	genes	inherits	

1. This radio isn't working. You need to _____ the batteries.

2. I don't know how to play that game. Please read the _____ to me.

3. Great news! He isn't going to die. The doctors have _____ him!

4. That house is expensive because it is in a _____ location, in the best part of town.

5. Sometimes, parents and children don't understand each other because they come from different _____.

6. The men in his family have been tennis champions for generations. The talent must be in their _____.

7. Doctors now realize that depression is an _____, with real physical causes.

8. I'm sorry. I didn't _____ that I hurt you.

9. Each _____ in the class must participate in at least one experiment.

10. Everyone has two types of blood _____: red and white.

11. The mechanic will call you when he _____ the cause of the problem.

12. Everyone was surprised when the news of his marriage _____. Nobody knew that he had a girlfriend.

13. Most schools in my country are coeducational. That is, they accept students of both _____.

Word Families

A Complete the chart with the correct forms of the words. Check your answers in your dictionary.

Noun	Verb	Adjective
		desirable
	prevent	
	cure	

B Complete the sentences with words from the chart. Be careful; you will not use all the words.

1. Sicknesses caused by insects are _____. If you protect yourself from insect bites, you won't get these sicknesses.

2. Don't worry. She's not going to die from that disease. It is _____.

3. His _____ to become a scientist is so strong that he spends every minute studying and conducting experiments.

4. Scientists are working hard to find a _____ for that disease.

5. The _____ of forest fires is the responsibility of the Department of Fire Safety.

6. Their father gives them whatever they _____.

C **Working with a partner, answer the questions. Make sure you use the correct form of the boldfaced words.**

1. Sometimes your **desires** for the future do not match the **desires** of your family or other people that you love. Has this ever happened to you? If so, what did you do? If not, what do you think you would do?

2. Make a list of diseases that are **preventable**. Talk about how you can **prevent** them.

3. Which diseases do you think scientists will find a **cure** for in your lifetime?

Studying Collocations

Certain prepositions follow certain verbs. Sometimes the preposition comes directly after the verb, and sometimes it comes after the object of the verb. In these sentences, the preposition comes after the object.

- He *prevented* us *from* finding out the truth.
- The doctor *cured* her *of* cancer.
- She *inherited* a lot of money *from* her grandmother.
- I damaged her computer, but I *replaced* it *with* a new one.

Write answers to these questions. Use the boldfaced words in your answers.

1. If you have children, what will you try to **prevent** them **from** doing?

_____

_____

2. Do you know anyone who has been **cured of** a serious disease?

_____

_____

3. Who will **inherit** your money and property **from** you?

   _____

   _____

4. Write about a time when you broke or lost something that belonged to someone else and you had to replace it. What did you **replace** it **with**?

   _____

   _____

PUTTING IT ALL TOGETHER

Discussion

Share your ideas in a small group. As you talk, try to use the vocabulary below. Each time someone uses a target word or phrase, put a check (✔) next to it.

come out	get rid of
desire/desirable/undesirable	illness
determine	individual
disease	inherit
gene/genetic	prevent/preventable
generation	trait

1. Decide which of the following news stories are true. Be ready to explain your answers to the class. After you have discussed all of the news stories, your teacher will tell you which ones are true.

   • Most farmers in the United States use special seeds to grow food. The genes of these seeds have been changed. The plants that grow from them grow faster and are larger than the plants grown from regular seeds. The plants also get fewer diseases.

   • Scientists are now able to take a few cells from a human heart, and grow a new heart from them. This new heart can then be used to replace the heart of someone with heart disease.

   • Scientists are now using genetic engineering to produce pigs with organs (for example, kidneys and hearts) that are genetically similar to human organs. In the future, doctors hope to be able to replace the diseased organs of human beings with these pig organs.

   • Scientists have discovered the gene for intelligence. Parents can now use genetic testing before their baby is born to find out whether their child is going to be intelligent or not.

2. Choose one of the true news stories above and talk about it in your group. Do you think using genetic engineering and/or testing in this way is a good thing or a bad thing? Why?

Writing

Complete one or both of these writing topics. When you write, use at least five of the target words from the chapter. Underline the target words in your paper.

1. Genetic testing now makes it possible for people to find out if they have a higher than average chance of getting certain genetic diseases. Write a paragraph or short essay discussing the advantages and disadvantages of knowing this information. You can start with the following sentence: *There are both advantages and disadvantages to knowing if you have a high risk for getting a genetic disease.*

2. Imagine that you are a manager at a large insurance company. You find out that very soon everyone who applies to your company for health insurance will be given a genetic test to determine how likely they are to develop a genetic illness. The test will tell you which people are most likely to develop a serious genetic disease in the future. In an e-mail to the other managers of the company, explain why you agree or disagree with this use of genetic testing.

CHAPTER 8

Designing the Future

GETTING READY TO READ

 A **First, answer the questions alone. Then compare your answers with a partner or in a small group.**

1. Look at the list of adjectives. If you could choose only three for your **son**, which would you choose and why? Put a check (✓) next to three, or write in your own.

   ____ strong   ____ thin   ____ handsome   ____ honest
   ____ intelligent   ____ funny   ____ kind   ____ successful
   other? _____

2. Now check the three adjectives that you would choose for your **daughter**.

   ____ strong   ____ thin   ____ beautiful   ____ honest
   ____ intelligent   ____ funny   ____ kind   ____ successful
   other? _____

The **boldfaced** words in the paragraph below appear in the reading. Which words are new to you? Circle them. Then, work with a partner. Read this paragraph introducing the topic of the reading, and match the words with their definitions. Be careful. There are two extra definitions.

Historically, parents could only hope that their child would be born with desirable moral traits such as **courage**. However, due to rapid progress in the field of genetics, very soon parents might be able to do much more than hope. They might **actually** be able to "design" their children before they are born. How? Some scientists believe that within the next fifty years, they will be able to **identify** the genes for everything from nose shape to intelligence. And after a gene for a particular **feature** is identified, scientists can use genetic engineering to make sure that a child is born with that trait.

Word	Definition
_____ **1.** historically	**a.** the ability to be brave and calm in a situation where most people would be afraid
_____ **2.** courage	
_____ **3.** actually	**b.** today
_____ **4.** identify	**c.** an important and noticeable characteristic of something
_____ **5.** feature	
	d. find out exactly what the cause or origin of something is
	e. in fact, although it may be strange
	f. in a story
	g. traditionally; in the past

READING

Read the text once without stopping.

Designing the Future

1   A young couple has decided that it is time for them to have a baby. So, what is the first thing they do? They go shopping! But not for clothes or furniture—that will come later. Before anything else, they must decide whether they want a girl or a boy. Now, it is time to consider their future child's **intellect**. Do they want an intellectually gifted child, or would a child with an average

level of intelligence be **acceptable**? Next, what about personality? Is **courage** important to them? Do they care if their child is shy? Finally, it is time to consider physical traits. What eye color would they prefer? What about height and weight? Do they want an **athletic** child, so that he or she can play tennis with Mom? There are so many **features** to choose from!

2   Of course, the situation described above does not **actually** happen today. But recent progress in genetic engineering[1] has **led** some scientists **to** believe that the day when parents can "shop" for their future child's physical, intellectual, and personality traits is rapidly **approaching**. It seems that almost every day scientists **identify** new genes and the traits that they control. Already, genetic testing can be used to identify gender very early in the development of the fetus.[2] The genes that mark for[3] a few serious genetic diseases can also be identified. And there are scientists who are convinced that very soon they will find the genes for a wide variety of traits—artistic talent, courage, a tendency toward depression, physical **appearance**—just about anything you can imagine. Reportedly, one scientist has even spoken of using genetic engineering to give future humans desirable traits that only animals have now—for example, a dog's powerful sense of smell, or an owl's[4] ability to see at night.

3   However, not everyone working in the field of genetics believes that parents will be making such choices anytime soon. Some believe that the more complex types of genetic engineering will not be possible for at least 100 years. Others are not at all **convinced** that our genes control characteristics such as intelligence and personality. And still others believe that the use of genetic engineering should be **restricted** to just those cases in which the health of the mother or her fetus is threatened.

4   Surveys show that the attitudes of the public on this subject have been changing, at least in the United States. In a telephone survey done in the United States in 1986, 42 percent thought that changing the genes of human cells was morally wrong. However, in the same survey done in 1996, that number had dropped to only 22 percent. Other recent surveys have shown that many parents would be willing to use genetic engineering to improve

---

[1] *genetic engineering* = the science of changing the genes of a plant or animal to make it stronger or more healthy

[2] a *fetus* = a young human or animal before birth

[3] *mark for* = signal or show the presence of (something)

[4] an *owl* = a bird that hunts at night and has large eyes and a loud call

(continued)

their child's chances of inheriting desirable traits, such as beauty or intelligence. And it is instructive to remember that **historically**, whenever the once unimaginable has become possible (think about cars, airplanes, and the Internet), it soon becomes common. That is why many believe that if the technology to "design" children exists, parents will use it in ever increasing numbers.

5   All of this **brings up** some difficult social and moral questions. What are the long-term[5] health risks of genetic engineering? Will too many parents choose to have children of the same gender leading to a **shortage** of boys or girls? What will happen to children whose parents cannot afford to give them the physical and mental **advantages** enjoyed by their genetically "designed" peers? How will society treat "imperfect" children? **In short**, will genetic engineering forever change the face of **humanity**?

---

[5] *long-term* = continuing for a long period of time into the future

Comprehension Check

Read these sentences. Circle T (true), F (false), or ? (can't determine the answer from the reading). If you circle F, change the sentence to make it true. Check your answers with a classmate. If your answers are different, look back at the reading.

1. Intelligence and personality are determined by our genes.   T   F   ?

2. It is now possible for parents to determine the sex of their child before it is born.   T   F   ?

3. Some parents are already using genetic engineering to determine what their future child will look like.   T   F   ?

4. In the future, some scientists expect to find the genes for almost all the traits that are passed from parents to their children.   T   F   ?

5. Even if genetic engineering makes it possible for parents to "design" their children, most parents won't use the technology because it is morally wrong.   T   F   ?

6. Genetic engineering to change children's physical appearance will have no effect on their health.   T   F   ?

EXPLORING VOCABULARY

Thinking about the Target Vocabulary

Guessing Strategy

Understanding punctuation can help you understand the meaning of unfamiliar words. The **dash** (—) is a type of punctuation. Writers use dashes to focus the reader's attention on important information. Often, writers put examples between two dashes. Look at the example.

*And there are scientists who are convinced that very soon they will find the genes for a wide variety of traits—artistic talent, **courage**, a tendency toward depression, physical **appearance**—just about anything you can imagine.*

In this case, the word before the dash is *traits*. The words after the dash are specific examples. Although you may not understand the exact meaning of the target words *courage* or *appearance*, you can guess from the context that they are both examples of traits.

Try It!

Read the sentence, and write a definition of the boldfaced target word.

Genetic engineering brings up serious social and moral issues—health risks, a possible **shortage** of boys or girls—so many people worry about using it.

A possible **shortage** of boys or girls is an example of _____

_____.

A Look at the target words and phrases. Which ones are new to you? Circle them here and in the reading. Then read "Designing the Future" again. Look at the context of each new word and phrase. Can you guess the meaning? Use the Guessing Strategy where possible.

Target Words and Phrases

intellect (1)	actually (2)	convinced (3)	shortage (5)
acceptable (1)	led to (2)	restricted (3)	advantages (5)
courage (1)	approaching (2)	historically (4)	in short (5)
athletic (1)	identify (2)	brings up (5)	humanity (5)
features (1)	appearance (2)		

B Complete the word-form chart with the target words and phrases as they are used in the reading. Write the base form of verbs and the singular form of nouns.

Nouns	Verbs	Adjectives	Other
intellect			

Using the Target Vocabulary

These sentences are **about the reading**. Complete them with the words and phrases in the box. Circle the words or phrases in the sentences that help you understand the meanings of the target words. Be careful. There are two extra words or phrases.

acceptable	athletic	humanity	lead to
advantages	brings up	identifying	restricted
appearance	convinced	in short	shortage
approaching	historically	intellect	

1. Some scientists believe that the day when parents will be able to choose what their future children look like is rapidly _____. Others think that it will take at least 100 years.

2. For some parents, choosing physical traits is important. They would like to be able to determine their children's height, or _____ ability.

3. It might also be possible for parents to determine their child's _____. Some parents will probably want their children to be gifted. Others will be happier with children of average intelligence.

4. People are starting to ask some very difficult questions about genetic engineering. Genetic engineering _____ some complex questions.

5. The technology to determine the gender of the fetus already exists. Some people worry that if too many parents choose one gender, there will be a _____ of the other gender.

6. Many people in the United States think that there is nothing wrong with using genetic engineering to design children with desirable traits. They think that this use of genetic engineering is

_____.

7. In the future, parents will probably be able to choose certain traits for their children. The physical traits that the parents choose will have an effect on their child's _____.

8. One scientist believes that we will be able to design people who have both human and animal traits. He doesn't think we will be _____ to just human traits.

9. Although some scientists are _____ that there are genes for almost all traits, others disagree. They don't think that genes control complex personality traits or intellect.

10. Some people are concerned that using genetic engineering to design the perfect child will _____ a society in which rich children have genetic _____ over poor children.

11. They worry that the use of genetic engineering to design babies could change the definition of what a human being is. _____, they worry that genetic engineering will have a negative effect on _____.

DEVELOPING READING SKILLS

Understanding Inference

Read the sentences from "Designing the Future." Then, read the two sentences that follow. Put a check (✔) next to the sentence in each set that is a reasonable inference based on the sentences from the reading. The numbers in parentheses are the paragraphs that the sentences come from.

1. But recent progress in genetic engineering has led some scientists to believe that the day when parents can "shop" for their future child's physical, intellectual, and personality traits is rapidly approaching. (2)

   _____ The technology for designing babies does not exist yet.

   _____ In the future, almost all parents will design their babies.

2. Reportedly, one scientist has even spoken of using genetic engineering to give future humans desirable traits that only animals have now. (2)

   _____ Human beings will soon be able to have traits that only animals have now.

   _____ Right now, scientists don't know how to make humans with animal traits.

3. However, not everyone working in the field of genetics believes that parents will be making such choices anytime soon. (3)

   _____ Nobody working in genetics believes that parents will want to choose their children's traits.

   _____ Some geneticists think that it will be a long time before the technology that will allow parents to design their babies is developed.

Summarizing

Complete this summary of "Designing the Future." Write as much as you can without looking back at the reading. Then, compare your summary to that of a classmate. If there are any differences, decide whose summary is more accurate. Finally, go back to the reading to check your summary and to add any missing information.

Because of genetic _____, many scientists believe that in

the future, parents will be able to _____. Already,

scientists know how to _____

_____

_____.

In the future, scientists expect to _____

_____.

When that happens, surveys show that many parents _____

_____

_____.

The use of genetic engineering to "design" children leads to some difficult

moral questions, for example: _____

_____

_____?

But the most important question is: _____

_____

_____?

EXPANDING VOCABULARY

Using the Target Vocabulary in New Contexts

**Complete the sentences with the target words and phrases in the box.
Be careful. There are two extra words or phrases.**

acceptable	athletic	historically	lead to
advantages	bring up	humanity	restricted
appearance	convinced	in short	shortage
approach	courage	intellect	

1. He can't throw a ball or run fast. He isn't very _____.
2. I had a lot of homework to do, but my sister _____ me to
   go to the movies with her.

3. The work of Austrian scientist Gregor Mendel, the father of genetics, was important for all of _____.

4. You look different. Your new haircut really changes your _____.

5. Travel to that region is _____. You can only go there if you get permission from the government.

6. Bad eating habits can _____ illness and other physical problems.

7. I'm sorry, but this paper is not _____. It is very messy and has many errors. You are going to have to write it again.

8. You should _____ your concerns in class. Your teacher will help you.

9. There is nothing wrong with her _____. She's a very smart woman.

10. There are many _____ to having a good education. For example, people who are well-educated usually earn more money than people with less education.

11. He is attractive, intelligent, and successful. _____, he's the perfect man for you!

12. It hasn't rained in almost a year. There is a water _____.

13. Slow down as we _____ the traffic light. My house is on the corner, just after the light.

Word Families

The adjective ending -ous means "full of." Therefore, the adjective courageous means "full of courage." The addition of certain suffixes, including -ous, can change the syllable stress on a word. You can look in your dictionary to find out which syllable is stressed. In most dictionaries, the symbol ' is placed at the beginning of the stressed syllable.

A Look at the pronunciation guides for the following words. Answer the questions.

1.
> **cour·age** /ˈkɚɪdʒ, ˈkʌr-/ *n* **1** [U] the quality of being brave when you are in danger, a difficult situation, etc.: *He didn't* **have the courage to** *face the media.* | *It must have* **taken a lot of courage** *for him to drive again after the accident.* —**courageous** /ˈkəˈreɪdʒəs/ *adj: a courageous decision* —**courageously** *adv*

  a. How many syllables are in the noun **courage**? _____
     Which syllable is stressed? _____

  b. How many syllables are in the adjective **courageous**? _____
     Which syllable is stressed? _____

2.
> **ad·van·tage** /ədˈvæɾɪdʒ/ *n* **1** [C,U] something that helps you to be better or more successful than others [≠ **disadvantage**]: *Her computer skills gave her an* **advantage over** *the other applicants.* | *He turns every situation* **to his advantage**. **2 take advantage of sth** to use a situation or thing to help you do or get something you want: *He* **took advantage of the opportunity** *given to him.* **3** [C] a good or useful quality that something has: *Good restaurants are one of the many* **advantages of** *living in a big city* **4 take advantage of sb** to treat someone unfairly or to control a particular situation in order to get what you want
> **ad·van·ta·geous** /ˌædvænˈteɪdʒəs, -vən-/ *adj* helpful and likely to make you more successful [≠ **disadvantageous**]

  a. How many syllables are in the noun **advantage**? _____
     Which syllable is stressed? _____

  b. How many syllables are in the adjective **advantageous**? _____
     Which syllable is stressed? _____

3.
> **anx·i·e·ty** /æŋˈzaɪəti/ *n* [U] a strong feeling of worry about something: *a lifestyle that creates stress and anxiety* | *workers'* **anxiety about** *being fired*
> **anx·ious** /ˈæŋkʃəs, ˈæŋʃəs/ *adj* **1** very worried about something or showing that you are worried: *June's* **anxious about** *the results of her blood test* | *an anxious look*

  a. How many syllables are in the noun **anxiety**? _____
     Which syllable is stressed? _____

  b. How many syllables are in the adjective **anxious**? _____
     Which syllable is stressed? _____

B Working with a partner, answer the questions. Use the **boldfaced** words in your answers. Make sure you stress the correct syllable.

1. When you feel **anxious**, what do you do to relax?

2. In life, which is more **advantageous**—physical beauty or intellectual ability? Why?

3. Are you a **courageous** person? Explain your answer with specific examples.

Studying Word Grammar

An **adverb** is a word that can be used to modify a verb, an adjective, another adverb, or an entire sentence. Look at the examples.

*They lost the game despite fighting **courageously** up until the very end.*	The adverb *courageously* modifies the verb *fighting*.
*It is important for children to be **intellectually** challenged.*	The adverb *intellectually* modifies the adjective *challenged*.
*My son is **very** athletically gifted.*	The adverb *very* modifies the adverb *athletically*.
***Historically**, whenever the once unimaginable has become possible, it soon becomes common.*	The adverb *historically* modifies the whole sentence that follows it.

Complete the sentences with the adverbs below.

actually   historically   humanely   in short

1. _____, women stayed at home and took care of the children. Today, however, many women work outside of the home.

2. It is not acceptable to hurt an animal on purpose. Animals should be treated _____.

3. Your artwork is creative, original, intelligent, and beautiful. _____, it's remarkable!

4. Most people think he's been playing the piano for years. _____, he just began playing three months ago.

PUTTING IT ALL TOGETHER

Discussion

Share your ideas in a small group. As you talk, try to use the vocabulary below. Each time someone uses a target word or phrase, put a check (✔) next to it.

acceptable	humanity
advantage/advantageous	identify
appearance	intellect/intellectual
athletic	lead to
courage/courageous	restricted
feature	shortage

1. Imagine that in the future you will be able to design your own son or daughter. Will you do it? Why or why not?

2. Read the last paragraph on page 106 again, and discuss your answers to the five questions.

Writing

Complete one or both of these writing topics. When you write, use at least five of the target words from the chapter. Underline the target words in your paper.

1. Imagine that in the future you will be able to design your own child. What traits do you want your son or daughter to have? Write a letter to your future child explaining why you wanted him or her to have these traits.

2. *The use of genetic engineering to make a child more intelligent or more attractive is morally wrong.* Do you agree or disagree with this statement? Write a short essay explaining your opinion.

A Terrible Inheritance, A Difficult Decision

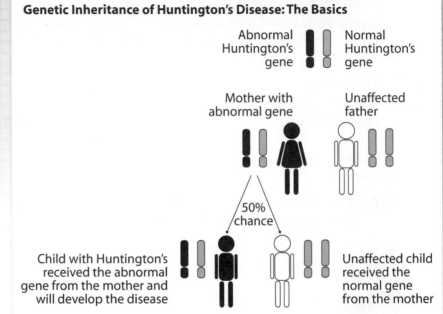

Genetic Inheritance of Huntington's Disease: The Basics

Genetic Inheritance of Huntington's Disease: The Basics

GETTING READY TO READ

 Talk with a partner or in a small group.

Look at the diagram and the title of the chapter reading. Discuss what you think the reading will be about. What does "a terrible inheritance" refer to? What is the "difficult decision"?

B **The boldfaced words and phrases in the paragraph below appear in the reading. Which words or phrases are new to you? Circle them. Then, work with a partner. Read this paragraph introducing the topic of the reading, and match the words with their definitions. Be careful. There are two extra definitions.**

Imagine that you have a 50 percent chance of getting a terrible genetic illness twenty years from today. Will you be tested for the disease? What **factors** will affect your decision? If there is no way to prevent, treat, or cure the disease, will you still want to be tested for the **harmful** gene? Is there any **benefit** in knowing that you will get the disease? Will that knowledge **poison** your life? Or will it help you to plan for and feel more **in charge of** your own future?

Word	Definition
1. factor	**a.** make a time period shorter; reduce
2. harmful	**b.** influence someone's thoughts or emotions in a bad way, or make them feel very unhappy
3. benefit	**c.** controlling or responsible for a group of people or an activity
4. poison	**d.** one of several things that influence or cause a situation
5. in charge of	**e.** something that you know is true because there is proof
	f. causing damage to something
	g. something that gives you advantages or improves your life in some way

READING

Read the text once without stopping.

A Terrible Inheritance, A Difficult Decision

1   If you were at risk for[1] developing a genetic disease, would you be tested for it? What **factors** would affect your decision? If there were no way to prevent, treat, or cure the disease, would you still want to be tested? As gene research **progresses**, these are questions that a growing number of people are facing. As many are discovering, there are no easy answers.

2   Meet Katharine Moser. Moser is an occupational therapist[2] at Terence Cardinal Cooke Health Care Center, a nursing home on the Upper East Side of Manhattan. In 2002, Moser's grandfather died at Cooke. He had Huntington's Disease, a **severe** genetic illness

---

[1] *at risk for* = in danger of

[2] an *occupational therapist* = someone who helps people with physical or emotional problems do different activities

(continued)

that attacks the brain. Victims of the disease usually begin to show symptoms[3] when they are 40 to 50 years old. Early symptoms can include emotional and behavioral changes such as depression and aggressive behavior. As the disease progresses, victims **suffer** from a loss of control over their movements, difficulty in thinking and talking, and severe emotional and psychiatric complications. After ten to twenty years of suffering, victims lose all ability to move and finally die.

3   There is no special **diet** that you can follow to prevent Huntington's. There is no medicine that doctors can **prescribe** to treat it, and there is no **operation** they can perform to fix it. If one parent suffers from Huntington's, his or her children have a 50 percent chance of inheriting the gene that causes the disease. And if you have the gene, you will definitely develop the illness. There is no **effective** treatment, and no one has ever **recovered** from it.

4   At the age of 23, Moser made the decision to be tested for Huntington's. Her decision was unusual. Since there is no treatment or cure, most people at risk for Huntington's do not see any **benefit** to being tested. And knowing that you will one day get the disease can be **harmful** to your mental health and your relationships. In fact, Moser's own mother did not agree with her daughter's decision. If her daughter had the harmful gene, that would mean that she had it, too. And she did not want to know. "You don't want to know stuff like that. You want to enjoy life."

5   Nancy Wexler, like Katharine Moser, comes from a family with a history of Huntington's. Her mother, grandfather, and three of her uncles died of the disease. And like Moser, Wexler's work brings her into close contact with victims of the disease. She is a neuropsychologist[4] at Columbia University and is **in charge of** the Hereditary Disease Foundation. She is an expert in Huntington's, and was involved in the discovery of the gene for the disease in 1993. That discovery led to the development of the genetic test that Moser decided to take years later.

6   Wexler, like Moser, had always **intended** to have the test when it became available. But when she was actually faced with the decision of whether or not to be tested, she realized that she did not want to know. If the test were positive for the gene, she felt that her life would be **poisoned** by the knowledge. "If you take the test, you have to be prepared to be really depressed," said Nancy. "I've been depressed. I don't like it."

---

[3] a *symptom* = a physical or psychological condition which shows that you have a particular illness

[4] a *neuropsychologist* = a doctor who has special training in the nervous system and how it affects someone's psychological health

7   Moser had the test in 2005. It was positive for the deadly gene. However, she says that she is not sorry that she was tested. "I'm the same person I've always been. It's been in me from the beginning." At first, it was difficult for her to be around the Huntington's patients at work. However, she now finds strength and purpose in working with them. She is also involved in raising money for research on Huntington's Disease. Mostly, she is busy living her life. "I have a lot to do. And I don't have a lot of time."

8   Sadly, Moser's mother has not spoken to her daughter since she found out the results of the test. In an interview her mother said, "It's a horrible illness . . . Now he [her husband] has a wife who has it. Did she think of him? Did she think of me? Who is going to marry her?"

9   Wexler has never been tested, but it seems that she has been more **fortunate** than Moser. She is now in her 60s, past the age when symptoms of the disease usually appear. As Wexler continues her research, Moser goes on with her life, working, playing tennis, going to church, learning to ride a unicycle,[5] spending time with her best friend, traveling . . . and hoping that the work of Wexler and others will lead to a cure before it is too late for her and thousands of others.

---

[5] a *unicycle* = a vehicle that is like a bicycle but has only one wheel

Comprehension Check

Read these sentences. Circle T (true), F (false), or ? (can't determine the answer from the reading). If you circle F, change the sentence to make it true. Check your answers with a classmate. If your answers are different, look back at the reading.

1. Huntington's Disease is a genetic illness that only affects women.   T (F) ?

2. Fifty percent of people with Huntington's recover from the illness.   (T) F ?

3. Most people at risk for Huntington's get tested for the gene.   T (F) ?

4. Nancy Wexler decided not to be tested for Huntington's. (T) F ?

5. Nancy Wexler will never get Huntington's.   T F (?)

6. Katharine Moser's mother has Huntington's.   (T) F ?

EXPLORING VOCABULARY

Thinking about the Target Vocabulary

Guessing Strategy

Antonyms are words that have opposite meanings. Look at the example.

Two children with the same disease receive the same medicine:
One child recovers; the other dies.

The contrast in this sentence is between the two verbs *recover* and *die*. They are antonyms. If you understand the meaning of *die*, you can guess that *recover* has an opposite meaning.

Try It!

Read the sentence, and write a definition of the boldfaced target word.

The symptoms of the illness are **severe**, but the illness itself is not very serious.

Severe means _____.

 A   **Look at the target words and phrase. Which ones are new to you? Circle them here and in the reading. Then read "A Terrible Inheritance, a Difficult Decision" again. Look at how the target words and phrase are used and think about their meanings.**

Target Words and Phrase

factors (1)	diet (3)	recovered (3)	intended (6)
progresses (1)	prescribe (3)	benefit (4)	poisoned (6)
severe (2)	operation (3)	harmful (4)	fortunate (9)
suffer (2)	effective (3)	in charge of (5)	

B Complete the word-form chart with the target words and phrase as they are used in the reading. Write the base form of verbs and the singular form of nouns.

Nouns	Verbs	Adjectives	Other
factor	suffer	severe	in charch of
progresse	prescribe	effective	
diet	recovered	harmful	
operation	poisont	fortunate	
	intended		

Using the Target Vocabulary

These sentences are **about the reading**. Complete them with the words and phrase in the box. Circle the words or phrase in the sentences that help you understand the meanings of the target words. Be careful. There are two extra words or phrase.

diet	in charge of	poisons	recovered
effective	intends	prescribe	severe
fortunate	operation	progresses	suffered

1. Huntington's Disease _progresses_ over a period of ten to twenty years until the sufferer finally dies.
2. No one has ever _recovered_ from Huntington's. There is no cure or treatment.
3. The symptoms of Huntington's are _severe_. Once the disease appears, it is impossible for sufferers to live a normal life.
4. Because Huntington's is caused by a gene, doctors cannot perform an _intents_ to cut it out of your body.
5. Doctors cannot _prescribe_ a drug to prevent it.
6. You can't slow down the disease by eating a special _diet_.
7. Katharine Moser's grandfather and Nancy Wexler's mother _suffered_ and eventually died from Huntington's.
8. Wexler was involved in developing a very _effective_ test for Huntington's disease. In fact, the test is 100 percent reliable.

9. Wexler is now past the age when most people begin to show symptoms, so she probably will not get Huntington's. She is more _____ than Moser, who tested positive for the disease.

10. Despite the bad news, Moser is facing her future with courage. She _____ to use the time that she has left to enjoy life, and to help others with the disease.

DEVELOPING READING SKILLS

Interpreting a Diagram

Readings about scientific or technical topics often include both text and **diagrams**. The diagrams usually illustrate a specific part of the text to make it easier to understand. Understanding the connection between a written text and a diagram is an important reading skill.

Reread "A Terrible Inheritance, a Difficult Decision." Then look at the diagram of Katharine Moser's family tree. Based on the reading and what you see in the diagram below, circle and label the figures that represent the people from Katharine's family who are mentioned in the reading. Write K (Katharine), KG (Katharine's grandfather), and KM (Katharine's mother).

Multiple Generations

Descendants of a person who has or had Huntington's disease, but who have not had a genetic test, are "at risk" for the disease. Because symptoms develop later in life, there are often many generations of at-risk descendants. Children of someone with Huntington's have a 50% chance of carrying the disease-causing gene. Their children have a 25% chance, and so on.

Affected individual

Untested child has 50% chance

Untested Grandchild has 25% chance

Katharine Moser's Family

Key Chance of having abnormal gene

100% 50% 25% 0%

Testing Status

+ tested positive

− tested negative

EXPANDING VOCABULARY

Using the Target Vocabulary in New Contexts

**Complete the sentences with the target words and phrases in the box.
Be careful. There are two extra words or phrases.**

diet	harmful	prescribed	severe
effective	in charge of	progressed	suffering
factor	poison	recovering	

1. You are eating too much. It isn't healthy. You need to change your
   diet.

2. Sitting too close to a television when you are watching it can be
   harmful to your eyes.

3. He has _progressed_ very quickly in his career. He has been at
   the company for only one year, but he's already in charge of three
   departments and 100 employees.

4. She saw mice in her apartment, so she is going to get something to
   poison them.

5. There is going to be a _severe_ snowstorm tonight. I think
   we should stay home.

6. He's a very _effective_ teacher. His students learn a lot from him.

7. Her job is very important. She is _recovering_ 1,000 workers.

8. He is _suffering_ from cancer, but fortunately, the type that he
   has is curable.

9. One _factor_ to consider when buying a car is the cost.

Word Families

A **Read these sentences, and write the target words that are in the same
word families as the boldfaced words.**

1. The patient's **recovery** was faster than his doctors had expected.
   Target word: _recover_

2. She had a bad cough, so her doctor wrote her a **prescription** for
   cough medicine.
   Target word: _prescribe_

3. I'm sorry. It was never my **intention** to hurt you.
   Target word: _intend_

4. I know my dog looks scary, but he would never bite anyone. He's **harmless**.
   Target word: _harm_

5. In this book, there is a **progression** of activities from easy to difficult.
   Target word: _progress_

6. Eating the right kinds of food is **beneficial** to your health.
   Target word: _benefit_

B **Match the words from Part A to their definitions. Be careful. There is one extra definition.**

___c___ **1.** recovery
___f___ **2.** prescription
___d___ **3.** intention
___b___ **4.** harmless
___a___ **5.** progression
___g___ **6.** beneficial

a. a change or development from one situation or state to another

b. not dangerous

c. the act of getting better after an illness

d. something that you plan to do

e. the patient who a doctor operates on

f. a piece of paper from your doctor that allows you to get the medicine you need

g. good for you

Studying Collocations

Medicine, like any other professional field, has specialized vocabulary that includes many collocations. Look at the **boldfaced** collocations in the examples.

- She **suffers from** high blood pressure.
- She is in the hospital, **recovering from** a serious illness.
- He has very high cholesterol, so he has to **follow a strict diet**.
- The doctor who **performed the operation** made a serious mistake.

A Rewrite the following sentences with the correct collocations. Write one word in each space.

1. My father has skin cancer.
   My father ___suffers___ ___from___ skin cancer.   *I'm recovering from my surgery*

2. After his illness, he got better in a week.
   He ___recovered___ ___from___ ___his___ ___illness___ in a week.

3. Dr. Smith will be in charge of the operation.
   Dr. Smith will ___performed the___ ___operation___.

4. His doctor told him to be very careful about what he eats.
   His doctor advised him to ___follow___ ___a___ ___strict___ ___diet___.

B Write answers to these questions. Use the **boldfaced** collocations in your answers.

1. If you were **suffering from an incurable illness**, would you want your doctor to tell you, or would you rather not know?

   _____

   _____

2. Why do children usually **recover from an illness** more quickly than elderly people?

   _____

   _____

3. Have you ever watched a doctor **perform an operation**? If so, describe it. If not, would you like to? Why or why not?

   _____

   _____

4. People who suffer from certain diseases have to **follow a strict diet**. Name a couple of these diseases, and make a list of the foods that are restricted for each one.

   _____

   _____

PUTTING IT ALL TOGETHER

Discussion

Share your ideas in a small group. As you talk, try to use the vocabulary below. Each time someone uses a target word or phrase, put a check (✔) next to it.

beneficial	factor	harmful	progress	severe
effective	fortunate	prescribe	recover	suffer from

1. Some people think that genetic testing can be dangerous. They worry that we don't know who will use the information and how they will use it. For example, a company might want you to get a genetic test before they will give you a job. Then, depending on the results of the test, they will decide whether to give you a job or not. Do you think companies should be allowed to do this?

2. Imagine a day when doctors and scientists will be able to prevent or cure all diseases. Will this be a completely positive thing? Can you imagine any problems that this might lead to?

Writing

Choose one or both of the Discussion questions above to write about. When you write, use at least five of the target words from the chapter. Underline the target words in your paper.

REVIEWING READING SKILLS AND VOCABULARY

Read the text. Do not use a dictionary.

1   Historically, it took individual farmers generations of experimentation to develop the strongest, healthiest, and fastest-growing variety of a crop. Today, however, due to rapid progress in gene research, farmers can buy seeds whose genes have been carefully changed in a laboratory. The crops that grow from these genetically engineered seeds grow faster and are stronger and less likely to suffer from disease than traditional crops. In short, they have all the traits that farmers used to spend generations developing. The food that is produced from these crops is called genetically modified (GM).

2   In the United States, it is almost impossible to find food that does not contain at least some GM products. Actually, it is very difficult to determine whether you are buying GM food. That is because food labels in the United States do not usually identify products that have been genetically modified. In Western Europe, however, things are very different. Walk into almost any supermarket in France, Great Britain, or Italy, and you will see labels on the food that read "GM-free." By reading the labels, customers can identify those products that have not been genetically modified.

3   Why the difference? Although scientists say that GM food is harmless, many Europeans do not believe it. They express concern about the possible negative effects of growing and eating GM food. They worry about the effect it might have on the health of individuals and the environment. Finally, many Europeans are especially sensitive to this issue because of the importance of food to their culture.

4   In the United States, however, scientists and farmers who produce GM food argue that it is not only harmless but actually beneficial to humanity. They claim that by growing GM crops, farmers can produce much more food in a shorter period of time. In that way, GM products can help prevent hunger in parts of the world suffering from food shortages.

127

Comprehension Check

Read these sentences. Circle T (true), F (false), or ? (can't determine the answer from the reading). If you circle F, change the sentence to make it true.

1. In the past, farmers had no way to develop healthier, faster-growing plants.   T   F   ?

2. Today, most farmers in the United States benefit from the progress that scientists have made in the field of genetic engineering.   T   F   ?

3. By reading food labels, customers in the United States can decide for themselves whether or not to buy food that contains GM products.   T   F   ?

4. Many western Europeans are worried that GM food could make them sick.   (T)   F   ?

5. It is difficult to find GM food in Europe today.   T   F   (?)

Guessing Meaning from Context

Answer these questions.

1. Look at the word *crops* in paragraph 1. Write some examples of crops.

    rice, corn, wheat · oats

2. What is the meaning of the word *modified* in paragraph 1?

   _____

3. Look at the word *labels* in paragraph 2. What information is often written on these kinds of labels?

   tag stiker

Understanding Major Points

Answer these questions about the major points in the reading. Use your own words. Do not copy from the text.

1. What is the definition of genetically modified food?

   _____

2. What are some of the benefits of genetically modified food?

   harmless,

3. What are some of the possible problems with genetically modified food?

   _____

EXPANDING VOCABULARY

Studying Word Grammar

Some verbs must have a noun immediately after them. This noun is called a **direct object**. Verbs that need a direct object are called **transitive verbs**. The verb "love" is a transitive verb.

		verb	direct object
Transitive:	I	love	ice cream.

Other verbs do not have a direct object. These verbs are called **intransitive verbs**. The verb "listen" is an intransitive verb: *He is listening to the radio*, or *He is listening*. We can't say *He is listening radio*.

		verb	object of the preposition
Intransitive:	He	is listening	to the radio.
	He	is listening.	

A Look at the boldfaced verbs in these sentences. Circle T (transitive verb), or I (intransitive verb).

1. Their research **is progressing** rapidly.   T   I

2. To **prevent** heart disease, you should eat a healthy diet.   T   I

3. I don't like to see anyone **suffer**.   T   I

4. When his grandmother died, he **inherited** her house.   T   I

B On a piece of paper, write your own sentences with the verbs from Part A.

Word Families

Look at these sentences.

> *Fortunately, your disease is not severe.*

> *Unfortunately, however, it is incurable.*

A **prefix** is a word part added to the beginning of a word. It changes the word's meaning. The prefixes *un-* and *in-* both mean *not*. Other common prefixes include *dis-*, which also means *not*, and *mis-*, which means *wrong* or *bad*.

Complete these sentences with your own ideas. There is more than one correct way to complete each sentence.

1. If your father gives you **unrestricted** use of his car, you can <u>use it any time you want</u>.

2. If your parents **disinherit** you, you won't _have a many_.

3. If you suffer a **misfortune**, your friends might _help you_.

4. If your way of doing something is **ineffective**, you should _change your action_.

5. If your boss tells you that your work is **unacceptable**, you should _change your work._.

PLAYING WITH WORDS

You can play the game Concentration alone, but it is more fun if you play with one, two, or three other students.

- **Step 1:** Choose 10 words from the unit that you are having trouble learning. Take 20 blank index cards, and make 10 cards with just the words written on them, and 10 cards with the definitions of the 10 words written on them.

- **Step 2:** Next, mix the cards up well, and lay them facedown on a large desk or table, four cards across and five cards down.

- **Step 3:** Now, turn over any two cards, and try to remember what is written on them and where they are. If they form a match—a word or phrase on one card, a matching definition on the other—pick them up from the board and keep them, and take another turn. However, leave the other cards exactly where they were. If the two cards you turn over do not match, turn them both back over. Now it's the next person's turn. Play until all of the cards have been matched up. The winner is the person who has the most cards.

BUILDING DICTIONARY SKILLS

Finding Collocations

Your dictionary is an excellent resource for learning collocations. Look carefully at the entire dictionary entry, including the example sentences, for patterns of words that occur together.

 These dictionary entries come from the *Longman Dictionary of American English*. Look carefully at the example sentences in the dictionary, and then complete the sentences below each dictionary entry. Write one word in each space.

> **in·struc·tion** /ɪnˈstrʌkʃən/ *n* **1 instructions** [plural] information or advice that tells you how to do something, how to use a piece of equipment or machine, etc. [= **directions**]: *Follow the instructions at the top of the paper.* | *Did you read the instructions first?* | *He gave us **instructions on/about how to** fix the toilet.* | *Inside you'll find **instructions for** setting up your computer.* | *He gave instructions to keep the ball on the ground, not to kick it high.* **2** [U] teaching in a particular skill or subject: *She's never had any formal **instruction** [= lessons or classes] in music.* — **instructional** *adj*

1. _____ the instructions on the label.

2. I fixed the light. The electrician _____ me instructions over the phone.

> **pre·scribe** /prɪˈskraɪb/ *v* [T] **1** to say what medicine or treatment a sick person should have: *Doctors commonly **prescribe** steroids **for** children with asthma.* **2** *formal* to state officially what should be done in a particular situation: *a punishment prescribed by the law*
>
> **pre·scrip·tion** /prɪˈskrɪpʃən/ *n* **1** [C] a piece of paper on which a doctor writes what medicine a sick person should have, or the medicine itself: *a **prescription for** painkillers* **2 by prescription** a drug that you get by prescription can only be obtained with a written order from the doctor [≠ **over the counter**]

3. My dentist _____ pain medicine _____ me.

4. My dentist wrote me a _____ _____ pain medicine.

> **di·et¹** /ˈdaɪət/ *n* **1** [C,U] the type of food that you eat each day: *Many kids don't get enough fruit in their diet.* | *The animals live on a **diet of** fruit and insects.* **2** [C] a plan to eat only particular kinds or amounts of food, especially because you want to get thinner or because you have a health problem: *a low-fat diet* | *No dessert for me –I'm **on a diet**.*
>
> **diet²** *v* [I] to eat less or eat only particular foods in order to lose weight: *Jill's always dieting.*

5. I can't have any ice cream. I am _____ _____ _____.

 On a piece of paper, write your own sentences about yourself and your life with the words from Part A.

Vocabulary Self-Test 1

Circle the letter of the word or phrase that best completes each sentence.

Example:

Scientists usually work in _____.

(**a.**) laboratories   **b.** literature   **c.** personalities   **d.** victims

1. That performer _____ received $10,000 for just one performance.

    a. rapidly   **b.** reportedly   **c.** morally   **d.** historically

2. The scientist conducted some _____ to find out how much sleep most teens need.

    a. experiments   **b.** equipment   **c.** championships   **d.** patterns

3. I'm tired because I _____ too late last night.

    a. stayed up   **b.** grew out of   **c.** stood out   **d.** burned out

4. The cat _____ her on the face.

    a. scratched   **b.** survived   **c.** cured   **d.** prevented

5. Poems are often written in _____.

    a. spin   **b.** replace   **c.** compete   **d.** rhyme

6. That team has won several _____.

    a. complaints   **b.** championships **c.** cells   **d.** features

7. Leave your little brother alone. Don't _____ him.

    a. pick on   **b.** bring up   **c.** drop out   **d.** stand up for

8. To be successful, it is important to have high _____.

    a. mystery   **b.** self-esteem   **c.** concern   **d.** diet

9. When your grandmother dies, you are going to _____ this house.

    a. progress   **b.** contribute   **c.** reduce   **d.** inherit

10. The government spends very little money on education. Almost 60 percent of the people in the country are _____.

    a. live   **b.** athletic   **c.** illiterate   **d.** anxious

11. Don't work so hard. You'll _____.

    a. stay up   **b.** burn out   **c.** in charge of   **d.** pick on

12. This is a _____ area. You cannot enter.

    a. talented   **b.** remarkable   **c.** moral   **d.** restricted

13. He is not doing well in school because he has a bad _____.

    a. appearance   **b.** individual   **c.** attitude   **d.** official

14. Stay in school. If you _____, you will never get a good job.

    a. recover   **b.** identify   **c.** prevent   **d.** drop out

15. He is _____ from a very serious disease.

    a. examining   **b.** reducing   **c.** conducting   **d.** suffering

16. She is very _____. She is good at most sports.

    a. economic   **b.** athletic   **c.** intellectual   **d.** characteristic

17. He went to the pharmacy to get the medicine that his doctor

    _____.

    a. suffered   **b.** examined   **c.** announced   **d.** prescribed

18. She is on a very restricted _____. She can only eat vegetables.

    a. appearance   **b.** background   **c.** diet   **d.** proof

19. They _____ to kill him if he didn't give them all of his money.

    a. poisoned   **b.** contacted   **c.** threatened   **d.** survived

20. _____, women have made less money than men.

    a. In charge of   **b.** On the basis of   **c.** Historically   **d.** Physically

21. She is in the hospital, recovering from a serious _____.

    a. cure   **b.** humanity   **c.** operation   **d.** victim

22. I'm your friend. I will always _____ you.

    a. stand by   **b.** pick on   **c.** grow out of   **d.** get rid of

23. I believe in freedom and _____ for all people.

    a. justice   **b.** courage   **c.** background   **d.** mystery

24. Because of its beauty, that painting _____.

    a. burns out   **b.** stands out   **c.** brings up   **d.** calls for

25. He won the competition _____ his illness.

    a. due to   **b.** on the basis of   **c.** despite   **d.** at least

26. We gave her the job because of her strong _____ in international business.

    a. pattern   **b.** instruction   **c.** background   **d.** challenge

27. Please stop making so much noise. I need to _____.

    a. concentrate   **b.** determine   **c.** identify   **d.** prescribe

28. Fortunately, the patient _____ from the illness.

    a. suffered   **b.** progressed   **c.** intended   **d.** recovered

29. She is the most _____ woman I know. She's not afraid of anything.

    a. beneficial   **b.** fortunate   **c.** courageous   **d.** depressed

30. His work is _____, but not brilliant.

    a. acceptable   **b.** severe   **c.** heavenly   **d.** evil

31. There are many _____ to getting a university education.

    a. complaints   **b.** concerns   **c.** traits   **d.** advantages

32. I'm so sorry I woke you up. I didn't _____ it was so early.

    a. identify   **b.** realize   **c.** intend   **d.** examine

33. Teenagers are usually very concerned about the opinions of their _____.

    a. experts   **b.** personalities   **c.** peers   **d.** perfectionists

34. You were very _____ to survive the fire.

    a. evil   **b.** original   **c.** fortunate   **d.** gifted

35. I wasn't _____ in the project. He did it by himself.

    a. fascinated   **b.** involved   **c.** related   **d.** threatened

36. You don't need to bring any _____. We have all the tools we need to do the job.

    a. technique   **b.** theory   **c.** equipment   **d.** challenge

See the Answer Key on page 275.

UNIT
4

GETTING EMOTIONAL

CHAPTER 10

Can You Translate an Emotion?

Children often have trouble controlling their emotions.

GETTING READY TO READ

A **Talk with a partner or in a small group.**

1. In general, is it easy or difficult for you to express your emotions? Which emotions do you often express? Which do you rarely express?

2. Who is the most emotional person you know? Describe him or her. Is the fact that he or she is so emotional positive or negative? Why?

B **The boldfaced words below appear in the reading. Which words are new to you? Circle them. Then, work with a partner. Read the definitions of the words, and write one word under each picture.**

> **anger** = a strong feeling of wanting to hurt or criticize someone because he or she has been unkind or done something bad to you
> **cheerfulness** = a happy, good feeling
> **disgust** = a strong feeling of dislike and disapproval
> **grief** = extreme sadness, especially because someone has died
> **guilt** = a strong feeling of being ashamed and sad because you know or believe you have done something wrong

1. ___Grief___
   grive

2. ___guilt___

3. ___disgust___

4. ___chorfulness___

5. ___anger___

READING

Read the text once without stopping.

Can You Translate
an Emotion?

1   In the Northwest of Canada, there is a group of people called the Utkuhikhalingmiut ("Utku"). According to anthropologist[1] Jean L. Briggs, author of the book *Never in Anger*, the Utku have no real word in their language for **anger**. And even more remarkable, they do not seem to ever get angry. The word that they use to describe

___

[1] an *anthropologist* = a person who studies people, their societies, beliefs, etc.

(continued)

the angry behavior of foreigners **translates** not as anger, but rather as "childishness."[2]

2   Similarly, the Ifaluk people of Micronesia seem to rarely get angry, and there is almost no murder in their culture. However, **in contrast** to the Utku, they talk about anger all the time and have many words to describe it. They consider anger to be evil—a demon,[3] in fact—and fear it.

3   The expression of **grief** and gratitude[4] is central to the Kaululi culture of Papua New Guinea. In contrast, people from the United States generally spend very little time talking about grief or gratitude. Research on American males shows that they are **particularly** uncomfortable expressing either emotion.

4   What is going on here? Aren't we all human beings? Don't we all feel the same basic emotions? This is a topic that philosophers,[5] scientists, religious leaders, and anthropologists, among others, have been arguing about for centuries. Many researchers today believe that a limited number of emotions are **universal**. However, there is not complete agreement on which emotions humans **indeed** share. Fear and anger are almost always included; **guilt**, joy, **shame**, **disgust**, and surprise are also considered by many to be universal. But then how can we explain the Utku and the Ifaluk?

5   Dr. Robert C. Solomon, professor of philosophy at the University of Texas at Austin, has argued that emotions are, at least in part, culture-specific. In one essay, he says that even among people from the same culture, it is difficult to get agreement on what an emotion is. For example, most anthropologists would not consider love to be an emotion, but if it is not an emotion, then what is it?

6   Another challenge is how to determine that two people are indeed feeling the same emotion. You can **observe** people's behavior, and ask them to describe their emotions, but it is impossible to directly observe what they are feeling. This becomes even more complex when you are trying to compare emotions across cultures.

7   We tend to **associate** certain behaviors with specific emotions, but of course our associations are based on what those behaviors mean in our own culture. For example, imagine you are a teacher

---

[2] *childishness* = behavior that is typical of a child

[3] a *demon* = an evil spirit

[4] *gratitude* = the feeling of wanting to express thanks for something kind that someone has done

[5] a *philosopher* = a person who studies or teaches about the world, life, death, etc.

with a Chinese student who has failed your class. Sadly, you learn that he **attempted** to hurt himself when he received his grade. If you are from the United States, you will probably describe his emotional state as depressed, for in U.S. culture, there is a belief that people who try to harm themselves are usually depressed. However, if you have some knowledge of Chinese culture, you might **recognize** your student's behavior as an expression of deep shame at having disgraced[6] his family.

8   Of course, this example is very simple—it does not mean that the Chinese do not ever experience depression, or that people from the United States do not feel shame. However, can someone from a culture that does not place the same value on family **honor** really understand this deep feeling of disgrace? In other words, is Chinese shame and American shame really the same emotion?

9   Another reason to believe that not all emotions are universal is the fact that different languages characterize emotions in different ways. For instance, in the ancient Indian languages of Sanskrit and Bengali, emotions are described as being either *sattva* (lightness), *rajas* (movement), or *tamas* (heaviness). Interestingly, two of the examples of *sattva*—**cheerfulness** and nobility[7]—are not generally considered to be emotions in English. Is this just a language difference? Or does it **reveal** that people across cultures do not share a similar emotional experience?

10   The mystery of whether emotions are universal or culturally specific is one that most likely will never be solved. That probably contributes to our fascination with the subject.

---

[6] *disgrace* = do something so bad that people lose respect for you

[7] *nobility* = the quality of being morally good or generous in a way that should be admired

Comprehension Check

Read these sentences. Circle T (true), F (false), or ? (can't determine the answer from the reading). If you circle F, change the sentence to make it true. Check your answers with a classmate. If your answers are different, look back at the reading.

1. All languages have words for the most basic human emotions.   T   F   ⓐ

2. In the Utku culture, people who express anger are considered childish.   Ⓣ   F   ?

3. The basic human emotions are universal, not culture-specific.   T   F   ⓐ

4. Because we cannot know exactly what other people are feeling, we observe their behavior and then try to guess what they are feeling. T F ?

5. The shame that an American feels is different from the shame that a Chinese person feels. T F ?

6. The word *sattva* means cheerfulness. T F ?

EXPLORING VOCABULARY

Thinking about the Target Vocabulary

Guessing Strategy

You learned in the Guessing Strategy for Chapter 4 that to avoid repeating words, writers often use synonyms. They also use words that have similar meanings, but are different word forms. Look at the example.

*Many researchers today believe that a limited number of emotions are **universal**. However, there is not complete agreement on which emotions humans indeed share.*

Based on the context, you can guess that the words *universal* and *share* have a similar meaning, even though *universal* is an adjective and *share* is a verb.

Try It!

Read the sentences, and write the word or words that are similar in meaning to the **boldfaced** target word.

His emotions are not hidden from anybody. He **reveals** whatever he is feeling.

Reveals is similar in meaning to _____.

A Look at the target words and phrase. Which ones are new to you? Circle them here and in the reading. Then read "Can You Translate an Emotion?" again. Look at the context of each new word and phrase. Can you guess the meaning? Use the Guessing Strategy where possible.

Target Words and Phrase			
anger (1)	universal (4)	disgust (4)	recognize (7)
translates (1)	indeed (4)	observe (6)	honor (8)
in contrast (2)	guilt (4)	associate (7)	cheerfulness (9)
grief (3)	shame (4)	attempted (7)	reveal (9)
particularly (3)			

B Complete the word-form chart with the target words and phrases as they are used in the reading. Write the base form of verbs and the singular form of nouns.

Nouns	Verbs	Adjectives	Other
anger			

Using the Target Vocabulary

The sentences on page 142 are **about the reading**. Complete them with the words and phrase in the box. Circle the words or phrases in the sentences that help you understand the meanings of the target words. Be careful. There are two extra words or phrases.

associate	honor	particularly	translate
attempted	in contrast	recognize	universal
cheerfulness	indeed	reveal	
disgust	observe	shame	

1. Are human emotions culturally specific, or are they _universal_ ?
2. Experts in many fields have _attempted_ to answer this question for years, but we still don't know the answer.
3. Answering the question is _particular_ difficult because we cannot "see" an emotion. We cannot _observe_ someone's feelings directly.
4. How do we know what others are feeling? We usually look at their behavior, and then _associate_ it with an emotion. In other words, we believe that actions _reveal_, or show, a person's true feelings.
5. However, the same behavior in one culture might mean something different in another. Therefore, it is not always easy to _recognize_ which emotions individuals from another country are expressing through their behavior.
6. For example, Americans think that people who deliberately try to hurt themselves are depressed. _In contr._, in Chinese culture, such behavior is often associated with _shame_ and guilt.
7. Because the Chinese believe that the reputation and _honor_ of a family are very important, a Chinese student who brings shame to his family by getting poor grades might consider harming himself.
8. Another problem is that it is not always easy to _translate_ the words of emotion from one language to another. _In sent_, in the Utku culture in Northwest Canada, there appears to be no word at all for anger.

DEVELOPING READING SKILLS

Understanding Inference

Answer the questions on page 143 in your own words. The answers are not written directly in the reading. You will need to infer them. There might be more than one correct way to answer each question.

1. In paragraph 3, the reading says that "American males . . . are particularly uncomfortable expressing either emotion." From this sentence, what can you infer about *females* in the United States?

   _____ less emoutions. _____

2. How do you think Utku parents react when their young children behave in an angry way? Be specific.

   _____

3. How do you think Ifaluk parents react when their young children behave in an angry way? Be specific.

   _____

Paraphrasing

When you **paraphrase** a sentence, you use different words. However, you do not change the meaning of the original sentence. Look at the paraphrase of this sentence from the reading.

   Original sentence: Grief and gratitude are central to the Kaululi culture of Papua New Guinea.

   Paraphrase: For the Kaululi people who live in Papua New Guinea, grief and gratitude are very important emotions.

Notice that you do not have to change *all* of the words when you paraphrase.

One sentence in each set paraphrases the sentence from the reading. Circle the correct answer.

1. Many researchers today believe that a limited number of emotions are universal.

   a. A lot of experts agree that most people experience at least a few of the same emotions, regardless of which country they come from.

   b. People who study human emotions think that all human beings share the same emotions.

2. However, there is not complete agreement on which emotions humans indeed share.

   a. But the emotions noted by one group of experts are completely different from those of another group of experts.

   b. But not all experts agree on which feelings are indeed universal.

3. This becomes even more complex when you are trying to compare emotions across cultures.

    a. It is particularly difficult to describe the emotions of two people who come from different cultures. ✓

    b. It is not easy to compare people who come from different parts of the world.

EXPANDING VOCABULARY

Using the Target Vocabulary in New Contexts

Complete the sentences with the target words and phrase in the box. Be careful. There are two extra words or phrases.

associate	honor	particularly	translate
attempt	in contrast	recognize	universal
disgust	indeed	reveal	
guilt	observe	shame	

1. It is an ____honor____ to be seated next to the president.

2. I'd rather not go to that movie. I'm not ____particularly____ interested in war films.

3. If you eat something that makes you sick, you will always ____associate____ that food with your illness.

4. Please wear a red coat so that I will ____recognize____ you in the crowd.

5. You are so courageous! I would be afraid to even ____attempt____ to climb that mountain!

6. This letter is too complex for me to ____translate____ My Spanish is not that good.

7. There are many feelings that may vary among cultures, but the need for love is probably ____universal____.

8. The doctor is almost certain that the patient has recovered, but he still wants to ____observe____ her for twenty-four hours.

homework.

9. *In fact* and ___indeed___ have the same meaning.

10. The competition lasts for a week. They will ___reveal___ the winner on the last day.

11. Tom felt terrible about the car accident. He felt both guilt and ___shameful___ that the little girl was hurt.

12. That drug can be harmful. This drug, ___in contre___, is harmless.

Word Families

Study the chart. Look at the adjective forms of the target words. Then, complete the sentences with words from the chart. Make sure you use the correct word forms. Be careful; you will not use all the words.

Noun: Names the emotion	Adjective: Describes the way someone feels	Adjective: Describes what/who causes the feeling
His **shame** at what he had done bothered him for the rest of his life.	You made her cry. You should be **ashamed** of yourself!	The way you treated her was **shameful**.
anger	angry	
shame	ashamed	shameful
cheerfulness	cheerful	cheerful OR cheery
disgust	disgusted	disgusting
guilt	guilty	

1. This soup smells ___disgusting___. I can't eat it!

2. After he stole the money, he felt ___guilty___, so he decided to give it back.

3. Her shame kept her quiet her entire life. She never revealed her ___shameful___ secret to anyone.

4. It's difficult to feel depressed around her because she's always so ___cheerful___.

5. Some people shout and throw things when they are ___angry___.

6. After I found a hair in my food, I was so ___disgusted___ that I couldn't eat.

7. The mother felt ___ashamed___ when her son was sent home from school for behaving badly in class.

Studying Word Grammar

You learned in Unit 3 that transitive verbs always have a direct object. Often, the direct object is a noun or pronoun. Look at the sentence using the transitive verb **recognize**.

                    pronoun   pronoun
*She didn't **recognize** me, but I **recognized** her.*

However, in some cases, the direct object is not a noun or pronoun. Look at the transitive verbs **attempt** and **observe**.

*We all **attempted** to help her, but unfortunately we couldn't.*

In the example above, *attempt* is followed by an **infinitive**: *to* + verb.

*The doctor **observed** that the patient was able to move his left leg.*

In the example above, *observe* is followed by a full **clause**: *that* + subject + verb. Different verbs have different patterns. In order to use a verb correctly, you need to learn the pattern(s) for that particular verb. If you are not sure, look in your dictionary.

A   **Look at the patterns in the box above for the verbs *recognize*, *attempt*, and *observe*. Then, read the sentences, and put a check (✔) next to those that are correct and an X next to those that are incorrect.**

____ **1.** When the police showed the victim several photographs, she recognized her attacker immediately.

____ **2.** The victim attempted identify her attacker, but she couldn't.

____ **3.** The police observed the man to behave in a strange way.

____ **4.** The researchers observed that all of the mice in the experiment had the same reaction to the chemical.

____ **5.** The police attempted to catch the man, but he escaped.

____ **6.** He tried to hide, but someone recognized him.

B   **Answer these questions in complete sentences. Use the boldfaced verbs. Make sure you use the correct patterns.**

1. Describe a time when you **attempted** to do something difficult, but failed.

I attempted to jump from very high wall and I broke my lay.

2. Choose a culture that you are familiar with. What differences have you **observed** between that culture and your own?

    _____

    _____

3. What would you do if you **recognized** your favorite actor on the street?

    I would say to him or her
    that he is the best.

PUTTING IT ALL TOGETHER

Discussion

Share your ideas in a small group. As you talk, try to use the vocabulary below. Each time someone uses a target word or phrase, put a check (✔) next to it.

anger/angry	in contrast
attempt	indeed
disgust/disgusted/disgusting	observe
grief	particularly
guilt/guilty	reveal
honor	shame/ashamed/shameful

1. Choose one of the emotions from the list above, and tell your group about a time when you or someone you know felt that way. Include details (for example, *who, what, where, when,* and *how*) to make your story come alive for your classmates.

2. Some people think that it is healthy to express emotions openly. Other people believe that it is best to control their emotions and not reveal them to others. What are the advantages and disadvantages of each approach?

Writing

Choose one or both of the Discussion questions above to write about. When you write, use at least five of the target words from the chapter. Underline the target words in your paper.

CHAPTER 11

Catching an Emotion

Will you catch his bad mood?

GETTING READY TO READ

 A **Talk with a partner or in a small group.**

1. Are you good at reading other people's faces? Can you usually guess how someone else is feeling?

2. Do you believe that feelings can be passed from one person to another, like a sickness can be passed from one person to another? Why or why not? Describe a time when you "caught" someone else's feeling.

B **Look at the boldfaced words and phrases in the sentences. Which words or phrases are new to you? Circle them. Then, work with a partner. Read the sentences and choose the correct definition of the boldfaced word or phrase.**

1. Many different cultures **make up** the world. Although some social rules are universal, others differ from one country to another.

   a. combine together to form a particular system or group

   b. confuse one thing with another

   c. paint or color something

2. In some cultures, parents teach their children to share their emotions with others. Expressing one's emotions is seen as a **virtue**.
   a. deep feeling
   b. difficult thing to do
   c. good quality in someone's character

3. In other cultures, children are taught to control their emotions from a very early age. Revealing one's feelings openly is **frowned upon**.
   a. disapproved of
   b. common and accepted
   c. unusual, but good

4. His thick, dark **eyebrows** make him look angry, but he isn't. He is actually a very cheerful person.
   a. eyes that are set too close together
   b. small hairs that grow along the edge of the eyelids
   c. the line of short hairs above your eyes

5. I know that she's not having a good time. She's smiling, but it's not a real smile. It's **artificial**.
   a. depressed
   b. not natural or real
   c. cheerful

READING

Read the text once without stopping.

Catching an Emotion

1   You wake up one day with a fever and a bad cough. Should you go to work? In the past, many employers would likely have said yes. Going to work even when you were sick showed your commitment to your job, and was considered a **virtue**. Missing work for any reason was **frowned upon**. Nowadays, however, employers would probably agree that the **proper** decision in this case would be to stay at home. After all, it is better for one sick employee to miss a day or two than to pass the illness on to everyone in the office. But now imagine this situation. You wake up

(continued)

in a bad **mood**. Should you be concerned about passing your mood on to your co-workers?

2   According to psychologist[1] and writer Daniel Goleman, the answer is yes. In his recent book, *Social Intelligence: The New Science of Relationships*, Goleman explains that our brains are social tools; that is, the human brain was designed for social interaction. Research has shown that the human brain contains cells called "mirror neurons."[2] According to Goleman, these neurons allow us to sense "both the move another person is about to make and their feelings, and instantaneously[3] prepare us to imitate[4] that movement and feel with them." Goleman goes on to say that "mirror neurons link brain-to-brain . . . if you put a person in a meeting who is either purposely upbeat[5] or downbeat,[6] it changes the whole group's collective mood for better or worse."

3   One example of passing one's emotions on to others is through laughter. One person starts laughing **out loud**, and even though we have no idea what the person is laughing at, we begin to laugh as well. When people are alone, on the other hand, they rarely laugh out loud, even when they read or hear a very **humorous** joke. This suggests that laughter is meant to be shared.

4   When someone laughs out loud, it is easy to recognize his or her emotional state. But most emotions are not expressed in such an obvious way. How are we able to recognize them? Brain research has shown that our ability to sense others' emotions is in our genes. We may not be **conscious** of it, but we are especially good at reading others' **facial expressions**. Even the most **reserved** people reveal some emotion on their faces. For example, a movement as small as a raised **eyebrow** can communicate a world of information.

5   Psychologist Paul Ekman is considered the world's leading expert on facial expressions. He has spent years identifying the **muscle** movements that **make up** the thousands of facial expressions that we use to communicate our emotions. Interestingly, Ekman's research has revealed that our facial expressions are not only a mirror of what we are feeling. Sometimes, just making a facial expression can cause us to

---

[1] a *psychologist* = someone who is trained in the way that people's minds work and the way that this affects their behavior

[2] a *neuron* = a type of cell that makes up the nervous system and sends messages in the brain about feelings, sights, smells, etc.

[3] *instantaneously* = immediately

[4] *imitate* = copy the way that someone behaves, speaks, moves, etc.

[5] *upbeat* = happy and confident that good things will happen

[6] *downbeat* = not hopeful that the future will be good

experience a particular emotion. For example, if you are in a bad mood, but put on an **artificial** smile, you will start to feel better faster. In other words, sometimes the facial expression actually starts the emotional process, rather than the other way around. So if you **greet** someone with a cheerful expression on your face, both of you will be more likely to feel cheerful.

6   Now let's return to our worker who wakes up in a bad mood. What should he do? The decision might depend on the workplace. If the atmosphere is generally positive and **harmonious**, he should get up and go to work; it is more likely that he will "catch" the positive mood of others than that he will pass on his negative mood. And if he smiles despite his bad mood, he will have an even greater chance of recovery.

7   On the other hand, if the workplace atmosphere is negative, it might mean that he's already "caught" the negative feelings of his co-workers. In that case, it might be a good idea for him to start looking for another job. And now that he understands how emotions are passed from one person to another, he should be more **choosy** about where he works. He should look for a healthy workplace where he is unlikely to "catch" negative feelings from his co-workers. At the same time, he should be more conscious of the effect that his own emotional state has on his co-workers. As Goleman says, "Mirror neurons make us far more neurally connected than we ever knew; this creates a pathway for emotional contagion.[7] If you really care about people, it gives a new spin to the term social responsibility: what emotional states are you creating in the people you're with?"

---

[7] *contagion* = a feeling or attitude that spreads quickly from person to person

Comprehension Check

Read these sentences. Circle T (true), F (false), or ? (can't determine the answer from the reading). If you circle F, change the sentence to make it true. Check your answers with a classmate. If your answers are different, look back at the reading.

1. If you are depressed, you should probably not go to work.   T   F   ?

2. Mirror neurons help us to recognize other people's feelings.   T   F   ?

3. Reserved people are particularly good at understanding how other people are feeling.   T   F   ?

4. We have very little control over our facial expressions.   T   F   ?

5. We learn how to read facial expressions from our parents.   T   F   ?

6. When people are alone, they don't laugh as much as when they are with other people.   T   F   ?

7. Our facial expressions can affect our emotions.   T   F   ?

EXPLORING VOCABULARY

Thinking about the Target Vocabulary

Guessing Strategy

Look carefully at an unfamiliar word. Does it look like another word you already know? If so, it might be a form of that word. Look at the example from the reading.

*We are especially good at reading others' **facial expressions**.*

Facial is the adjective form of the noun *face*. *Expression* is the noun form of the verb *express*. A facial expression is a look on a person's face that shows what that person is thinking or feeling.

Try It!

Read the sentences and answer the questions.

In some cultures, expressing emotions is accepted. In other cultures, expressing emotion is **frowned upon**.

    1. What word is similar to **frowned**?_____

    2. What does that word mean? _____

    3. What does **frowned upon** mean?_____

 Look at the target words and phrases on page 153. Which ones are new to you? Circle them on page 153 and in the reading. Then read "Catching an Emotion" again. Look at how the target words and phrases are used and think about their meanings.

Target Words and Phrases

virtue (1)	conscious (4)	artificial (5)
frowned upon (1)	facial expressions (4)	greet (5)
proper (1)	reserved (4)	harmonious (6)
mood (1)	eyebrow (4)	choosy (7)
out loud (3)	muscle (5)	
humorous (3)	make up (5)	

B Complete the word-form chart with the target words and phrases as they are used in the reading. Write the base form of verbs and the singular form of nouns.

Nouns	Verbs	Adjectives	Other
virtue			

Using the Target Vocabulary

These sentences are **about the reading**. Complete them with the words and phrases in the box. Circle the words or phrases in the sentences that help you understand the meanings of the target words. Be careful. There are two extra words or phrases.

artificial	frowned upon	mood	reserved
choosy	greet	muscles	
conscious	harmonious	out loud	
facial expressions	humorous	proper	

1. When humans _____ each other, they almost always look at each other's faces. It is the polite, _____ thing to do.

2. But there is another reason that we look at each other's faces. We want to know what the other person is feeling and thinking, so we observe each other's _____.

3. There are hundreds of _____ in the human face. Moving just one of them can reveal what we are feeling.

4. If you are in a good _____, your cheerful face will speak louder than any words.

5. You don't need to express your emotions _____. Your face will speak for you.

6. Even _____ people who tend to hide their emotions reveal more than they think on their faces.

7. According to psychologists, many of us do not realize the power of our own emotions. We are not _____ of how our feelings affect others.

8. When you hear something _____, you usually smile or laugh. That puts you in a good mood. You then pass that mood on to others around you.

9. Humor and laughter help create _____ relationships between people. People who laugh together feel more relaxed and happy around each other.

10. We also pass our bad moods on to each other. That is why we should be _____ about who we spend time with. If you have a choice, spend your time with people with a positive attitude.

DEVELOPING READING SKILLS

Understanding Major Points

Talk with a partner. Answer these questions. Do not look back at the reading. After you finish talking, write down your answers as completely as you can. Don't worry about grammar or spelling. Just focus on putting the major points into your own words. Be careful. Some of the answers are not stated directly in the reading. You will need to infer the answer.

1. What does Goleman mean when he says that our brains are "social tools"?

2. What do mirror neurons do, and why are they important?

3. How do we "read" other people's emotions?

4. What does Goleman mean when he says, "If you really care about people, it gives a new spin to the term social responsibility: what emotional states are you creating in the people you're with"?

Understanding Reference Words

A **reference word** is a word that takes the place of a noun, a noun phrase, or a clause. Pronouns (such as *he, she, it,* and *them*) are reference words. A reference word usually comes after a noun, a noun phrase, or a clause, and refers back to it. The words *this, that, these, those, that, which, who,* and *whom* are also reference words.

What do the boldfaced reference words mean in these sentences? Look back at the reading, and circle the correct answers. The number in parentheses is the paragraph number where the sentence appears.

1. Goleman goes on to say that "mirror neurons link brain-to-brain . . . if you put a person in a meeting **who** is either purposely upbeat or downbeat, it changes the whole group's collective mood for better or worse." (2)

   In this sentence, *who* refers to

   a. a person. **b.** a meeting. **c.** a group.

2. This suggests that laughter is meant to be shared. (3)

   In this sentence, *this* refers to

   a. the fact that people rarely laugh out loud when they are alone. **b.** the fact that people read or hear a humorous joke and laugh. **c.** the fact that people are alone.

3. How are we able to recognize **them**? (4)

   In this sentence, *them* refers to

   a. people who laugh out loud. **b.** most emotions. **c.** his or her emotional state.

4. We may not be conscious of **it**, but we are especially good at reading others' facial expressions. (4)

   In this sentence, *it* refers to

   a. our ability. **b.** brain research. **c.** our genes.

5. Even the most reserved people reveal some emotion on **their** faces. (4)

   In this sentence, *their* refers to

   a. others' emotions. **b.** other people. **c.** reserved people.

6. He has spent years identifying the muscle movements **that** make up the thousands of facial expressions that we use to communicate our emotions. (5)

In this sentence, *that* refers to

a. the muscle movements.
b. the thousands of facial expressions.
c. our emotions.

7. On the other hand, if the workplace atmosphere is negative, **it** might mean that he's already "caught" the negative feelings of his co-workers. (7)

In this sentence, *it* refers to

a. the fact that the worker wakes up in a bad mood.
b. the workplace atmosphere.
c. his co-workers feelings.

EXPANDING VOCABULARY

Using the Target Vocabulary in New Contexts

Complete the sentences with the target words and phrases in the box. Be careful. There are two extra words or phrases.

artificial	frowned upon	make up	proper
choosy	greet	mood	reserved
conscious	harmonious	muscle	virtue
eyebrows	humorous	out loud	

1. When you travel, it is important to know which behaviors are _____ in that culture, and which behaviors are inappropriate. That way, you will know how to behave politely.
2. My uncle has very thick _____ and a big moustache.
3. In some traditional cultures, a woman going out alone at night is still _____.
4. I don't like food with _____ ingredients. I like to eat healthy, natural food.

5. If you want to survive in this economy, you can't be
_____ about which job you take. You should feel
fortunate to have a job!

6. Most people would probably agree that honesty is a
_____.

7. It is faster to read silently than to read _____.

8. In some European cultures, it is proper to _____ a friend
with a kiss on the cheek.

9. _____ stories can be particularly difficult to translate.
That is because what is funny in one culture may not be funny in
another.

10. I'm sorry I'm late. I was so involved in my work that I wasn't
_____ of the time.

11. You go to the party without me. I'm not in the _____
for being around a lot of people.

12. People from England tend to be more _____ than
Americans. The English tend to keep their feelings to themselves
rather than expressing them openly.

13. England, Scotland, Ireland, and Wales _____ the United
Kingdom.

Word Families

Some adjectives are formed by adding -y to the end of a word. Look
at the example.

*My daughter is only three years old, but she is already very **choosy**.
For example, she won't let me choose her clothes. She likes to
choose her own.*

Sometimes, the meaning of the adjective will be very close to the
meaning of the original word, but in some cases, you will need to
use the context to guess what the adjective means. Notice that the
spelling sometimes changes when you add -y.

Complete the sentences with the adjectives below.

airy   juicy   moody   picky   smelly   watery

1. No one likes to invite her for dinner because she's such a _____ eater. It's impossible to remember the types of food that she won't eat.

2. These oranges are delicious! They are so sweet and _____.

3. I can't drink this coffee. It's too _____. I like stronger coffee.

4. This room is so bright and _____. And look at the beautiful view!

5. Some people do not like strong cheese. They think that it is too _____.

6. My brother is very _____. He can be cheerful one minute, and depressed the next.

Studying Phrasal Verbs

There are several phrasal verbs that are formed with the verb *make* and the particle *up*. Each one has a different meaning.

Read the definitions for *make up* and the sentences that follow. Write the letter of the meaning next to each sentence.

a. prepare or arrange something by putting things together

b. work or study at times when you do not usually work, so that you can do all the work that you should have done at an earlier time

c. become friendly again with someone after you have had an argument

d. invent a story, explanation, etc.

e. combine together to form a particular system, result, etc.

_____ 1. I missed the exam because I was sick. Can I **make** it **up**?

_____ 2. That isn't a true story. He **made** it **up**.

_____ 3. My husband and I had a fight last week, but yesterday we **made up**.

_____ 4. I'll **make up** a list of things we need for the party, and then we can go shopping.

_____ 5. There are many muscle movements that make up our facial expressions.

PUTTING IT ALL TOGETHER

Discussion

Share your ideas in a small group. As you talk, try to use the vocabulary below. Each time someone uses a target word or phrase, put a check (✔) next to it.

conscious	greet	humorous	out loud
facial expression	harmonious	mood/moody	reserved

1. Brain research has shown that our ability to "read" other people's emotions is genetic. Assuming that this is correct, why is this ability so important that it is in our genes? How does being able to read others' emotions help us survive?

2. Which of the following jobs call for the ability to read other people's emotions correctly? Rank the jobs. Explain your rankings to your group.
   1 = doesn't call for any ability to read other people's emotions correctly
   2 = calls for a little ability
   3 = calls for a lot of ability

   _____ an interpreter _____ a nurse _____ a teacher

   _____ a salesperson _____ a police officer _____ a judge

   _____ an athlete _____ an actor _____ a waiter

   _____ a disc jockey (DJ) _____ a lawyer _____ a painter (artist)

Writing

Complete one or both of these writing topics. When you write, use at least five of the target words from the chapter. Underline the target words in your paper.

1. Write an essay. Describe how people in your culture express emotions. Consider the following questions when writing your essay:
   - How open are people about expressing their emotions? Is expressing one's emotions considered a virtue, or is it frowned upon?
   - How do people express their emotions? On their faces? With their bodies, for example with their hands? By talking?

2. Choose a profession, and explain how the ability to read other people's emotions can contribute to one's success in that profession.

CHAPTER 12

Road Rage

Angry drivers can be dangerous.

GETTING READY TO READ

 A How aggressive is your driving? Answer the questions shown in the chart. (If you don't drive, choose someone you know and answer based on what you have observed of that person's driving.) First, complete the chart alone. Then, compare your answers in a small group.

How often do you . . .	Very often	Sometimes	Rarely	Never
drive faster than the speed limit?				
not stop at a red light?				
not stop at a stop sign?				
shout or gesture angrily at other drivers?				
sound your horn or flash your lights to make a slower driver get out of the way?		✓		

The **boldfaced** words and phrases below all appear in the reading. Which words or phrases are new to you? Circle them. Then, work with a partner. Read the definitions of the words, and complete the sentences below the pictures with the words.

gesture = tell what you mean or feel by moving your arms, hands, or head

pregnant = having an unborn baby growing in your body

pull in front of = move a car, truck, etc., in front of someone or something

slammed = hit someone, something, or a part of one's body against a surface, quickly and with a lot of force

witness = someone who sees an accident or crime and can describe it

1. She is eight months _pregnang_.

2. She _slammed_ the door in his face.

3. The police officer is asking the _witness_ what happened.

(n, v)

4. Drivers often _gesture_ when they are angry.

5. You should be careful when you _pull in front of_ another car.

162–172
homework.

READING

Read the text once without stopping.

Road Rage

1   The women were driving their cars just outside the U.S. city of Cincinnati, Ohio. Rene Andrews, 29, was six-months **pregnant** with her first child. Tracie Alfieri, 23, was the mother of two. Suddenly, Andrews **pulled in front of** Alfieri. Alfieri **gestured** angrily at Andrews, sped up, and drove her Pontiac past and in front of Andrews' Volkswagen, prosecutors[1] say. Alfieri, police say, then **slammed** on the brakes.[2] Andrews swerved[3] to the right and crashed into a truck parked on the side of the road. She was seriously **injured**—and she lost her unborn child.

2   Alfieri's lawyer, Timothy Schneider, says she stepped on the brakes because there was traffic ahead. However, the court found Alfieri guilty of aggravated vehicular homicide[4] and aggravated vehicular assault.[5] The judge ordered her to spend eighteen months in prison. After six months, she was allowed to leave prison to take care of a sick daughter.

3   The prosecutor of the case says his office has dealt with plenty of cases involving aggressive driving, but none that ended as violently as this one. "Alfieri's conduct[6] was so aggravated . . . it was so bad, that a **witness** to it followed her all the way to work to get her license number," prosecutor Joseph Deters says.

4   Two years after the accident, Andrews was still recovering. She and her husband have nearly $200,000 in medical bills. "She's hoping that she can still have children, but she doesn't know," Robin Levine, Andrews' lawyer says.

5   The term "road rage" has no exact **legal** definition, but it is commonly used when "a driver or passenger attempts to kill,

---

[1] a *prosecutor* = a lawyer who is trying to prove in a court of law that someone is guilty of a crime

[2] *brakes* = equipment that makes a vehicle (car, truck, etc.) go more slowly or stop

[3] *swerve* = turn suddenly and dangerously while driving

[4] *aggravated vehicular homicide* = the crime of killing someone with a car because you were driving in a dangerous way

[5] *aggravated vehicular assault* = the crime of attacking someone with a car

[6] *conduct* = the way someone behaves

injure, or intimidate[7] a pedestrian[8] or another driver or passenger or to **damage** their **vehicle** in a traffic **incident**," (*Canadian Medical Association Journal,* October 1, 2002). In recent years, English-language newspapers around the world have been publishing many **sensational** stories on cases like that of Andrews and Alfieri, and there has been a lot written about the cause of this "new" aggression on the roads. The explanations **range** from an increase in traffic to the anxiety people feel due to rapid technological change.

6   However, some researchers doubt that this is actually a "new" problem. They believe that the recent attention given to road rage is the result of the media's desire to sell more papers or increase their number of viewers. These researchers **accuse** the media of inventing the term "road rage" to sensationalize what is not a societal problem, but rather a personal **tragedy** affecting a very limited number of individuals.

7   It is difficult to determine whether or not aggressive driving is increasing. Because there is no legal definition of road rage, incidents are reported differently from town to town. Still, the U.S. Department of Transportation **calculates** that two-thirds of traffic deaths in the United States are at least partly caused by aggressive driving. In a 2002 Canadian study, 88 percent of drivers surveyed admitted to aggressive driving—such as speeding or going through yellow lights—in the previous year, an increase of 3 percent over the year before. And a recent survey done for Axa Direct, a British **insurance** company, showed that three out of every four drivers or passengers had experienced some form of road rage. However, it is important to note that only 1 percent reported having actually experienced a physical attack.

8   One thing that all researchers would likely agree on, however, is that the best way to deal with road rage is to prevent it from ever happening. In the United States, researchers are conducting tests with a simple machine called "The Flash" to see if it will help reduce incidents of aggressive driving. Drivers participating in the experiment will get a green light to put in their vehicle's back windows, and a button to **flash** it on and off. One flash means "Please," as in "Please let me get in front of you," two flashes means "Thank you," and three flashes means "I am sorry." Before drivers in an area start using "The Flash," there will be advertisements to educate the public about its use. The hope is that if drivers can communicate even just these few basic ideas and feelings to each other, there will be less of a tendency for them to react to each other with rage.

---

[7] *intimidate* = make someone afraid, often by using threats, so that she or he does what you want

[8] a *pedestrian* = someone who is walking instead of driving a car or riding a bicycle

Comprehension Check

Read these sentences. Circle T (true), F (false), or ? (can't determine the answer from the reading). If you circle F, change the sentence to make it true. Check your answers with a classmate. If your answers are different, look back at the reading.

1. Road rage is a crime in the United States, Canada, and Britain. T F ?
2. All aggressive drivers have been involved in accidents. T F ?
3. It is not clear whether incidents of road rage have been increasing in recent years. T F ?
4. Researchers studying road rage say that it is due to two main causes. T F ?
5. Road rage is a new problem. T F ?
6. Studies show that aggressive driving is not very common. T F ?
7. The use of "The Flash" will become popular among drivers in the United States. T F (?)

EXPLORING VOCABULARY

Thinking about the Target Vocabulary

Guessing Strategy

You can sometimes guess the meaning of a word or phrase by imagining the scene that it describes. Look at the example, and form a picture in your mind for the **boldfaced** words and phrases.

*Two cars were traveling next to each other on a large highway. Suddenly, one car **pulled in front of** the other. The driver of the second car had to **slam** on the brakes to avoid hitting the first car.*

To check your "picture," ask yourself questions. For example: *What can one car suddenly do to another car that is traveling next to it? What can a driver do to avoid hitting another car?*

Try It!

Read the sentence, and write a definition of the **boldfaced** target word.

The car in front of me was moving too slowly, so I **flashed** my lights to signal that I wanted to pass.

Flash means _____.

A Look at the target words and phrase. Which ones are new to you? Circle them here and in the reading. Then read "Road Rage" again. Look at the context of each new word and phrase. Can you guess the meaning? Use the Guessing Strategy where possible.

Target Words and Phrase

rage (title)	witness (3)	range (5)
pregnant (1)	legal (5)	accuse (6)
pulled in front of (1)	damage (5)	tragedy (6)
gestured (1)	vehicle (5)	calculates (7)
slammed (1)	incident (5)	insurance (7)
injured (1)	sensational (5)	flash (8)

B Complete the word-form chart with the target words and phrase as they are used in the reading. Write the base form of verbs and the singular form of nouns.

Nouns	Verbs	Adjectives	Other
rage			

Using the Target Vocabulary

These sentences are about the reading. Circle the meaning of each boldfaced word. Then circle the words or phrases in the sentences that help you understand the meanings of the target words.

1. Road **rage** is an expression that is used to describe the behavior of some drivers who become very, very mad at another driver. *Rage* means

   a. guilt.　　　**b.** anger.　　　**c.** disrespect.

2. Rene Andrews was pregnant when she was seriously **injured** in a road rage incident. As a result, she lost her baby. *Injured* means

   a. angry.　　　**b.** hurt.　　　**c.** in trouble.

3. Tracie Alfieri is the name of the other driver involved in the **incident** that resulted in the loss of Rene Andrews's unborn child. An *incident* is something

   a. that happens　　**b.** that happens　　**c.** unusual, serious,
   more than one　　　by mistake.　　　or violent that
   time.　　　　　　　　　　　　　　　happens.

4. The police **accused** Alfieri of slamming on her brakes and causing Andrews's accident. When you *accuse* someone of doing something, you

   a. say that the　　**b.** are guilty.　　**c.** send the person
   person did　　　　　　　　　　　to prison.
   something wrong.　　　　　　　　　　*to a gic.*

5. What happened to Alfieri and Andrews was a terrible **tragedy**. Their lives will never be the same again. A *tragedy* is

   a. an extremely　　**b.** a story that　　**c.** extreme anger.
   sad event.　　　　　is not true.

6. The incident involving Alfieri and Andrews was written about in many newspapers. These types of **sensational** stories are common in newspapers. Something that is *sensational* is

   a. intended to　　**b.** not particularly　　**c.** sad and depressing.
   shock or excite　　　interesting.
   people.

7. The court decided that Alfieri had used her **vehicle** as a weapon to injure Andrews. It is not **legal** to use your car in that way. That is why Alfieri was sent to prison. Examples of *vehicles* include

   a. guns and knives.   b. cars and trucks.   c. injuring and killing.

   Legal means

   a. morally wrong.   b. a good idea.   c. allowed by law.

8. The term *road rage* is not only used to describe incidents in which one driver injures another. It is also used when one driver **damages** another driver's car. *Damage* means to

   a. completely destroy.   b. cause harm to.   c. get into an accident.

9. It is difficult to **calculate** exactly how many traffic accidents are due to road rage, because there is no legal definition of road rage. When you *calculate* something, you

   a. reduce it a little.   b. deal with it.   c. measure it using numbers.

10. The definition of road rage includes acts that **range** from scratching someone's car to causing someone's death. *Range* means

    a. result in.   b. be serious.   c. vary.

11. **Insurance** companies want to find out more about the connection between aggressive driving and traffic accidents. That's because they pay for damages or injuries their clients cause while they are driving. Automobile *insurance* companies

    a. pay for the damage if their client gets in an accident.   b. help their clients avoid traffic accidents.   c. borrow money if their clients get into an accident.

12. Aggressive drivers typically **flash** their lights at slower drivers to make them get out of the way. When you *flash* your lights, you

    a. keep them on all day.   b. turn them on when it gets dark.   c. turn them on and then immediately off.

DEVELOPING READING SKILLS

Understanding Inference

Answer these questions in your own words. The answers are not written directly in the reading. You will need to infer them.

1. Do you think that Tracie Alfieri and Rene Andrews knew each other before the incident occurred? Explain why you think that way.

   _____

   _____

   _____

2. Did Alfieri stop her car when Andrews's car went off the road? Explain.

   She didn't. _____

   _____

   _____

3. What specifically will the advertisements about "The Flash" teach the public?

   _____

   _____

   _____

Paraphrasing

Remember that when you paraphrase what someone else has written, you change the structure of the sentence and some of the words, but you do not change the meaning of the original sentence. If the original sentence is long or complex, you might need more than one sentence to paraphrase it.

 One sentence in each set paraphrases the sentence from the reading. Circle the correct answer.

1. However, some researchers doubt that road rage is actually a "new" problem.

   a. But there are researchers who believe that road rage has existed for a long time.

   b. But some researchers don't believe that road rage exists.

2. They believe that the recent attention given to road rage is the result of the media's desire to sell more papers or increase their number of viewers.

   a. Some researchers think that people in the media want more people to buy their newspapers or watch their television shows. That is the only reason they focus so much on road rage.

   b. Some people in the media think that if they write about road rage a lot, the number of road rage incidents will increase. When that happens, their newspapers or TV stations will make more money.

3. In a 2002 Canadian study, 88 percent of drivers surveyed admitted to aggressive driving . . . an increase of 3 percent over the previous year.

   a. In the year 2002, 88 percent of Canadian drivers told researchers that they had driven aggressively. In the previous year, the percentage of aggressive drivers was 3 percent higher.

   b. In the year 2001, in one survey of drivers in Canada, 85 percent said that they had driven aggressively during that year. In a survey the following year, that figure had climbed to 88 percent.

B **Paraphrase these sentences from the reading. The numbers in parentheses are the paragraphs that the sentences come from.**

1. It is difficult to determine whether or not aggressive driving is increasing. (7)

   _____ devision _____ compute _____

2. Still, the U.S. Department of Transportation calculates that two-thirds of traffic deaths in the United States are at least partly caused by aggressive driving. (7)

   _____

   _____

   according to devision of Transportation
        compute

EXPANDING VOCABULARY

Using the Target Vocabulary in New Contexts

Complete the sentences with the target words in the box. Be careful.
There are two extra words.

accuse	gesture	legal	tragedy
calculate	incident	rage	vehicle
damaged	injured	range	witness
flashed	insurance	sensational	

1. If you want ___legal___ advice, you should go to a lawyer.
2. Shakespeare's *Romeo and Juliet* is a ___tragedy___. Both characters die at the end.
3. He was in a ___rage___ because he discovered that someone had stolen his computer.
4. When I was in the hospital, my health ___insurance___ paid for everything.
5. I worked a lot of extra hours last week. I need to ___calculate___ what my paycheck will be.
6. There was an unfortunate ___incident___ at the store where I work last night. Two employees started fighting, and the police had to come to separate them.
7. Without proof, you can't ___accuse___ him of stealing your wallet.
8. He was ___injured___ in the game last night, so he can't play tonight.
9. You need a special license to drive a ___vehicle___ with more than four wheels.
10. He's a doctor, but his interests ___range___ from medical research to rap music.
11. I'm sorry I ___damaged___ your stereo. Is there anything I can do to make up for it?

12. The doctor ___flashed___ a light in the unconscious woman's eyes to try to get her to react.

13. I think it's disgusting when reporters write ___sensation___ stories about violent crimes.

Word Families

A **root** of a word is a part of a word with a specific meaning. For example, the target word **sensational** contains the root *sen*, which comes from the Latin word meaning "sense" or "feel." Like other roots, *sen* appears as a part of many words, but it is not used alone.

Read these sentences. The boldfaced words all contain the root *sen*. Can you guess what the words mean? Write a definition for each one. Compare your definitions with a classmate's. Then, check your definitions in a dictionary.

1. I don't like **sentimental** birthday cards. I prefer humorous cards.

_____

2. After the accident, he lost all **sensation** in his left hand.

_____

3. When anyone comes close to the house, the outside lights come on immediately because they are connected to a motion **sensor**.

_____

Studying Collocations

There are many collocations associated with driving. In this chapter, you learned the collocation **pull in front of**.

Read the following sentences and look at the pictures. Can you guess the meaning of the boldfaced phrases? Write one phrase next to each picture.

1. She **pulled off** the road to make a call.

2. The movie is at 7:00, so I'll **pick you up** at 6:30.

3. The other driver gestured angrily when we **cut him off**.

4. At the next corner, **take a left**. My house is the first one on the right.

5. This is a **one-way street**!

1. She's picking up her boyfriend

2. She has pulled off the road.

3. He   one-way street.

4. take a left

5. cut sm. off.

PUTTING IT ALL TOGETHER

Discussion

Share your ideas in a small group.

1. Design a television advertisement to introduce "The Flash" to the public. Use at least five of the target words from the chapter. Perform your advertisement for the class.

2. Complete the scale showing how aggressive you think drivers are in different regions of the world. Use the abbreviations listed below. You do not have to use all of the positions on the scale, and you can place more than one region in the same position. When you finish, compare your group's scale to those of other groups. Be ready to explain your answers. As you talk, try to use the vocabulary below. Each time someone uses a target word or phrase, put a check (✓) next to it.

accuse	incident	legal	range
damage	injured	pull in front of	vehicle
gesture	insurance	rage	witness

How aggressive do you think drivers are in different regions of the world?

Eastern Europe (EE)   Middle East (ME)
Western Europe (WE)   North America (NA)
Far East (FE)   Central and South America (CSA)
Southeast Asia (SEA)

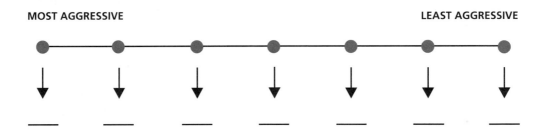

MOST AGGRESSIVE   LEAST AGGRESSIVE

Writing

Complete one or both of these writing topics. When you write, use at least five of the target words from the chapter. Underline the target words in your paper.

1. Imagine that you live in a city where there have recently been several serious incidents of road rage. Write a letter to the city official who is in charge of traffic. Make suggestions about what the city or town can do to reduce the number of road rage incidents.

2. What do you think about the punishment that Tracie Alfieri received? Was it severe enough? Was it too severe? Write an essay expressing your opinion. Include specific reasons to support your ideas. If you use information from the reading, paraphrase it—do not copy it.

Wrap-up

REVIEWING READING SKILLS AND VOCABULARY

Read the text. Do not use a dictionary.

1   People with expressive faces are probably not surprised when others sometimes "read their minds." However, even those who are not at all reserved can usually control their facial expressions if they make a conscious attempt. But imagine what your life would be like if anyone observing you could know exactly what you were thinking and feeling. What if your every emotion—guilt, shame, shock, anger, disgust, fear—immediately flashed across your face, for the whole world to witness? For people who suffer from a condition known as chronic blushing, this unfortunate situation is an everyday reality.

2   Of course, it is normal for our faces to become hot and get red when we are embarrassed. However, for people who suffer from chronic blushing, this normal physical reaction to stress is so constant and severe that it can damage their personal and professional lives. Consider, for example, a young television news announcer just starting out in her career. She has always blushed easily, but suddenly, she notices that whenever she reports on a tragic, sensational, or even humorous incident, her face, neck, and ears all turn a deep red. At first she deals with the problem by putting heavy makeup on her face before going on television. Unfortunately, the makeup gives her an artificial appearance, and she begins to lose popularity with television viewers.

3   The story of the television news announcer is just one of many that reveal the negative effects that chronic blushing can have on one's life. So, what can someone who suffers from this condition do? For minor cases, makeup works quite well. For serious cases, there is an operation that can get rid of blushing. However, it is a major operation that most doctors will perform only after the patient has explored other solutions.

Comprehension Check

Read these sentences. Circle T (true), F (false), or ? (can't determine the answer from the reading). If you circle F, change the sentence to make it true.

1. Most people are able to hide their feelings if they try hard enough.   T   F   ?

2. Blushing is very common.   T   F   ?

3. People who blush too much can sometimes have personal and professional problems.   T   F   ?

4. Chronic blushers are much more emotional than other people.   T   F   ?

5. According to the writer, people who suffer from chronic blushing should have an operation to correct the problem.   T   F   ?

Guessing Meaning from Context

Answer these questions.

1. What is *chronic blushing*? (paragraph 2)

   _____

2. What is *makeup*? (paragraph 2)

   _____

3. What does *minor* mean? (paragraph 3)

   _____

4. What target word from the unit is the adjective *tragic* related to? What does *tragic* mean? (paragraph 2)

   _____

Understanding Inference

Use inference to answer these questions.

1. What are three jobs in which chronic blushing might be a serious problem? For each job, explain how chronic blushing might be a serious disadvantage.

   _____

   _____

2. Imagine a case in which a doctor refused to perform an operation to "cure" someone's blushing problem. Describe the case using specific details.

_____

_____

Paraphrasing

Paraphrase these sentences from the text.

1. People with expressive faces are probably not surprised when others sometimes "read their minds."

_____

_____

2. Of course, it is normal for our faces to become hot and get red when we are embarrassed.

_____

_____

3. However, it is a major operation that most doctors will perform only after the patient has explored other solutions.

_____

_____

EXPANDING VOCABULARY

Studying Collocations

Read these sentences, and look carefully at the pattern for each verb.

a. Our company can **insure** you **against** fire but not against damage due to wind.

Pattern = **insure** someone or something **against** something

b. He **accused** me **of** being dishonest.

Pattern = **accuse** someone **of** something (or of doing something)

c. I always **associate** the smell of rain **with** my farm.

Pattern = **associate** something or someone **with** something or someone else

d. Could you please **translate** this **from** English **into** Chinese?

Pattern = **translate** something **from** something (a language) **into** something else (another language)

e. The cost of a house in this town **ranges from** $175,000 **to** $400,000.

Pattern = something **ranges from** something (an amount or size) **to** something else (another amount or size)

On a separate piece of paper, answer these questions in complete sentences. Use the boldfaced verb and preposition combinations.

1. If you live on the beach, what should you be **insured against**?

2. If the police **accused** you **of** something you didn't do, what would you do?

3. What smell(s) do you **associate with** your childhood?

4. Is it easy or difficult for you to **translate something from** your first language **into** English?

5. In your city, what is the cost of renting a one-bedroom apartment? (Use **range from** . . . **to** in your answer.)

Word Families

Some words can be nouns or verbs, with no change in spelling.

Complete the sentences with the words in the box. Identify whether the word is used as a noun or a verb. Circle n. (noun) or v. (verb).

damage	gesture	honor	range

1. Why did you _____ at me? n. v.

I'm not familiar with the _____ that you used. n. v.

2. How did you _____ my computer? n. v.

The _____ will be expensive to repair. n. v.

3. They had a party to _____ their employees. n. v.

The employees were proud of the _____. n. v.

4. The salary _____ in their department is quite wide. n. v.

The salaries _____ from $35,000 to $100,000. n. v.

PLAYING WITH WORDS

Look back at the lists of target vocabulary on pages 141, 153, and 165. In a small group, write as many target words and phrases as you can under each category shown in the chart below. Be ready to explain your answers. Some words might fit under more than one category, and some words might not fit under any category.

Things you can touch and see	Ways of showing your emotions
vehicle	

Bad feelings, behavior, or qualities	Good feelings, behavior, or qualities
	honor

BUILDING DICTIONARY SKILLS

Finding Words in the Dictionary

When you look up a word, you can find information about other words in the same word family in the same entry or in nearby entries. For example, look at the dictionary entries below.

con·scious /ˈkɑnʃəs/ *adj* **1** [not before noun] noticing or realizing something [= **aware**]: *I became **conscious of** the fact that someone was watching me.* **2** awake and able to understand what is happening [≠ **unconscious**]: *Owen was still conscious when they arrived at the hospital.* **3** **conscious effort/decision/attempt etc.** a deliberate effort, decision, etc.: *Vivian had made a conscious effort to be friendly.* **4** thinking that something is very important: *fashion-conscious teenagers* | *She's very **conscious of** safety.* —**consciously** *adv*

con·scious·ness /ˈkɑnʃəsnɪs/ *n* [U] **1** the condition of being awake and understanding what is happening: *Charlie fell down the stairs and **lost consciousness**.* | *It was two weeks before he **regained consciousness**.* **2** someone's mind, thoughts, and ideas: *research into human consciousness* **3** the state of knowing that something exists or is true [= **awareness**]: *The march is intended to **raise** people's **consciousness** about women's health issues.*

Below the entry for the target word **conscious**, you find the entry for the related noun **consciousness**. You also find the adverb form **consciously**, and an adjective with the opposite meaning, **unconscious**.

Look up the words in the box in your dictionary and find other forms of each word. Fill in the blanks with the correct forms of the words.

accuse	injure	observe	tragedy
associate	legal	recognize	translate
calculate	muscle		

1. Your ___calculations___ are correct, but your final answer is incorrect. Check your numbers again.

2. Your _____ is not very serious, but you won't be able to use your hand for a few days.

3. He has strong, _____ legs because he rides his bicycle every day to work.

4. The doctor made a _____ mistake, and as a result his patient died.

5. Can you help me with this _____? My Spanish isn't very good.

6. After watching the animals for several hours, the researcher wrote down her _____ in a notebook. Later her assistant typed them for her.

7. He said he knew her, but I think he was lying. When he saw her, there was no _____ on his face.

8. You can't do that! It's _____!

9. The police will never believe your _____. You have no proof!

10. If you belong to the Automobile _____ and you have a problem with your car while you are on a trip, you can call them for help.

MAN AND BEAST

ცხოველი

Is Music Universal?

Many whales communicate with each other with "whale songs."

GETTING READY TO READ

Do you think the following statements are true or false? Write T (true) or F (false). Compare your answers with a partner.

  1. There is one universal definition of music.

  2. It is possible that historically, humans learned how to play music before they learned how to speak.

  3. A wide variety of animal species not only make but also seem to enjoy music.

  4. Whale "songs" are completely different from human songs.

  5. Some animals make their own musical instruments and play them.

  6. There is one part of the brain that is used specifically for music.

9412

 B The **boldfaced** words and phrases in the paragraph below appear in the reading. Which words are new to you? Circle them. Then, work with a partner. Read this paragraph introducing the topic of the reading, and match the words with their definitions. Be careful. There are two extra definitions.

There is a lot of evidence that humans' love for music is quite **ancient**, perhaps even as old as the human race. However, there is now evidence that not only humans but also many other **species** of animals have a basic **appreciation** for music. In the **journal** *Science*, several **biologists** have written about how the brains of humans and animals react to music in very similar ways. The researchers hope that their work on the way that music affects the brain will lead to developments that could one day help **the deaf** to hear.

Word	Definition
_c_ **1.** biologists	**a.** a group of animals or plants of the same kind that can breed (have babies) with each other
_e_ **2.** journal	
_a_ **3.** species	**b.** belonging to a long time ago; very old
_f_ **4.** appreciation	**c.** scientists who study living things
_g_ **5.** the deaf	**d.** people who can't see
_b_ **6.** ancient	**e.** a magazine for professionals in a particular field, for example science
	f. an understanding of the importance or meaning of something
	g. people who can't hear
	h. interesting

READING

Read the text once without stopping.

Is Music Universal?

1   It has long been said that music is universal, but now science is proving just how deeply true that statement really is. Like most people, scientists cannot define exactly what music is, but they know it when they hear it. One group of scientists has shown that human **appreciation** of music may be shared by whales, birds,

(continued)

homework
183
193

and even rats; that it is remarkably **ancient**; and that studying why animals and humans appreciate music may help us better understand how the brain works.

2   In research published in 2001 in the **journal** *Science,* several scientists have shown that in very basic ways other **species** share music appreciation and that this appreciation may be one of humanity's oldest activities. Through such research, scientists hope they may come to understand the human mind better, perhaps even learning **key** information about how to deal with damage to the **auditory system**.

3   Jelle Atema is a **biologist** and coauthor of one of the *Science* papers.[1] Like several of the researchers involved in the *Science* papers, Atema is both a scientist and a musician. In addition to his work in biology, he plays the flute.[2] He has carefully made exact copies of ancient bone flutes in order to play them. He wants to determine the kinds of sounds that early humans may have made. Another of the researchers, Harvard Medical School's Mark Jude Tramo, is also a talented guitarist.

4   "Do musical sounds in nature reveal a profound[3] **bond** between all living things?" asks one of the papers. There is a lot of **evidence** that perhaps it does. For example, the "songs" of one type of whale follow many of the same, **precise** rules that are nearly universal in human music. The general **structure** of whale music is remarkably similar to that of human music. For example, the two species share a similar tonal[4] **scale**, and their songs involve the introduction and variation of a central **theme**.

5   Many species of birds sing in ways that also follow the rules of human song, including the ways that songs are passed from one generation to another or are shared by a group of peers. Many use note scales similar to those used by humans, even though an **endless** variety of such scales is possible. Some even make instruments and play them. For example, one type of bird uses a **hollow** log[5] as a **drum**, beating on it with a small stick it breaks off from a tree!

6   Music goes back to the earliest ages of human prehistory,[6] and flutes have been found that may be 53,000 years old. The

---

[1] a *paper* = a piece of writing by researchers who have made a study of a particular subject

[2] a *flute* = a musical instrument shaped like a pipe, that you play by holding it across your lips and blowing into it

[3] *profound* = having a strong influence or effect

[4] *tonal* = having a particular quality of musical sound

[5] a *log* = a thick piece of wood cut from a tree

[6] *prehistory* = the time in history before anything was written down

technology used to make these ancient instruments was much more advanced, Atema says, than that used at the same period to produce tools. "To see that they spent so much time [making instruments] means music was important to them," he says. The ability to make music, some scientists believe, may even be older than language.

7   Tramo, a neurologist[7] at Harvard Medical School and Massachusetts General Hospital, says he is fascinated by the complexity of the human brain's reaction to music. "There is no 'music center' in the brain," he wrote. Nearly every thinking part of the brain is involved in listening to music, and when we move to the music many of the areas controlling movement are involved too. "Imagine how much of the brain lights up when we dance!"

8   Tramo sees the research on music as a process leading to a better understanding of how the brain works. By learning exactly how the brain processes and "understands" the specific features that music is made of, a more complete understanding of how the brain **makes sense of** the world around us may develop. In the same way, other scientists are using the way the brain reacts to **visual** arts as a way of understanding the way the human visual system works.

9   Tramo believes that "That understanding . . . is going to help scientists in their efforts to help **the deaf** to hear, and help the blind to see."

---
[7] a *neurologist* = a doctor who studies and treats the nervous system and the diseases related to it

Comprehension Check

Read these sentences. Circle T (true), F (false), or ? (can't determine the answer from the reading). If you circle F, change the sentence to make it true. When you finish, go back and compare your answers to the way you answered on page 182. Then, check your answers with a classmate. If your answers are different, look back at the reading.

1. There is one universal definition of music.   T   F   ?

2. It is possible that historically, humans learned how to play music before they learned how to speak.   T   F   ?

3. A wide variety of animal species not only make but also seem to enjoy music.   T   F   ?

4. Whale "songs" are completely different from human songs.   T   F   ?

5. Some animals make their own musical instruments
   and play them.   T   F   ?

6. There is one part of the brain that is used specifically
   for music.   T   F   ?

EXPLORING VOCABULARY

Thinking about the Target Vocabulary

Guessing Strategy

Sometimes, a word is followed by a descriptive phrase that can help
you guess its meaning. Look at the example.

*The scientist submitted an article to the **journal,** writing about
music's effects on babies' development.*

From the descriptive phrase after the word *journal*, you should be
able to figure out that a journal is something that contains written
articles.

Try It!

**Read the sentences, and write a definition of the boldfaced
target word.**

Some even make instruments and play them. For example, one
type of bird uses a hollow log as a **drum**, beating on it with a
small stick it breaks off from a tree!

Drum means _____.

 A Look at the target words and phrases on page 187. Which ones are new
to you? Circle them here and in the reading. Then read "Is Music
Universal?" again. Look at the context of each new word and phrase.
Can you guess the meaning? Use the Guessing Strategy where possible.

Target Words and Phrases

appreciation (1)	auditory (2)	precise (4)	hollow (5)
ancient (1)	system (2)	structure (4)	drum (5)
journal (2)	biologist (2)	scale (4)	makes sense of (8)
species (2)	bond (4)	theme (4)	visual (8)
key (2)	evidence (4	endless (5)	the deaf (9)

B Complete the word-form chart with the target words and phrases as they are used in the reading. Write the base form of verbs and the singular form of nouns.

Nouns	Verbs	Adjectives	Other
appreciation			

Using the Target Vocabulary

These sentences are **about the reading**. Circle the meaning of each **boldfaced** word or phrase. Circle the words or phrases in the sentences that help you understand the meanings of the target words.

1. Scientists have recently found **evidence** that some animals produce music very similar to human music. One example is the fact that whale songs follow many of the same musical patterns as human songs. *Evidence* is used to

   a. conduct an experiment.   **b.** prove a theory.   **c.** make music.

2. There is an **endless** variety of musical patterns. It is therefore surprising that human songs and whale songs are so similar. If something is *endless*, it

   a. hurts your ears because it is so loud.

   b. is very large or very long.

   c. is so difficult that no one can understand it.

3. An example of a similarity between whale music and human music is the **scale** that they both use. Although the number of possible musical **scales** is in fact endless, both whales and humans "sing" with the same notes. A musical *scale* is

   a. a combination of a variety of animal sounds.

   b. a musical note that is sung for a long time.

   c. a series of notes that go from lower to higher or from higher to lower in a set pattern.

4. Like humans, whales begin their songs with a **theme**, make some changes to it, and then come back to the original **theme** before ending the song. The *theme* of a piece of music is

   a. the main subject of it.

   b. the first note of it.

   c. the most popular song in it.

5. In fact, both whale and human music follow many of the same, very **precise** rules. If a rule is *precise*, it is

   a. exact and correct in every detail

   b. important in a very general way.

   c. interesting and beautiful.

6. Another fascinating similarity between human and animal music is that some animals actually make musical instruments. For example, one bird uses a stick to hit an empty piece of wood, or **drum**. A *drum* is a musical instrument that

   a. sounds like a bird's song.

   b. is played by hitting it with the hand or an object.

   c. makes a very soft, continuous sound.

7. Interestingly, the bird only uses the stick to hit a **hollow** piece of wood. It never chooses a solid piece of wood. A *hollow* piece of wood is
    a. very heavy.   **b.** extremely dry.   **c.** empty inside.

8. All of this evidence of musical similarities between animals and humans suggests that the **bond** between us and other living things is deeper than we thought. A *bond* is a
    a. connection.   **b.** difference.   **c.** suggestion.

9. By studying how the brains of both humans and animals process music, scientists hope to learn **key** information about the way the brain works in general. *Key* information is
    a. very difficult.   **b.** very important.   **c.** very new.

10. Scientists hope to use this information to help people who are deaf. They hope to learn how to repair damage to parts of the **auditory system**, such as the inner ear. The *auditory system* includes
    a. the parts of the body that have been injured.   **b.** the parts of the body that enable us to hear.   **c.** the internal (inside) parts of the body.

11. While some scientists are working to help the deaf, others are working to help the blind. They are trying to better understand the way the human **visual** system works. Our *visual* system is in charge of
    a. what and how we see.   **b.** what and how we hear.   **c.** what and how we move.

12. Scientists want to know how the brain **makes sense of** the visual and auditory information it receives. When you *make sense of* something, you
    a. understand how it works.   **b.** improve the way it works.   **c.** hear it and watch it.

13. Despite progress in science and technology, scientists still do not completely understand the **structure** of the human brain. If they could understand the brain's *structure*, they would understand
    a. the way it is organized.   **b.** what happens when we die.   **c.** how to control it.

DEVELOPING READING SKILLS

Understanding Main Ideas, Major Points, and Supporting Details

An **outline** gives you an overall idea of the structure and most important information in a text. You can look at an outline of a reading and immediately recognize the relationship among the main ideas, major points, and supporting details. When you write an outline, you should use single words or phrases rather than full sentences.

This is an outline of the information contained in paragraphs 4 and 5 of "Is Music Universal?" Fill in the missing information in the outline. The Roman numeral I is for the main idea, the letters A and B are for the major points, and the numbers 1, 2, 3, and 4 are for the supporting details.

I. _Summarizing_ _____

    A. <u>Structure of whale & human music very similar</u>

        1. _____

        2. _____

    B. _____

        1. _____

        2. <u>Share songs with peers</u>

        3. _____

        4. _____

Summarizing

Use the information from your outline to write a summary of paragraphs 4 and 5 of the reading. Do not look back at the text.

EXPANDING VOCABULARY

Using the Target Vocabulary in New Contexts

Complete the sentences with the target words and phrase in the box. Be careful. There are two extra words or phrases.

appreciation	drums	key	structure
auditory	endless	make sense of	system
biologist	evidence	precise	themes
bond	hollow	scale	visual

1. He was in a car accident and suffered severe _____ damage. Now he's deaf.

2. The _____ between mother and child is very strong. Even when they live far away from each other, they always feel a connection.

3. He went to a special school for _____ arts. He studied painting and design.

4. What is the highest note that you can sing on a C major _____?

5. That movie seemed _____! I was really bored.

6. This lamp looks heavy, but actually it's very light because it's _____.

7. If you are having trouble dancing to the music, just listen for the _____ .

8. I can't _____ these instructions. Can you help me?

9. The police can't prove he robbed the bank because they don't have any _____.

10. Honor for one's parents is a _____ feature of Chinese culture.

11. Courts, lawyers, and judges are key parts of the legal _____.

12. Because of client complaints, the management is changing the company _____. They will have fewer supervisors and more customer service help.

13. I don't like movies that deal with serious _____. I prefer movies that make me laugh.

14. Please check your calculations. The measurement must be _____.

Word Families

In Chapter 12, you learned that a root is a part of a word with a specific meaning. The target word **biologist** contains the root *bio*, which means "life." The target words **visual** and **auditory** contain roots, too: *vis* means "see"; *audi* means "hear."

 Read these sentences. Match the boldfaced words with their definitions.

1. My night **vision** is not very good. I need to wear glasses when I drive after dark.

2. The **audience** loved his performance. Everyone in the theater stood up and clapped when he finished.

3. Do you need any **audiovisual** equipment for your presentation?

4. In the past ten years, scientists have made a lot of progress in the field of **biotechnology**.

5. Do you think the professor will let me **audit** her course? I don't need a grade; I just want to attend her lectures.

Word	Definition
_____ **1.** vision	**a.** the people watching or listening to a concert, speech, movie, etc.
_____ **2.** audience	**b.** the ability to see
_____ **3.** audiovisual	**c.** study a subject at college without getting a grade for it
_____ **4.** biotechnology	**d.** the use of living things such as cells in science and industry
_____ **5.** audit	**e.** involving the use of recorded pictures and sound

B Working with a partner, answer the questions using the **boldfaced words.**

1. Is your night **vision** as good as your day **vision**?

2. Have you ever performed in front of a live **audience**? If not, would you like to? Why or why not?

3. In which professions are **audiovisual** presentations common?

4. What kinds of research are being done in the field of **biotechnology**?

5. In universities in your country, is it possible to **audit** classes? What are the advantages and disadvantages of auditing a class?

Studying Collocations

There are many collocations with the word **system**. A **system** is a set of related or connected things that work together. The human body, for example, has systems that consist of organs that work together. The **auditory** and **visual** systems are two of the body's systems. Other systems of the body include the circulatory system and the digestive system. There are also government systems. The educational system and the legal system are two important government systems.

Work with a partner. Write each word under the category on page 194 that you associate the word with. Some words may go in more than one category. For example, you may associate the word *knowledge* with just the educational system. Somebody else might put it in all four categories, because knowledge is important to all of the systems. Be ready to explain your associations.

athlete	instructor	literature	prevent
blood	judge	misidentify	proof
diet	justice	peer	research
disease	knowledge	physical	stomach
evidence	laboratory	poison	victim
freedom	lawyer	prescribe	witness
heart			

Educational System	Circulatory System	Digestive System	Legal System
knowledge	heart	stomach	

PUTTING IT ALL TOGETHER

Discussion

Share your ideas in a small group. As you talk, try to use the vocabulary below. Each time someone uses a target word or phrase, put a check (✔) next to it.

appreciation/appreciate	drum	structure
audience	make sense of	system
auditory	scale	theme
bond	species	

1. How is music important to individuals? To society? Make a list of all the ways people use music. For example, you could write: *People use music to relax.* Try to think of at least six things.

2. Now make a list of all the ways animals use music. Can you think of anything that animals might use music for that humans do not?

Writing

Complete one or both of these writing topics. When you write, use at least five of the target words from the chapter. Underline the target words in your paper.

1. Do some research at the library or on the Internet on whale songs or bird songs. Then, write a short report on what you have learned. Do not copy from the research—paraphrase.

2. Imagine that you have traveled to a planet where music does not exist. Write a letter to a friend on earth explaining what life is like without music.

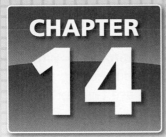

Our Dogs Are Watching Us

Can dogs read our minds?

GETTING READY TO READ

 Talk with a partner or in a small group.

1. Do you now, or have you ever had a pet? If so, tell your group about your pet. If not, would you like to have a pet? Why or why not?

2. Do you think that it is possible for animals and people to have an emotional connection? Explain your answer.

3. Which animals are best at communicating with people? Complete the chart.

dogs   horses   cats   birds   other (your ideas): _____

Very good at communicating with people	Can communicate with people, but not very well	Can't communicate with people

195

B The **boldfaced** words and phrases in the paragraph below appear in the reading. Which words are new to you? Circle them. Then, work with a partner. Read this paragraph introducing the topic of the reading, and match the words with their definitions. Be careful. There are two extra definitions.

Can dogs **read the minds** of their human owners? To anyone who owns a dog, the answer is **obvious**: Yes! Now, scientists have done some interesting experiments to **back up** the theory that as dogs **evolved** from their wolf ancestors over thousands of years, they developed a simple, yet **striking** characteristic. They learned to look at people's faces, something that wolves rarely or never do.

Word	Definition
_____ **1.** read (someone's) mind	**a.** unusual or interesting enough to be noticed
_____ **2.** obvious	**b.** develop by changing slowly over time
_____ **3.** back up	**c.** difficult to see
_____ **4.** evolve	**d.** guess what someone is thinking
_a_ **5.** striking	**e.** easy to notice or understand
	f. grow
	g. show that something is true

READING

Read the text once without stopping.

Our Dogs Are Watching Us

ADAPTED FROM: Ingram, Jay. "Dogs keep eyes on the prize by watching us." *Toronto Star* 18 May 2003: E06.

1   A few months ago, I reported a study of the abilities of dogs to **read the minds** of their owners. Well, not exactly. They were not really reading minds; they were reading human body language to figure out which of two containers actually had food hidden in it. Now, experimenters have conducted more research in an attempt to identify the single skill that dogs have but other animals lack.

2   In experiments reported in November 2002, scientists compared dogs, wolves,[1] and **chimpanzees**. The tests involved hiding food in one of two containers, then pointing at, looking at, or both pointing at and tapping[2] on the container with the food.

3   While dogs were quick to figure out which container held what they were looking for, neither the wolves nor the chimps understood what the experimenters were trying to communicate. The inability of the chimps to perform better than the dogs was surprising, considering the **overall** intelligence of chimpanzees. But the differences between dogs and wolves were fascinating because of the relationship between the two.

4   Wolves gave rise to[3] dogs several thousand years ago, and while the physical differences between the two are the most **obvious**, there are clearly mental differences, too. This experiment suggested those differences are in the area of social interaction with humans. A team of Hungarian scientists has found what they think is the key: Dogs look at people's faces. It sounds simple, but there are experiments to **back up** the claim.

5   The Hungarian team made sure that the wolves were **socialized** to humans by having them live with people twenty-four hours a day from the time they were four days old. This meant that the dogs and wolves **were** equally **used to** human voices and gestures. By **familiarizing** the wolves and dogs to humans, the researchers hoped to **eliminate** the effect that the animals' anxiety might have on the experiment. The socialization seems to have worked. Some of the wolves were able to understand some of the human gestures, although overall they still were not as good as the dogs.

6   They then conducted the experiment that revealed the key difference between the two animals. Both dogs and wolves were trained to get a piece of meat in two ways. They were taught how to lift the **lid** of a container to get at the meat inside and how to pull a rope (tied around a piece of meat) out of a cage.[4] When the animals had figured out how to do both, the scientists tricked them: The lid was **fastened** down and the rope was tied to the cage. It was now impossible for them to get at the food.

---

[1] a *wolf* = a wild animal that looks like a dog and lives and hunts in groups

[2] *tap* = gently hit your finger against something

[3] *gave rise to* = were the species that (dogs) evolved from

[4] a *cage* = a structure made of wires or bars in which birds or animals can be kept

(continued)

7   What happened? I'm sorry I can't report that the dogs learned to untie the rope or use a screwdriver[5] to open the container, but they did do something the wolves didn't do—they kept looking at the people in the room, apparently[6] waiting for some sort of sign to help them get the meat.

8   The differences between the two animals were **striking**. In both tests, seven out of nine dogs kept **checking out** the person, while only two out of seven wolves did. The researchers claim that this act of looking at human faces is a "genetic predisposition" in dogs. It is one of the **innate** differences between the two species and therefore must have been one of the first steps in the process of **domestication** thousands of years ago.

9   I would like to see this new piece of evidence applied to previous observations and theories about how dogs were domesticated. Some researchers have theorized that as dogs evolved from wolves, their behavior became more **immature**. For instance, dogs exhibit[7] submissive[8] behaviors that wolves do not, as if adult dogs are more like baby wolves. But the tests conducted by the Hungarian researchers were done when the animals were only a few months old, so you would think that if dog behavior is basically the same as that of young wolves, the wolves in this experiment might have looked at their owners, too.

10   I can add to this research from my own experience. My dog also looks at people to get food: He makes sure I'm not looking at him, then steals my sandwich. That's what I call highly **evolved** behavior.

---

[5] a *screwdriver* = a tool with a long, thin metal end, used for turning screws (a piece of metal used to keep two pieces of wood or metal together)

[6] *apparently* = according to the way something looks or someone appears

[7] *exhibit* = show or display

[8] *submissive* = always willing to obey someone

Comprehension Check

Read these sentences. Circle T (true), F (false), or ? (can't determine the answer from the reading). If you circle F, change the sentence to make it true. Check your answers with a classmate. If your answers are different, look back at the reading.

1. The experiments proved that dogs are more intelligent than chimpanzees.   T (F) ?

2. The experiments showed that there are very specific differences between dogs and wolves.   T F ?

3. The experiments showed that wolves and dogs are
   not related.   T (F) ?

4. The dogs who looked at the experimenters were given
   a piece of meat as a reward.   T   F   ?

5. The behavior of young wolves and young dogs is
   basically the same.   T   F   ?

6. Some researchers believe that dogs have a special
   ability to understand human beings.   T   F   ?

EXPLORING VOCABULARY

Thinking about the Target Vocabulary

Guessing Strategy

You learned in the **Guessing Strategy** for Chapter 10 that words
can have similar meanings even if they are not the same word form.
Look at the example.

> The Hungarian team **socialized** the wolves to humans by having
> them live with people twenty-four hours a day from the time
> they were four days old. By **familiarizing** the wolves and dogs to
> humans, the researchers hoped to eliminate the effect that the
> animals' anxiety might have on the experiment.

Based on the context, you can guess that the words *socialized* and
familiarizing have a similar meaning, even though one is a verb in
the past tense, while the other is a gerund.

Try It!

**Read the sentences, and write the word that is similar in meaning
to the boldfaced target word.**

> There are several **striking** differences between dog and wolf
> behavior. For example, researchers noticed that dogs look at
> human faces, while wolves don't.
>
> **Striking** is similar in meaning to _____.

A Look at the target words and phrases. Which ones are new to you? Circle them here and in the reading. Then read "Our Dogs Are Watching Us" again. Look at the context of each new word and phrase. Can you guess the meaning? Use the Guessing Strategy where possible.

Target Words and Phrases

read the minds (1)	were used to (5)	checking out (8)
chimpanzees (2)	familiarizing (5)	innate (8)
overall (3)	eliminate (5)	domestication (8)
obvious (4)	lid (6)	immature (9)
back up (4)	fastened (6)	evolved (10)
socialized (5)	striking (8)	

B Complete the word-form chart with the target words and phrases as they are used in the reading. Write the base form of verbs and the singular form of nouns.

Nouns	Verbs	Adjectives	Other
	read the mind		

Using the Target Vocabulary

The sentences on page 201 are **about the reading**. Complete them with the words and phrases in the box. Circle the words or phrases in the sentences that help you understand the meanings of the target words. Be careful. There are two extra words or phrases.

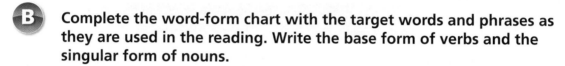

checked out	evolve	innate	overall
chimpanzees	familiarize	lid	socialized
domestication	fastening	obvious	were used to
eliminate	immature		

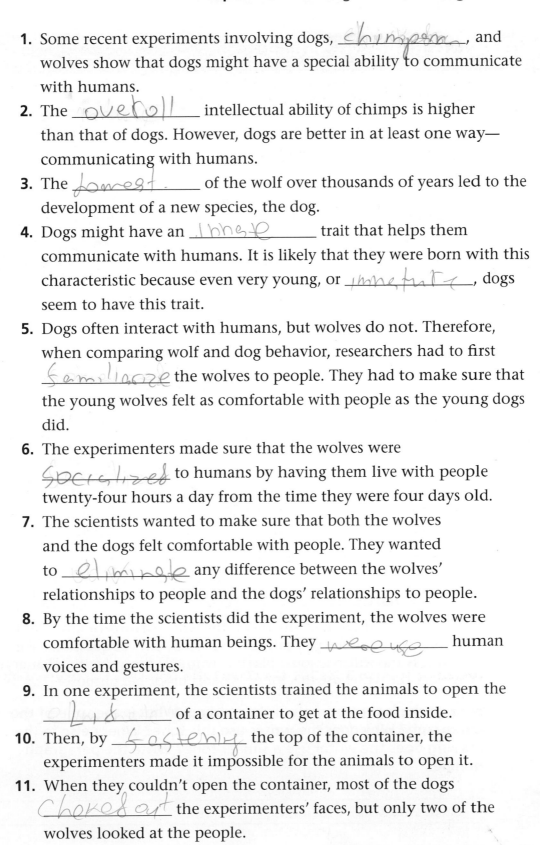

1. Some recent experiments involving dogs, _chimpan_, and wolves show that dogs might have a special ability to communicate with humans.

2. The _overall_ intellectual ability of chimps is higher than that of dogs. However, dogs are better in at least one way—communicating with humans.

3. The _lowest_ of the wolf over thousands of years led to the development of a new species, the dog.

4. Dogs might have an _innate_ trait that helps them communicate with humans. It is likely that they were born with this characteristic because even very young, or _immature_, dogs seem to have this trait.

5. Dogs often interact with humans, but wolves do not. Therefore, when comparing wolf and dog behavior, researchers had to first _familiarize_ the wolves to people. They had to make sure that the young wolves felt as comfortable with people as the young dogs did.

6. The experimenters made sure that the wolves were _socialized_ to humans by having them live with people twenty-four hours a day from the time they were four days old.

7. The scientists wanted to make sure that both the wolves and the dogs felt comfortable with people. They wanted to _eliminate_ any difference between the wolves' relationships to people and the dogs' relationships to people.

8. By the time the scientists did the experiment, the wolves were comfortable with human beings. They _were use_ human voices and gestures.

9. In one experiment, the scientists trained the animals to open the _lid_ of a container to get at the food inside.

10. Then, by _fastening_ the top of the container, the experimenters made it impossible for the animals to open it.

11. When they couldn't open the container, most of the dogs _looked at_ the experimenters' faces, but only two of the wolves looked at the people.

DEVELOPING READING SKILLS

Understanding Details

Look at the illustrations. Put a check mark below those that illustrate something from the reading.

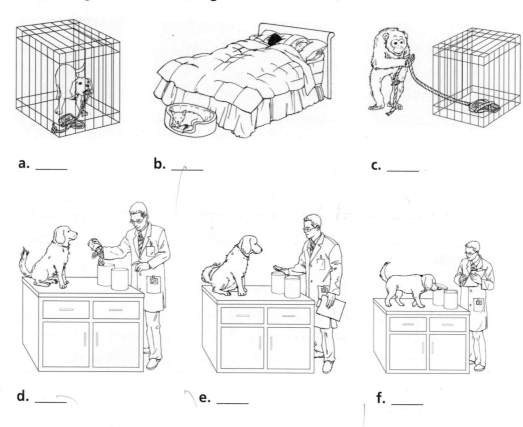

a. _____

b. _____

c. _____

d. _____

e. _____

f. _____

Recognizing Tone

One important element of any text is the writer's **tone**, or attitude. To identify a writer's tone, you can ask yourself a series of questions. For example: Is the writer serious? playful? worried? funny? critical? angry? sad? Why does the writer use this tone? What is his or her purpose?

Look at the last paragraph of the reading. What is the tone of the paragraph? Why does the writer use this tone? Where else in the reading does the writer use a similar tone? Write the paragraph number.

_____

_____

_____

EXPANDING VOCABULARY

Using the Target Vocabulary in New Contexts

Complete the sentences with the target words and phrases in the box. Be careful. There are two extra words or phrases.

am used to	domestication	immature	overall
back up	eliminated	innate	socialization
check out	familiarize	lid	striking
chimpanzees	fasten		

1. Please _____fasten_____ your seat belt. The plane is about to land.

2. Humans and _____chimpanzees_____ are very similar genetically. In fact, they are our closest animal relative.

3. Some researchers believe that an appreciation for music is an _____innate_____ human trait.

4. Please make sure the _____lid_____ of the trash can is tightly closed.

5. The _____domestication_____ of horses made it possible for humans to travel over longer distances.

6. The _____socialization_____ of young children is an important goal of any educational system. In school, children are taught to interact with their peers.

7. Any player who breaks the rules will be _____eliminated_____ from the game.

8. When I got my new computer, it took me about a week to _____familiarize_____ myself with all of its different features.

9. Your _____immature_____ behavior is not acceptable. You are not a little boy anymore.

10. Scientists don't understand precisely how the brain makes sense of music, but they do have a good understanding of the _____overall_____ structure of the auditory system.

11. Hey, _____check out_____ this website. It's really interesting.

12. When I first moved from New York to London, it was difficult for me to drive on the left side of the road, but now I _____am used to_____ it.

Word Families

In Chapters 10 and 12 you learned about paraphrasing. When you paraphrase, one of the ways to change the structure of the original sentence without changing its meaning is to use a different form of one of the words in the original sentence. Look at the example.

Original sentence: *It took thousands of years for dogs to **evolve** from wolves.*

Paraphrase: *The **evolution** of the dog from its wolf ancestor took many, many years.*

Study the chart. Then look at the sentences below. In each set of sentences, b is a paraphrase of a. Complete the paraphrases with the appropriate forms of the words from the chart. Make sure that your paraphrases are grammatically correct and have the same meaning. Be careful; you will not use all the words.

Noun	Verb	Adjective
domestication	domesticate	domestic
evolution	evolve	evolved
familiarity	familiarize	familiar
immaturity		immature
socialization	socialize	social

1. a. Scientists used to believe that dogs were just a _____ form of the wolf.

    b. Until recently, scientists saw dogs as just wolves that ancient humans were able to domesticate.

2. a. The immaturity that can be observed in adult dog behavior can be compared to the way that very young wolves act.

    b. The immature behavior of mature dogs is similar to the behavior of wolves that are very young.

3. a. The dogs and the wolves had to have the same degree of familiarity with humans before the experiment began.

b. Both the dogs and the wolves had to be equally _familiar_
with people before the researchers could start the experiment.

4. a. It is much easier to _socialize_ a dog to humans than it is
to do the same with a wolf.

b. The _socialization_ of wolves to people is far more difficult
than getting a dog to adapt to people.

5. a. The _evolution_ of a species is a process that involves many
genetic changes.

b. It takes a large number of changes in the genes of a species for it to
evolve.

Studying Word Grammar

The phrase **used to** can be used with both *be* and *get*, but the
meaning is different. Look at the examples.

*I am the oldest of six children, so I **am used to** sharing my things.
In contrast, my husband was an only child. He **is used to** having his
own things. When we first got married, it wasn't easy to **get used
to** each other's habits.*

When you *are used to* something, you *are already* familiar with it.
When you *get used to* something, you *become familiar with it over a
period of time.* The same grammar patterns follow both *be* and *get
used to*.

*I **am used to sharing** everything.* *My husband had to **get used to** sharing his things with me.*	*be* or *get* + *used to* + gerund (verb + *-ing*)
*I had to **get used to my husband's habits**.* *It took a long time, but now we **are used to each other**.*	*be* or *get* + *used to* + direct object (noun, pronoun, or noun phrase)

accustomed.

Complete the sentences with *get* or *be*. Use the correct form of the verb.

1. I've tried, but I can't ___get___ used to eating with chopsticks.

2. Don't worry. It's difficult at first, but you will ___get___ used to driving on the left side.

3. At first, going to work so early was difficult for him, but now he ___is___ used to it.

4. I can't sleep at night if it's too quiet. I come from a big city, so I ___am___ used to falling asleep with a lot of traffic noise.

 Working with a partner, answer the questions. Make sure you use the correct form of the **boldfaced** words.

1. When two people get married, what are some of the things that they have to **get used to** about each other?

2. If you move to another country, what do you think will be the most difficult thing for you to **get used to**?

3. What is something that was difficult for you to do at first, but that now you **are used to** doing?

PUTTING IT ALL TOGETHER

Discussion

Share your ideas in a small group. As you talk, try to use the vocabulary below. Each time someone uses a target word or phrase, put a check (✔) next to it.

check out	innate
chimpanzee/chimp	obvious
domestic/domestication/domesticate	read someone's mind
evolve/evolution	socialize/socialization
familiar/familiarity/familiarize	striking
immature/immaturity/maturity/mature	

1. Do you believe that animals and humans can communicate with each other? What kinds of things can they and can't they communicate? Explain your answers with specific examples.

2. Your teacher will give your group blank copies of the questionnaire on page 207. Survey at least ten pet owners (per group). Present your results to the class.

Gender of survey respondent:	☐ Male	☐ Female
1. What kind of pet do you have? ☐ dog ☐ cat ☐ bird ☐ fish ☐ other (please specify): _____		
2. How long have you had your pet? ☐ less than a year ☐ 1–3 years ☐ 4–6 years ☐ more than 6 years		
3. How many pets have you owned in your life? ☐ just 1 ☐ 2 ☐ 3 or more		
4. How did you get your pet? ☐ I bought it. ☐ It was a gift. ☐ I found it. ☐ I got it from an animal shelter.* ☐ Other? _____		
5. How often do you talk to your pet? ☐ very often ☐ sometimes ☐ rarely ☐ never		
6. How well do you think your pet understands what you are thinking? ☐ very well ☐ some ☐ a little ☐ not at all		
7. How well do you think your pet understands what you are feeling? ☐ very well ☐ some ☐ a little ☐ not at all		
8. How much can your pet communicate to you about what it wants or needs? ☐ a lot ☐ some things ☐ not much ☐ nothing		
9. Do you think your pet loves you? ☐ yes ☐ maybe ☐ no		

*an *animal shelter* = a building for animals without a place to live

Writing

Complete one or both of these writing topics. When you write, use at least five of the target words from the chapter. Underline the target words in your paper.

1. Write a report based on your group's survey of pet owners. Try to explain the trends or patterns that you noticed in the data.

2. Do you think that the type of research reported on in the reading is important? Why or why not? Write an essay expressing your opinion about the value of this type of research.

CHAPTER 15

The Mind of the Chimpanzee

Jane Goodall with a baby chimp

GETTING READY TO READ

 A Talk with a partner or in a small group.

1. What skills do you think chimpanzees have? Put a check next to all that apply.

   ____ invent names for common objects

   ✓ understand human language

   ✓ paint pictures

   ✓ recognize people after a long separation

   ____ use human language

   ✓ divide objects into categories

2. Chimpanzees are often used in laboratories in medical research projects. Some people believe that this is morally wrong and governments should not allow it. What do you think?

B The **boldfaced** words and phrases in the paragraph below appear in the reading. Which words are new to you? Circle them. Then, work with a partner. Read this paragraph introducing the writer of the text, and match the words with their definitions. Be careful. There are two extra definitions.

Jane Goodall is a scientist who has spent her life living among and studying the behavior of our closest relative in the animal world—the chimpanzee. She has observed chimps for longer than any other scientist, and has spent endless hours **analyzing** the behavior of chimpanzees in **the wild**. She has also worked closely with other researchers who conduct experiments using domesticated chimps. In many of these experiments, the chimps are encouraged to stretch their minds to the limit, in order to see exactly how far their intellectual abilities can take them. Jane Goodall's work has led to discoveries that are **meaningful** not only to those involved in protecting wild animals, but also to anyone with an interest in human behavior.

Word	Definition
_c_ **1.** analyze	**a.** an area that is natural and not controlled or changed by people
_a_ **2.** the wild	**b.** crazy and without limits
_d_ **3.** stretch	**c.** examine or think about something carefully in order to understand it
_e_ **4.** meaningful	**d.** use as much of something as is available
	e. serious, useful, or important
	f. unusual and exciting

pg 209 216.

READING

Read the text once without stopping.

The Mind of the Chimpanzee

ADAPTED FROM: Goodall, Jane. "The Mind of the Chimpanzee." *Through a Window*. Boston: Houghton Mifflin, 1990.

1   In the middle of the 1960s, Beatrice and Allen Gardner started a project that, along with other similar research, taught us a lot about the chimpanzee mind. They bought an **infant** chimpanzee and began to teach her the signs[1] of ASL, the American Sign Language used by many of the deaf in Canada and the United States. The

---
[1] a *sign* = a hand symbol used by the deaf to communicate

(continued)

Gardners achieved remarkable success with their student, Washoe. Not only did she learn signs easily, but she quickly began to put them together in **meaningful** ways. It was clear that when she saw or used a sign, she formed a picture in her mind of the object it represented. If, for example, she was asked in sign language to get an apple, she would go and find an apple that was **out of sight** in another room.

2   When news of Washoe's achievements were first announced to the scientific community, there was a lot of **protest**. The results of the research **implied** that chimpanzees had the ability to learn a human language, and suggested that chimps might **possess** intellectual skills similar to those of humans. Although many were fascinated and excited by the Gardners' discoveries, many more **bitterly** criticized the whole project. The **controversy** led to many other language projects, and the resulting research provided additional information about the chimpanzee's mind.

3   The fact that chimpanzees have excellent memories surprised no one. So it was not particularly remarkable when Washoe gave the name-sign of Beatrice Gardner, her surrogate mother,[2] after a separation of eleven years. Actually, it was no greater an achievement than the memory of dogs who recognize their owners after separations of almost as long.

4   Chimpanzees also possess premathematical skills: They can, for example, easily tell the difference between *more* and *less*. They can put things into specific categories according to a particular characteristic. Therefore, they have no difficulty in separating a **pile** of food into fruits and vegetables at one time, and at another, dividing the same pile of food into *large* and *small*, even though this calls for putting some vegetables with some fruits.

5   Chimpanzees who have been taught a human language can **combine** signs creatively in order to describe objects for which they have no sign. Washoe, for example, **puzzled** the people taking care of her by asking many times for a *rock berry*. **Eventually** they discovered that she was referring to a sweet type of nut that she had been given for the first time a short time before. Another language-trained chimp described a cucumber[3] as a *green banana*, and another referred to an Alka-Seltzer[4] as a *listen drink*. They can

---

[2] a *surrogate mother* = someone who takes the place of a person or animal's biological mother

[3] a *cucumber* = a long, thin rounded vegetable with a dark green skin, usually eaten raw

[4] an *Alka-Seltzer* = a type of medicine that is put in water and then drunk, and that makes a sound when it is put in water

even invent signs. One chimp had to be put on a leash[5] when she went outside. One day, ready to go outside but having no sign for *leash*, she showed what she wanted by holding a bent finger to the ring on her collar.[6] This sign became part of her vocabulary.

6   Some chimpanzees love to draw, and especially paint. Those who have learned sign language sometimes give a name to their artwork, "This apple"—or sweet corn, or bird, or whatever. The fact that the paintings often look, to our eyes, remarkably different from the objects themselves either means that the chimpanzees are not very good artists or that we have a lot to learn about chimpanzee art!

7   People sometimes ask why such complex intellectual powers have evolved in the chimpanzee when their lives in **the wild** are so simple. The answer is, of course, that their lives in the wild are not so simple! They use—and need—all their mental skills during normal everyday life in their complex society. Chimpanzees always have to make choices—where to go, or with whom to travel. They need highly developed social skills— particularly males who want to become leaders. And low-ranking[7] chimpanzees must learn to hide their intentions or to do things in secret if they want to survive. Indeed, the study of chimpanzees in the wild suggests that their intellectual abilities evolved over thousands of years to help them deal with daily life.

8   It is easier to study intellectual skill in the lab where, through carefully designed tests and the proper use of rewards, chimpanzees can be encouraged to **stretch** their minds to the limit. It is more meaningful to study the subject in the wild, but much harder. It is more meaningful because we can better understand the environmental pressures that led to the evolution of intellectual skills in chimpanzee societies. It is harder because, in the wild, almost all behaviors are complicated by endless variables;[8] years of observing, recording, and **analyzing** replace planned testing; the number of research subjects can often be counted on the fingers of one hand; the only experiments are nature's own, and only time— eventually—may lead to their being repeated.

---

[5] a *leash* = a piece of rope, leather, etc., fastened to an animal's (usually a dog's) collar in order to control it

[6] a *collar* = a band put around an animal's neck

[7] *low-ranking* = having a very low social position in a group

[8] a *variable* = something that may vary in different situations

Comprehension Check

Read these sentences. Circle T (true), F (false), or ? (can't determine the answer from the reading). If you circle F, change the sentence to make it true. Check your answers with a classmate. If your answers are different, look back at the reading.

1. The Gardners got an infant chimpanzee as a pet.   T   F   ?
2. Chimpanzees cannot learn how to use language.   T   F   ?
3. The Gardners taught Washoe how to use ASL because she is deaf.   T   F   ?
4. Some people protested because they didn't think that the Gardners were taking good care of Washoe.   T   F   ?
5. Dogs have better memories than chimpanzees.   T   F   ?
6. Chimpanzees sometimes hide what they are thinking.   T   F   ?
7. It is much easier to study a chimp in the laboratory than in the wild.   T   F   ?

EXPLORING VOCABULARY

Thinking about the Target Vocabulary

Guessing Strategy

The use of similar structures in two sentences or phrases can provide important keys to understanding the meaning of unfamiliar vocabulary. Look at the example.

> *The results of the research **implied** that chimpanzees had the ability to learn a human language, and suggested that chimps might **possess** intellectual skills similar to those of humans.*

You can see a similarity between the phrase *implied that chimpanzees had the ability* and the phrase *suggested that chimps might possess intellectual skills* . . . By comparing the structure of the two phrases, you can infer that the target word *imply* is similar in meaning to *suggest*, and the target word *possess* is similar in meaning to *had*.

Try It!

Read the sentences, and write a definition of the boldfaced target word.

> Jane Goodall believes in speaking out against the hunting and killing of wild chimps for food. She supports **protesting** the inhumane treatment of chimpanzees in medical laboratories.

> **Protesting** means _____.

 A Look at the target words and phrases. Which ones are new to you? Circle them here and in the reading. Then read "The Mind of the Chimpanzee" again. Look at the context of each new word and phrase. Can you guess the meaning? Use the Guessing Strategy where possible.

Target Words and Phrases

infant (1)	implied (2)	pile (4)	the wild (7)
meaningful (1)	possess (2)	combine (5)	stretch (8)
out of sight (1)	bitterly (2)	puzzled (5)	analyzing (8)
protest (2)	controversy (2)	eventually (5)	

B Complete the word-form chart with the target words and phrases as they are used in the reading. Write the base form of verbs and the singular form of nouns.

Nouns	Verbs	Adjectives	Other
infant			

Using the Target Vocabulary

These sentences are **about the reading**. Complete them with the words and phrase in the box. Circle the words or phrase in the sentences that help you understand the meaning of the target words. Be careful. There are two extra words or phrases.

analyze	eventually	out of sight	protest
bitter	imply	pile	puzzled
combined	infant	possess	stretch
controversy			

1. Washoe is the name of a chimpanzee who was adopted by a human family when she was very small. She was an _____ when they got her.

2. The Gardners wanted to find out if Washoe (and other chimps) might _____ the intellectual ability to learn and use language.

3. After they had taught Washoe sign language, the Gardners designed an experiment to test her understanding. They asked her to get an apple that was in another room, _____. Washoe left the room, and came back with the apple.

4. Washoe could understand language. But could she use language to communicate? One day, Washoe _____ the people taking care of her when she invented her own sign, asking for a "rock berry." At first, no one could make sense of Washoe's sign, but _____ they figured out that she had invented a sign for a type of sweet nut.

5. Washoe _____ two signs that she knew, "rock" and "berry," to make a new word.

6. Not everyone in the scientific community was happy about the news of Washoe's achievements with language. In fact, there was a lot of _____ against the work that the Gardners and others were doing.

7. Some scientists were not comfortable with the idea that chimps could learn a language. If that were true, it would suggest, or _____, that chimps might possess intellectual skills similar to those of humans.

8. There was a lot of disagreement among scientists. It was a scientific
   _____.

9. Scientists on both sides disagreed strongly with each other. They
   sometimes got into _____ arguments.

10. Fortunately, the controversy led to more research. In other
    experiments, chimps proved that they could perform complex tasks,
    such as separating one _____ of objects into a number
    of different categories.

DEVELOPING READING SKILLS

Understanding Major Points and Supporting Details

A Which of these sentences are major points and which are supporting details? Write MP (major point) or SD (supporting detail).

   MP 1. The lives of wild chimpanzees are very complex.

   ____ 2. Chimpanzees recognize people that they haven't seen in years.

   ____ 3. Chimpanzees can learn how to communicate with humans.

   ____ 4. Chimps have been taught some of the signs of ASL.

   ____ 5. Chimps are artistically creative.

   ____ 6. Chimps have good memories.

   ____ 7. All chimps learn what their position in chimp society is.

   ____ 8. Laboratory chimps like to draw and paint, and they give names to their "artwork."

   ____ 9. Chimps understand the meaning of *more* and *less*.

   ____ 10. Chimps have some math skills.

B Complete the chart with the information from Part A. Write the details next to the major points they support.

Major Point	Supporting Detail(s)
The lives of wild chimpanzees are very complex.	

Understanding Main Ideas

Answer this question.

What is the main idea of "The Mind of the Chimpanzee"?

_____

_____

Summarizing

Use the information from the previous two exercises, Understanding Major Points and Supporting Details and Understanding Main Ideas, to write a summary of the reading. Do not copy—paraphrase.

EXPANDING VOCABULARY

Using the Target Vocabulary in New Contexts

Complete the sentences with the target words and phrases in the box. Be careful. There are two extra words or phrases.

bitter	implying	pile	puzzles
combine	infant	possess	the wild
controversy	meaningful	protest	
eventually	out of sight		

1. When she was an _____, her doctors discovered a problem with her auditory system. Now she's three years old and almost totally deaf.

2. You are very gifted, but I'm not sure if you _____ the characteristics that make someone a truly great musician.

3. In English, we have an expression "_____, out of mind." It means that when you do not see someone for a long time, you have a tendency to forget him or her.

4. Please put the dirt in a _____ in a corner of the garden.

5. The newspaper received over 10,000 letters of _____ against the war.

6. There is a big _____ over uniforms at that school. About half of the parents want their children to wear them, and the other half don't.

7. I understand why you're angry, but your _____ comments are not going to improve the situation.

8. To make that cake, first _____ the flour and sugar in a large bowl.

9. Your answer _____ me. I can't make sense out of it.

10. Are you _____ that he stole the money? If that's what you're trying to say, you'd better have some evidence to prove it.

11. We can wait. He'll come home _____.

Word Families

Study the chart. Then look at the sentences below and complete the paraphrases with the appropriate forms of the boldfaced words. Make sure that your paraphrases are grammatically correct and have the same meaning as the original sentence. Be careful. You will not use all the words.

Noun	Verb	Adjective
analysis	analyze	analytical
controversy		controversial
implication	imply	
possession	possess	possessive
puzzle	puzzle	puzzling, puzzled
the wild		wild

1. You didn't **analyze** the problem very well.
   Your _____ analysis _____ of the problem was not very good.

2. He is someone who likes to **analyze** everything.
   He is an _____ individual.

3. There was a **controversy** over the president's decision.
   The president's decision was _____.

4. What are you **implying**?
   What is the _____ of what you just said?

5. He lost everything he **possessed** in the fire.
   The fire destroyed his _____.

6. Some children don't like to share their **possessions** with anyone else.

They are _____ of the things that belong to them.

7. His angry reaction **puzzled** me.

I was _____ by the angry way that he reacted.

His anger was a _____ to me.

8. It is important to protect animals living in **the wild**.

We should protect _____ animals.

Studying Word Grammar

Some adjectives become nouns when the definite article *the* is in front of them. Look at the examples.

*The lives of chimpanzees in **the wild** are not so simple.*

*They taught an infant chimpanzee the language used by **the deaf**.*

In these sentences, the adjectives *wild* and *deaf* are used as nouns. Nouns of this kind refer to an entire category, not just one individual. Certain adjectives describing nationalities can also be used in this way. Look at the example.

***The French** are famous for their talented chefs.*

Be careful. Only nationalities that have no plural form are used in this way. For example, we do not say *the American* to refer to the people of the United States. Rather, we use the plural noun with no article—*Americans* (not *the* Americans).

Talk with a partner. Discuss what the people below are famous for.

- The Spanish
- The Swiss
- The Chinese
- The Japanese
- The _____ (your idea)

PUTTING IT ALL TOGETHER

Discussion

Share your ideas in a small group.

1. As scientists discover more and more similarities between humans and animals, it may become difficult to define what distinguishes human beings from other animals. Make a list of the characteristics that you believe make us human. As you talk, try to use the vocabulary below. Each time someone uses a target word or phrase, put a check (✓) next to it.

analyze/analysis	**meaningful**
controversy/controversial	**possess/possession**
eventually	**protest**
imply/implication	**puzzle/puzzled/puzzling**
intend/intention/intentional	**the wild/wild**

2. In paragraph 5 of the reading, the writer describes how some chimps that have been taught sign language create their own, very clever signs for everyday objects—for example, "green banana" (cucumber). Choose five everyday objects, and invent your own "signs" for them. Each sign should be made of two simple words. For example, the sign for a *pencil* could be "writing stick." When you finish, see if the students in other groups can guess what your "signs" mean.

Writing

Complete one or both of these writing topics. When you write, use at least five of the target words from the chapter. Underline the target words in your paper.

1. Do some research either in the library or on the Internet on Jane Goodall and her work. Write a one- to two-page report about her.

2. Write an essay describing the characteristics that you believe distinguish human beings from other animals. As you are writing, consider your answers to question 1 in the Discussion section above. You can use information from the readings in Chapters 13, 14, and 15 to support your ideas, but do not copy—paraphrase.

REVIEWING READING SKILLS AND VOCABULARY

Read the text. Do not use a dictionary.

1   On September 28, 2003, a 300-pound gorilla named Little Joe escaped from a city zoo in the United States. During his escape, the eleven-year-old gorilla attacked and injured a two-year-old girl and her babysitter. Fortunately, their injuries were not serious, and Little Joe was eventually captured by police and returned to the zoo. However, those who witnessed the incident will not soon forget it. Said Mark Matthews, a firefighter who lives close to the zoo, "I saw the gorilla sitting at the bus stop. Everybody was scared, including the police."

2   Rhonda Devance also spotted the gorilla, but she couldn't make sense out of what she was seeing. "I thought it was a person. I thought it was a guy with a big black jacket and a snorkel on."

3   John Dorris, who as a long-time police officer is fairly used to strange incidents, said, "I thought I'd seen it all in eighteen years."

4   The structure where Little Joe lives was thought to be escape-proof, so zoo officials were puzzled at how easy it was for him to get out. However, they were not at all puzzled by the escape attempt itself. At eleven years old, Little Joe can be compared to a human teenager who has reached physical maturity but is still intellectually and emotionally immature. It is common for apes at that age to become restless and seek more freedom. Indeed, experts familiar with Little Joe say that overall, he is a perfectly normal, healthy ape.

5   Not surprisingly, Little Joe's brief taste of freedom has led to protest from those who believe that it is inhumane to keep wild animals in zoos.

Comprehension Check

Read these sentences. Circle T (true), F (false), or ? (can't determine the answer from the reading). If you circle F, change the sentence to make it true.

1. Little Joe escaped from the zoo because zoo workers were not watching him closely enough.   T   F   ?

2. John Dorris was surprised when he saw the escaped gorilla.   T   F   ?

3. Little Joe's behavior is unusual.   T   F   ?

4. Little Joe got on a city bus.   T   F   ?

5. People who think it is morally wrong to keep animals in zoos have used Little Joe's story to support their opinion.   T   F   ?

Guessing Meaning from Context

Find the words in the reading, and match each word to its definition. Be careful. Two definitions will not be used.

Word	Definition
_____ 1. capture	**a.** try to find or get something
_____ 2. spot	**b.** something that people wear on their face in order to breathe under water
_____ 3. snorkel	**c.** notice or recognize something that is unusual or difficult to see
_____ 4. escape-proof	**d.** avoid something that you are afraid of
_____ 5. ape	**e.** a very large nose
_____ 6. restless	**f.** catch and keep someone or something
_____ 7. seek	**g.** not allowing someone or something to get out of somewhere
_____ 8. inhumane	**h.** unable to stop moving because you are impatient, anxious, or bored
	i. a large monkey without a tail or with a very short tail, such as a gorilla
	j. treating people or animals in a way that is unkind or cruel

Paraphrasing

Paraphrase these sentences from the text.

1. Rhonda Devance also spotted the gorilla, but she couldn't make sense out of what she was seeing.

   _____

   _____

2. The structure where Little Joe lives was thought to be escape-proof, so zoo officials were puzzled at how easy it was for Little Joe to get out.

   _____

   _____

3. However, they were not at all puzzled by the escape attempt itself.

   _____

   _____

EXPANDING VOCABULARY

Studying Collocations

Look at the sentence containing the target word **bitter**.

The announcement of the government's decision to go to war led to **bitter** protest.

The word *bitter*, meaning extremely angry or unpleasant, is part of several collocations.

Complete the sentences with the correct collocation from the box.

bitter argument	bitter end	bitter wind
bitter disappointment	bitter protest	

1. She had no hat or coat to protect her from the _____.
2. The two brothers haven't spoken to each other since they had a _____ over money.
3. The fact that Tom did not graduate from college was a _____ to his parents.

4. Despite the _____ of people living in the area, the city cut down all the trees to make room for a new parking lot.

5. The movie seemed endless, but we stayed until the _____.

Word Families

Look at this sentence.

> Please do not **unfasten** your seat belts until the plane has come to a complete stop.

You learned in Unit 3 that the prefix *un-* means "not." But when the prefix *un-* is added to a verb, for example **fasten**, it means more than just "not." It means that something has already been done. In the example, the people on the plane have already fastened their seatbelts. In other words, before you can **undo** something, you need to **do** it.

On a separate piece of paper, answer these questions in complete sentences. Use the boldfaced words.

1. When you get back home after a trip, do you **unpack** immediately, or do you wait until the next day?

2. Have you ever locked yourself out of your car or your house? How did you finally **unlock** the door and get in?

3. When you go away on a long trip, is it a good idea to **unplug** your electrical appliances (for example, your toaster, coffee maker, or computer)? Why or why not?

4. Have you ever done anything in your life that you would like to **undo** if you could?

PLAYING WITH WORDS

Complete the puzzle with words you studied in Chapters 13–15.

Across

2. a group of animals or plants of the same kind that can breed with each other

4. having an empty space inside

5. to develop by gradually changing or to make something do this

6. to join together the two sides of something so that it is closed

7. a very intelligent small African ape

8. a cover for a pot, box, or container

9. a baby

10. confused and unable to understand something

Down

1. a scientist who studies living things

2. a series of musical notes that have a fixed order and become gradually higher or lower in pitch

3. a magazine for professionals in a particular field, for example science and music

5. facts, objects, or signs that make you believe that something exists or is true

10. a large group of similar things collected or thrown together

BUILDING DICTIONARY SKILLS

Finding the Correct Meaning

Many words have more than one meaning. Look at the dictionary entries below. Read each sentence and write the number of the meaning.

> **bit·ter** /ˈbɪtɚ/ *adj* **1** angry and upset because you feel something bad or unfair has happened to you: *I feel very **bitter about** what happened.* | *a bitter old man* **2** [only before noun] making you feel very unhappy and upset: *a **bitter disappointment*** | *She knew **from bitter experience** that they wouldn't agree.* **3** a bitter argument, battle, etc. is one in which people oppose or criticize each other with strong feelings of hate or anger: *a bitter legal battle over custody of the children* **4** having a strong taste, like coffee without sugar **5** extremely cold: *a bitter wind* | *We had to walk home in **the bitter cold**.* **6 to/until the bitter end** continuing until the end even though this is difficult: *We will **fight until the bitter end** to defend our land.* —**bitterness** *n* [U]

1. a. _____ He is **bitter** about losing his job.

   b. _____ This medicine has a **bitter** taste.

> **wild¹** /waɪld/ *adj* **1** wild animals or plants live or grow in a natural state, without being controlled by people [≠ **tame**]: *wild horses* | *wild flowers* → NATURAL¹ **2** showing strong uncontrolled emotions such as excitement, anger, or happiness: *a wild look in her eyes* | *wild laughter* | *The kids were **wild with** excitement.* **3** (*spoken*) exciting, interesting, or unusual: *Sarah's party was wild.* | *a wild haircut* **4** [only before noun] done or said without knowing all the facts or thinking carefully about them: *a wild guess* **5 be wild about sth/sb** (*informal*) to like something or someone very much: *I'm not too wild about his movies.* **6** a wild card in a game can represent any card that you want it to be **7** a wild area of land is in a completely natural state and does not have farms, towns, etc. on it

2. a. _____ I had a **wild** experience last night.

   b. _____ How can you make such a **wild** accusation? You have no proof!

   c. _____ I'm not **wild** about mushrooms. Please don't put any in my salad.

> **stretch**[1] /strɛtʃ/ v **1** [I,T] **also stretch out** to become bigger or looser as a result of being pulled, or to make something become bigger or looser by pulling it: *My sweater has stretched all out of shape.* **2** [I,T] to reach out your arms, legs, or body to full length: *Maxie got up and stretched.* | *Klein stretched out his hand to Devlin.* → see picture on page A22 **3** [I] to spread out over a large area, or continue for a long period: *The line of people stretched around the corner.* | *The project will probably stretch into next year.* **4** [I] if cloth stretches, it changes shape when you pull or wear it, and becomes its original shape when you stop: *The shorts stretch to fit.* **5** [T] to pull something so that it is tight: *Stretch a rope between two trees.* **6 be stretched (to the limit)** to have hardly enough money, supplies, energy, time, etc. to do something: *Our resources are already stretched to the limit.* **7 stretch your legs** (informal) to go for a walk

3. a. _____ My new jeans are a little tight, but they will **stretch**.

 b. _____ Before you do any physical exercise, it's a good idea to **stretch**.

 c. _____ I'm going outside. I need to **stretch** my legs.

> **scale**[1] /skeɪl/ n **1** SIZE [singular, U] the size or level of something, when compared to what is normal: *The scale of the problem soon became clear.* | *There has been housing development on a massive scale since 1980.* | *a large/small scale research project* **2** MEASURING SYSTEM [C usually singular] a system for measuring the force, speed, amount, etc. of something, or for comparing it with something else: *The earthquake measured 7 on the Richter scale.* | *Your performance will be judged on a scale of 1 to 10.* **3** RANGE [C usually singular] the whole range of different types of people, things, ideas, etc. from the lowest level to the highest: *Some rural schools have 50 students while at the other end of the scale are city schools with 5,000 students.* **4** FOR WEIGHING [C] a machine or piece of equipment for weighing people or objects: *The nurse asked me to get on the scale.* → see picture at WEIGH **5** MEASURING MARKS [C] a set of marks with regular spaces between them on an instrument that is used for measuring: *a ruler with a metric scale* **6** MAP/DRAWING [C,U] the relationship between the size of a map, drawing, or model and the actual size of the place or thing that it represents: *a scale of 1 inch to the mile* **7** MUSIC [C] a series of musical notes that have a fixed order and become gradually higher or lower in PITCH **8** ON FISH [C usually plural] one of the small flat pieces of hard skin that cover the bodies of fish, snakes, etc. → see picture on A2

4. a. _____ The doctor asked the patient to step on the **scale** so he could check her weight.

 b. _____ Before you cook the fish, you must remove the **scales**.

 c. _____ Please rate each essay on a **scale** from one to five, with one for the best one and five for the worst one.

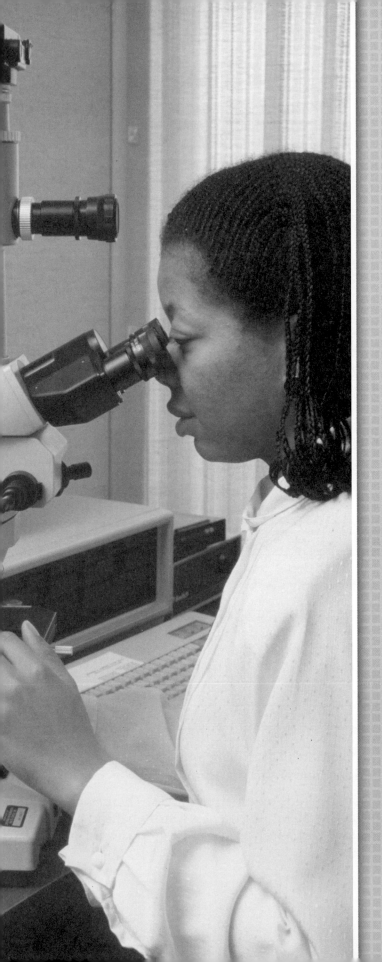

THE PEOPLE BEHIND THE SCIENCE

CHAPTER 16

A Woman's Fate

Dr. Jeong-Wha Choi and one of her inventions

GETTING READY TO READ

A **Talk with a partner or in a small group.**

Based on the photograph above and the paragraph in Part B, imagine what the reading will be about, and write three questions you expect to be answered.

1. _____

2. _____

3. _____

B **Read the first paragraph of "A Woman's Fate." Write the words or phrases that match the definitions below the paragraph.**

The attractive, well-dressed woman holds up a pair of gloves. There seems to be nothing remarkable about them. But there is a story behind these gloves. It involves a war, a little girl who wanted to be a housewife, a determined mother, a talented student, three prestigious universities, and a unique ability to see the big picture.

Definition	Word or Phrase
1. Clothing worn on your hands, with separate parts to cover each finger	_____
2. Having a strong desire to continue to do something even when it is difficult	_____
3. Admired and respected as one of the best or most important	_____
4. Unusually good and special; the only one of its kind	_____
5. Look at a situation and understand the most important issues	_____

READING

Read the text once without stopping.

A Woman's Fate

1   The attractive, well-dressed woman holds up a pair of **gloves**. There seems to be nothing remarkable about them. But there is a story behind these gloves. It involves a war, a little girl who wanted to be a housewife, a **determined** mother, a talented student, three **prestigious** universities, and a **unique** ability to **see the big picture**.

2   Jeong-Wha Choi was born in 1946 in Seoul, Korea. The only girl in a family of four children, Choi lost her father in the Korean War. Her mother went to work as a nurse to support her family. In Korea at that time, it was unusual for a woman to work outside the home, and as a child Choi was very sensitive to her mother's absence. Although an excellent student, she **resisted** her mother's attempts to interest her in a career in medicine. She knew exactly what she wanted to do with her life, and it did not involve medical school. Choi's dream was to be a stay-at-home wife and mother. Choi's mother, however, was determined that her children attend university. Choi agreed, but with one condition—she would not study medicine; she would study home economics.[1]

___
[1] *home economics* = the scientific study of the interaction of individuals, families, and communities with their work, social, and personal environments

(continued)

3   Choi entered prestigious Seoul National University, and did very well in her studies. Her professors encouraged her to go on to graduate school,[2] but with no intention of having a career, Choi was not interested. Fate, however, had different plans.

4   While Choi waited for a **suitable** husband to appear, she took a job with the government as a child welfare[3] worker. But after she had been at her job for only six months, one of her **former** professors offered her a job as an assistant to the department of Home Economics. It was an interesting opportunity, and she accepted.

5   Choi spent almost five years in the department. While she was there, she learned a lot about clothing and textiles.[4] Reading through international publications, she became fascinated by a field that did not even exist in South Korea at that time—clothing physiology. (Clothing physiology is the study of the biological **function**, or work, of clothing, specifically how clothing can contribute to or **interfere** with the healthy functioning of the human body.)

6   Although she had always dreamed of being a wife and mother, Choi accepted the fact that perhaps it was not her fate to marry. She therefore began to look for a graduate program where she could study clothing physiology. Japan seemed to be the best choice. She taught herself as much Japanese as she could by reading textbooks and looking through Japanese fashion magazines, and in January 1973, left South Korea for Japan.

7   Choi expected that it would be at least a year before she would be ready to take the university entrance exam. To her surprise, however, she passed after only two months of study. In March 1975, just two short years after her arrival in Japan, Choi graduated with a degree in clothing physiology from prestigious Nara Women's University. She then went on to get a Ph.D.[5] from the School of Medicine at Kobe University in Kobe, Japan.

8   As her research topic, Choi examined how Korean traditional clothing compares to Western clothing in two ways: thermal adaptability (how well the clothing allows the body to control temperature) and mobility (how well the clothing suits the

---

[2] *graduate school* = a college or university where you can study for a master's degree or a Ph.D.

[3] *welfare* = the system by which the government provides money, free medical care, etc., for people who cannot provide for themselves

[4] a *textile* = any kind of cloth, including cloth that is made from natural or synthetic (= artificial) fabric, for example, a mechanically or chemically bonded fabric

[5] a *Ph.D.* = a doctorate degree from a university

wearer's movement). Choi's research **confirmed** that Korean traditional clothing, while beautiful, did not do very well on a physiological level.

9   In September 1979, Choi returned to Seoul National University, this time as an assistant professor in the same department where she had studied and worked years before. She has since done important research on the effects of clothing on the wearer's quality of life. She and her research team conduct scientifically controlled experiments to precisely measure the ways in which clothing affects mental, physical, and occupational[6] health and **well-being**. And that's what brings us back to those gloves.

10   As a scientist, one of Choi's strengths is her ability to notice problems that others do not, and then **come up with** solutions. On a visit to the South Korean countryside, Choi noticed the green **stains** and painful cracks on the farmers' hands. After analyzing the farmers' work habits and needs, she returned to her laboratory to design a glove suitable for their work. In coming up with the final design, Choi considered a range of factors, from **sweating** rate to worker productivity.[7] The gloves that she and her research team invented are made of a thin, light material that "breathes," making it comfortable enough for all-day wear. The fingers of the glove are covered in a material that stops the fingers from **slipping**. At the same time, the material is thin enough for the farmers to feel what they are doing. Choi and her research group have since patented[8] their invention, and their gloves are worn today by **agricultural** workers all over South Korea. The gloves have also begun to attract the attention of those in other professions, including pharmacists who find that the gloves are perfectly suited to their work.

11   Eventually, Choi did marry and have two children, but she is hardly a stay-at-home wife and mother. She lives in Seoul with her family and is a professor in the Department of Clothing and Textiles, College of Human Ecology,[9] at Seoul National University. She has published many papers in her field and has patents and patents pending[10] on a variety of inventions.

---

[6] *occupational* = relating to a job

[7] *worker productivity* = the rate at which goods are produced, and the amount produced

[8] *patent* = get an official document that says that you have the right to make or sell a new invention and that no one else is allowed to do so

[9] *ecology* = the scientific study of the way in which plants, animals, and people are related to each other and to their environment

[10] *pending* = not yet decided, agreed on, or finished

Comprehension Check

Read these sentences. Circle T (true), F (false), or ? (can't determine the answer from the reading). If you circle F, change the sentence to make it true. Check your answers with a classmate. If your answers are different, look back at the reading.

1. When Choi was young, her mother did not live with her family.   T   F   ?
2. Choi was a better student than her brothers.   T   F   ?
3. Choi intended to work only until she got married.   T   F   ?
4. Choi decided to become a fashion designer.   T   F   ?
5. Choi spent two years learning Japanese.   T   F   ?
6. Choi wishes that she were a stay-at-home wife and mother.   T   F   ?

EXPLORING VOCABULARY

Thinking about the Target Vocabulary

Guessing Strategy

In Chapter 3, you learned that the signal word *or* can help you guess the meaning of unfamiliar words. Look at the example.

*Clothing physiology is the study of the biological **function**, or work, of clothing, specifically how clothing can contribute to or **interfere** with the healthy functioning of the human body.*

function = work
interfere ≠ contribute to

Remember: The punctuation with the word *or* helps you guess meaning.

Try It!

Read the sentences, and write a definition of the boldfaced target words.

1. At her **former**, or previous, job she worked for the government.

   Former means _____.

2. I couldn't decide whether to agree to his plan or **resist** it.

   Resist means _____.

A Look at the target words and phrases. Which ones are new to you? Circle them here and in the reading. Then read "A Woman's Fate" again. Look at the context of each new word and phrase. Can you guess the meaning? Use the Guessing Strategy where possible.

Target Words and Phrases

fate (title)	resisted (2)	well-being (9)
gloves (1)	suitable (4)	come up with (10)
determined (1)	former (4)	stains (10)
prestigious (1)	function (5)	sweating (10)
unique (1)	interfere (5)	slipping (10)
see the big picture (1)	confirmed (8)	agricultural (10)

B Complete the word-form chart with the target words and phrases as they are used in the reading. Write the base form of verbs and the singular form of nouns.

Nouns	Verbs	Adjectives	Other
fate			

Using the Target Vocabulary

These sentences are **about the reading**. Complete them with the words and phrases in the box. Circle the words or phrases in the sentences that help you understand the meanings of the target words. Be careful. There are two extra words or phrases.

agricultural	function	slip
coming up with	interfere	stains
confirm	prestigious	suitable
fate	resisted	sweating
former	seeing the big picture	well-being

1. As a child, Jeong-Wha Choi decided that she would not have a career. However, it seems that being a housewife was not her

   _____ .

2. When she was a young girl, Choi _____ her mother's attempts to interest her in a career in medicine. Instead, she wanted to study home economics.

3. A few months after Choi finished her studies at Seoul National University, one of her _____ professors offered her a job.

4. When Choi started her research on traditional clothing, she was not sure whether her results would _____ or disprove the theory that Korean traditional clothing was warmer than modern clothing.

5. Because Choi is interested in analyzing problems and _____ solutions, a career in science is especially _____ for her.

6. As a scientist, Choi wants to know if a particular type of clothing increases or decreases the wearer's health and comfort. She is interested in the clothing's effect on the physical and mental _____ of the wearer.

7. Some of Choi's projects involve Korean _____ workers, or farmers.

8. When Choi visited agricultural workers in Korea, she noticed the green _____ that they had on their hands from cutting plants.

9. When agricultural workers are cutting plants, they need to be able to hold the plants firmly so that the plants don't _____.

10. When Choi and her team designed gloves to help farmers in their work, they carefully considered the _____, or work, of the gloves.

11. She wanted her gloves to be comfortable for farmers to wear even in the hot sun. Therefore, she measured the farmers' _____ rate when they were wearing the gloves and when they weren't.

12. She did not want the gloves to _____ with the farmers' work. Rather, she wanted the gloves to make the farmers' work easier.

DEVELOPING READING SKILLS

Understanding Text Organization

To understand a reading that involves several different time periods, it is important to be able to put the important events into the correct time order.

Number the following events in the correct order. If you cannot determine from the reading when an event occurred, write a question mark (?).

_____ **a.** Choi graduated with a Ph.D.

_1_ **b.** The Korean War occurred.

_____ **c.** Choi studied home economics.

_____ **d.** Choi worked for six months as a child welfare worker.

_____ **e.** Choi learned Japanese.

_____ **f.** Choi discovered the field of clothing physiology.

_____ **g.** Choi started working for her former professors.

_____ **h.** Choi conducted research on traditional Korean clothing.

_____ **i.** Choi became a professor at Seoul National University.

_____ **j.** Choi got married.

Recognizing Point of View

It is important to understand how a writer feels or thinks about a topic. Often, writers do not state their opinions, or points of view, directly. Rather, the reader needs to infer a writer's point of view.

Circle the statement that best expresses the writer's point of view.

1. The writer admires Jeong-Wha Choi.

2. The writer thinks that all women should have careers.

3. The writer thinks that Jeong-Wha Choi should not have had children.

Summarizing

Use the information from the previous two exercises, Understanding Text Organization and Recognizing Point of View, to write a summary of the reading. Do not copy—paraphrase.

EXPANDING VOCABULARY

Using the Target Vocabulary in New Contexts

Complete the sentences with the target words and phrases in the box. Be careful. There are two extra words or phrases.

agricultural	former	resist	sweat
came up with	function	slip	unique
confirm	glove	stain	well-being
fate	interfere	suitable	

1. I washed the shirt many times, but I couldn't get rid of the coffee

_____.

2. That coat is not _____ for this cold weather. Why don't you buy a heavier one?

3. Be careful. The sidewalk is icy. You could _____ and fall.

4. Please don't _____ in my personal life. I can solve my own problems.

5. I know that I shouldn't eat ice cream because I'm on a diet, but I can't _____.

6. I made less money at my _____ job than at the job I have now.

7. It wasn't your fault. There was nothing you could do. It was

   _____ .

8. Good doctors care about the _____ of their patients.

9. Please _____ your reservation by calling the airline 24 hours before departure.

10. The economy of that country is based on _____ products, particularly coffee, rice, and fruit.

11. It took them a long time, but eventually they _____ a name for their company.

12. I don't understand your _____ here. What exactly do you do?

13. I _____ a lot when it's hot.

Word Families

The prefix *inter-* means "between." Look at the sentence.

*I don't think you should **interfere** in their argument. You will only make things worse.*

In this sentence, the word *interfere* means "come between."

Complete the sentences with the words below.

interaction	interpersonal	interstate
interlocking	interrelated	

1. That company has offices in both New York and California so they have to pay _____ taxes.

2. In a puzzle, you must put together the _____ pieces.

3. This job calls for excellent _____ skills. If you have trouble getting along with others, this is not the right job for you.

4. Research has confirmed that the more _____ there is between teachers and students, the more the students learn.

5. Those two fields are _____. What happens in one field always affects the other.

Studying Phrasal Verbs

The phrasal verb **come up with** means "to think of an idea, plan, reply, etc." There are many phrasal verbs that are formed with the verb *come*.

Read the sentences. Think about the meaning of the boldfaced phrasal verbs. Then write answers to the questions.

a. The project was going well until last week. We **came up against** some unexpected problems.

b. They were best friends until that woman **came between** them.

c. I don't feel very well. I think I'm **coming down with** a cold.

d. I **came across** an article in the newspaper that I thought might interest you.

1. What difficulties have you **come up against** in learning English?

   _____

   _____

2. Has anything or anyone ever **come between** you and your best friend? Explain.

   _____

   _____

3. What is the best thing to do if you feel that you are **coming down with** a cold or other illness?

   _____

   _____

4. When you are reading and **come across** a word that you are unfamiliar with, what should you do?

   _____

   _____

PUTTING IT ALL TOGETHER

Discussion

Share your ideas in a small group. As you talk, try to use the vocabulary below. Each time someone uses a target word or phrase, put a check (✔) next to it.

come up with	former	suitable	well-being
confirm	function	unique	

Come up with an invention that will be useful in everyday life. When you are ready, present your invention to the class. Explain the problem that the invention solves, as well as the way that it functions. Be prepared to answer questions from the class.

Writing

Complete one or both of these writing topics. When you write, use at least five of the target words from the chapter. Underline the target words in your paper.

1. Imagine that you want to convince someone to produce the invention that you and your group have come up with. Write a letter to possible investors (people who might give you money to produce the invention). Your letter should include the following information:

   • What the invention was designed for

   • Who the invention was designed for

   • How the invention functions

   • Why people will want to buy this invention

2. What was the most important invention of the past 100 years? Write an essay describing the invention, who invented it, and why it was so significant. If you get information for your report from the Internet or the library, give your teacher a list of the websites, articles, and books that you used in your research. Write the report in your own words. Don't copy—paraphrase.

The Father of Vaccination

Edward Jenner (1749–1823) vaccinates his son.

GETTING READY TO READ

 A **Talk in a small group or with the whole class.**

1. Put a check (✓) next to the diseases that you are familiar with. If you are not familiar with one of the diseases, ask your classmates or look it up in your dictionary.

    ____ influenza (flu)   ____ smallpox   ____ chicken pox

    ____ HIV (AIDS)   ____ cancer   ____ malaria

2. For some diseases, your doctor can give you an injection[1] that will protect you from the disease. This injection is called a *vaccination*. Which of the diseases above can be prevented with a vaccination? Circle them. When you finish, check your answers with your teacher.

___

[1] an *injection* = the act of giving a drug by using a special needle

B The **boldfaced** words in the sentences below appear in the reading. Which words are new to you? Circle them. Then, read the sentences about the reading. Decide whether the pairs of words after each sentence have similar or different meanings. Write S (similar) or D (different).

1. Edward Jenner studied medicine in London because he wanted to become a **physician**.

    _____ physician / doctor

2. In the eighteenth century, physicians were trained in **surgery** so that they could operate on their patients.

    _____ surgery / operation

3. In those days, smallpox was a deadly disease. However, some people were fortunate, and got only a **mild** form of the disease.

    _____ mild / severe

4. Some people would **deliberately** attempt to get a mild form of the disease, so that later they wouldn't get a more severe case.

    _____ deliberately / intentionally

5. When Jenner started his experiments on smallpox, many other physicians criticized him. However, Jenner **ignored** the criticism, and continued his work.

    _____ ignored / paid attention to

READING

Read the text once without stopping.

The Father of Vaccination

1   In a small town in England in the middle of the eighteenth century, an eight-year-old boy named Edward Jenner was intentionally **infected** with a deadly disease. He was then locked in a barn² with other children who had been similarly infected. There they remained until they either died or recovered. Fortunately for humanity, Jenner survived.

2   Child **abuse**? No—variolation. A common **practice** in the eighteenth century, variolation involved **deliberately** infecting a

² a *barn* = a large farm building in which animals are kept

(continued)

healthy person with smallpox, a highly **contagious** disease that killed one in three infants and young children. It was believed that healthy people infected with the pus[3] of patients sick with **mild** cases of smallpox would develop only a mild form of the disease. Those individuals would then be protected from smallpox for the rest of their lives. Although variolation was the only effective **means** of fighting smallpox at that time, it was quite dangerous. About 10 percent of those variolated came down with a severe case of smallpox.

3   Edward Jenner would never forget his terrible days in the barn. Perhaps that was what led him to choose medicine as a career. In 1761, at just thirteen, Jenner began his medical studies. By 1770, he was studying anatomy[4] and **surgery** under John Hunter at St. George's Hospital in London. With Hunter, Jenner was trained in the scientific method, which his instructor described simply as "Why think; why not try the experiment?"

4   After two years in London, Jenner returned to his hometown. He was a popular doctor, due to his gentle personality and surgical skill. One common **request** was for variolation. Jenner performed the **procedure** many times, although he used a less severe method than the one that he had suffered through as a child. Jenner observed that some of his variolated patients never developed even a mild case of smallpox. Because of his training in the scientific method, he wanted to understand why these particular individuals were able to resist the disease. He discovered that they had all previously had cowpox, a mild illness passed from cows to humans. Cowpox affected mostly people who worked closely with cows. Jenner observed that cowpox, while much less severe than smallpox, was in many ways similar to it. He was also aware of a traditional belief that people who had cowpox never got smallpox. Based on his observations, Jenner came up with a theory. He believed that cowpox not only protected against smallpox, but could be passed from one human being to another as a deliberate means of protection.

5   In May 1796, Jenner finally got the chance to test his theory. He learned that a young woman from a local farm, Sarah Nelmes, had cowpox. Jenner asked the parents of an eight-year-old boy named James Phipps for **permission** to conduct a risky experiment on their son. Jenner chose James because he had never had cowpox or smallpox. Jenner removed pus from Sarah's hand and spread it on scratches he had made on the boy's arms. As expected, the

---

[3] *pus* = a thick yellowish liquid produced in an infected part of the body

[4] *anatomy* = the scientific study of the structure of human or animal bodies

boy developed a mild case of cowpox, but recovered rapidly. Jenner was now ready for the second, much riskier stage of his experiment. On July 1, 1796, Jenner variolated Phipps with pus from a smallpox patient. Jenner and other scientists and **physicians** waited anxiously for the results. Some were excited about Jenner's experiment, but many others accused him of taking too great a risk.

6   In fact, James Phipps never developed smallpox. This was clear evidence to support Jenner's theory, but more data were needed. Jenner experimented successfully on thirteen more patients, and at the end of 1796 wrote a report describing his work for the Royal Society.[5] However, it was **turned down** for publication. According to those who **reviewed** it, Jenner's theory was too much of a challenge to the accepted medical beliefs of the time.

7   Jenner **ignored** the criticism and continued experimenting. In 1798 he published his own book based on twenty-three cases in which vaccination (named for the *vaccinnia* virus[6] of cowpox) resulted in lasting protection against, or immunity to, smallpox. Although many people continued to criticize Jenner, some well-known London physicians were starting to vaccinate their patients. By the beginning of the nineteenth century, the practice of vaccination had spread throughout the world.

8   Eventually, Jenner's contributions to science were formally recognized. However, he never made an attempt to get rich through his discovery. Instead, he spent much of his time working, without pay, to spread the good news about vaccination. In 1977, the last known victim of smallpox recovered. No new cases appeared, and in 1980, the World Health Assembly announced that "the world and its peoples" were **free of** smallpox.

[5] the *Royal Society* = a group of respected physicians and scientists in London who review the research of other scientists

[6] a *virus* = a very small living thing that causes diseases that can be passed from one person or animal to another

Comprehension Check

Read these sentences. Circle T (true), F (false) or ? (can't determine the answer from the reading). If you circle F, change the sentence to make it true. Check your answers with a classmate. If your answers are different, look back at the reading.

1. When Edward Jenner was a boy, he got smallpox.   T   F   ?

2. Jenner decided to become a doctor because of his terrible experience with smallpox as a child.   T   F   ?

3. Because of his early experiences, Jenner refused to variolate his patients.   **T   F   ?**

4. Jenner discovered a cure for smallpox.   **T   F   ?**

5. At first, Jenner's work on vaccination was not accepted by the medical community.   **T   F   ?**

6. Jenner's work is important because it led to both the elimination of smallpox and the discovery of how vaccines work.   **T   F   ?**

EXPLORING VOCABULARY

Thinking about the Target Vocabulary

Guessing Strategy

The signal word *but* shows that a writer is contrasting two words or ideas. If you understand the contrast the writer is making, it can help you guess the meaning of unfamiliar words. Look at the example.

*Children who had a **mild** form of the disease usually survived, but those with a severe case almost always died.*

In this sentence, the contrast is between a mild form of the disease and a *severe* case. In Chapter 9 you learned that *severe* means "very serious." From this sentence, you can see that *mild* is the antonym of *severe*. Therefore, *mild* means "not serious."

Try It!

Read the sentence, and write a definition of the boldfaced target word.

That journal often accepts articles from well-known writers, but they **turned down** his paper because he had never published anything before.

Turn down means _____.

A Look at the target words and phrases. Which ones are new to you? Circle them here and in the reading. Then read "The Father of Vaccination" again. Look at the context of each new word and phrase. Can you guess the meaning? Use the Guessing Strategy where possible.

Target Words and Phrases

vaccination (title)	mild (2)	physicians (5)
infected (1)	means (2)	turned down (6)
abuse (2)	surgery (3)	reviewed (6)
practice (2)	request (4)	ignored (7)
deliberately (2)	procedure (4)	free of (8)
contagious (2)	permission (5)	

B Complete the word-form chart with the target words and phrases as they are used in the reading. Write the base form of verbs and the singular form of nouns.

Nouns	Verbs	Adjectives	Other
vaccination			

Using the Target Vocabulary

The sentences on page 246 are **about the reading**. Complete them with the words and phrases in the box. Circle the words or phrases in the sentences that help you understand the meanings of the target words. Be careful. There are two extra words or phrases.

abuse	infected	practice	reviewing
contagious	means	procedure	turned down
free of	permission	request	vaccination
ignoring	physician		

1. Before Jenner made his discovery, it was common medical
   _____ for doctors to deliberately infect children with smallpox.

2. Were the doctors who infected the children guilty of
   _____? No, they were just trying to protect them from
   developing a severe case of the disease.

3. Although they knew it was risky, parents requested the practice
   because at that time it was the only _____, or way, to
   protect their children from getting a severe case of the disease.

4. The _____, called variolation, involved putting a child into
   contact with a person who was infected with a mild case of the disease.

5. Because smallpox is a _____ disease, most children who
   had contact with someone suffering from smallpox would get sick.

6. However, not all children who were _____ with smallpox
   died. Those who got a mild form of the disease often recovered.

7. When physician Edward Jenner asked the Phipps family if he could
   use their son in an experiment, it was just a _____.
   They did not have to agree to it, but they did. They gave Jenner
   _____ to conduct the experiment.

8. As a result of those early experiments, Jenner eventually developed a
   medical procedure called _____.

9. However, Jenner's discovery was not immediately accepted.
   Indeed, when Jenner attempted to publish his research, he was
   _____ by the prestigious medical journals.

10. The Royal Society didn't do a good job of _____ Jenner's
    research. They just looked at it quickly and decided that his ideas
    were too new.

11. Fortunately, Jenner continued his research. Today, due to his work,
    the world is _____ the deadly disease of smallpox.

DEVELOPING READING SKILLS

Understanding Reference Words

In Chapter 11 you learned that a reference word takes the place of a noun or noun phrase. Reference words are often pronouns, such as *he, she,* and *it,* but in fact, almost any word can be a reference word. Look at the **boldfaced** words in the sentences.

> Jenner observed that some of his variolated patients never developed even a mild case of smallpox. Because of his training in the scientific method, he wanted to understand why **these particular individuals** were able to resist **the disease**.

In these sentences, the boldfaced words replace, or refer back to, something already mentioned in the text. The noun phrase *these particular individuals* refers back to some of *Jenner's variolated patients,* and *the disease* refers back to *smallpox.*

What do the boldfaced words refer to? Look back at the reading, and write your answers.

1. He was then locked in a barn with other children who had been similarly infected. **There** they remained until they either died or recovered. (paragraph 1)

   There = _____

2. With Hunter, Jenner was trained in the scientific method, **which his instructor** described simply as "Why think; why not try the experiment?" (paragraph 3)

   which = _____

   his instructor = _____

3. Jenner performed the procedure many times, although he used a less severe method than **the one** that he had suffered through as a child. (paragraph 4)

   the one = _____

4. In fact, James Phipps never developed smallpox. **This** was clear evidence to support Jenner's theory, but more data were needed. (paragraph 6)

   This = _____

5. However, he [Jenner] never made an attempt to get rich through **his discovery**. (paragraph 8)

   his discovery = _____

Understanding Main Points and Important Details

Complete the chart with information from the reading. If the reading does not contain the information, write a question mark (?). The completed chart should tell the story of Edward Jenner's life and work.

When?	What?	Where?	Who?
When Jenner was 8 years old			
		St. George's Hospital in London	
1772–May 1796			
May–July 1796			
End of 1796			The Royal Society
1797–1798			
1798			
1798–beginning of the nineteenth century			
1977			
	Announced that the disease of smallpox had been eliminated	?	World Health Assembly

Summarizing

Write a summary of the reading. Do not look back at the reading. Use the information in the chart as a guide.

EXPANDING VOCABULARY

Using the Target Vocabulary in New Contexts

Complete the sentences with the target words in the box. Be careful. There are two extra words or phrases.

abuse	infected	practice	reviewed
contagious	means	procedure	turned down
deliberately	mild	request	vaccinations
free of	permission		

1. His boss turned down his _____ for a pay increase.

2. For the well-being of the hospital staff, patients suffering from _____ diseases must be identified immediately and kept in a separate area.

3. The writer who _____ the movie was very critical.

4. I asked my boss for _____ to leave early.

5. We don't have the _____ to pay for a prestigious university for our son.

6. He was _____ for the job because his experience wasn't suitable.

7. Everyone should have a childhood _____ abuse.

8. That cut on your hand is _____. It's not getting better. You should ask a physician to look at it.

9. Could you please explain the _____ for getting a driver's license?

10. Before traveling to another country, your physician must confirm that you have received all of the required _____.

11. The police have evidence that her severe injuries were intentional. They are due to deliberate _____.

12. It is not my usual _____ to interfere in domestic arguments.

Word Families

Some words contain both a root and a prefix. For example, the target word **procedure** contains the root *ced*, which means "go" or "move," as well as the prefix *pro-*, which means "according to." The definition of a *procedure* is "something that follows a set of rules"— in other words, something that goes or moves forward according to certain rules.

Read the sentences. Using both context and what you know about the meaning of the root *ced* and the prefixes *inter-* (between or among), *pre-* (before) and *re-* (back or again), write a definition of each boldfaced word. Then, compare your definitions with a partner's. When you are finished, look the words up in your dictionary.

1. If the parents cannot agree on whether or not their daughter should have surgery, her physician will have to **intercede**.

intercede: _____

2. As we drove away from the coast, the sound of the ocean **receded**.

recede: _____

3. Variolation, a dangerous medical procedure, **preceded** the far safer practice of vaccination.

precede: _____

Studying Collocations

The adjective **mild** and its antonym **severe** are used in several common collocations.

Read the sentences. Think about the meaning of the boldfaced collocations. Then write answers to the questions. Use complete sentences.

a. There is going to be a **severe storm** tomorrow. If you can, stay at home.

b. My husband is very **mild-mannered**. He almost never gets angry.

c. Most American food has a very **mild taste**. I prefer food with a stronger flavor.

d. Don't worry. You just have a **mild cold**.

e. When the president announced his plan to raise taxes, he came up against **severe criticism**.

f. He's in such **severe pain** that he can't walk.

g. After the dentist removes the tooth, you might experience some **mild pain**.

1. What is the most **severe** storm you have ever experienced? Describe it.

_____

_____

2. How does a **mild-mannered** person behave?

_____

_____

3. Do you prefer food with a **mild** taste or a spicy taste?

_____

_____

4. Have you ever had a **mild** case of a serious disease? Explain.

_____

_____

5. Have you ever received **severe** criticism for something you've done? Explain.

_____

_____

6. What can you do to deal with **mild** pain? **severe** pain?

_____

_____

PUTTING IT ALL TOGETHER

Discussion

Share your ideas in a small group. As you talk, try to use the vocabulary below. Each time someone uses a target word or phrase, put a check (✔) next to it.

abuse	means	procedure
contagious	mild	request
deliberately	permission	surgery
free of	physician	turn down
infect	practice	vaccination/vaccine

1. One problem with testing new vaccines is that it is risky to use an untested vaccine on human beings. Today, there are laws that limit scientists' ability to conduct such experiments. However, those laws did not exist in Edward Jenner's time. Discuss the advantages and disadvantages of laws that limit scientists from conducting experiments on human beings. Under what circumstances is it acceptable to allow experiments on humans? Under what circumstances is it unacceptable?

2. What medical advances do you think will occur in your lifetime? Consider the following questions in your discussion: Which diseases will be cured? For which diseases will a vaccine be developed? Will life expectancy (how many years a human being, on average, lives) increase? By how many years?

Writing

Complete one or both of these writing topics. When you write, use at least five of the target words from the chapter. Underline the target words in your paper.

1. Conduct research either in the library or on the Internet on vaccines that scientists are currently working to develop. Write a report on your findings. Write the report in your own words. Do not copy—paraphrase. Give your teacher a list of the websites, articles, and books that you used in your research.

2. Write an essay based on question 1 in the Discussion section above.

CHAPTER 18

A Nose for Science

Luca Turin

GETTING READY TO READ

 A **Talk with a partner or in a small group.**

1. Do you like to wear cologne?[1] If so, do you always wear the same kind, or do you change what you are wearing depending on the situation? Are there any situations for which wearing cologne is not appropriate? Explain.

2. Which sense is the most important to you—sight, hearing, speech, touch, taste, or smell? The least? Why?

---
[1] *cologne* = a liquid that smells slightly like flowers or plants, which you put on your neck and wrists

Read the paragraph and answer the questions.

One of France's most famous royal couples was King Louis XVI and his wife, Marie Antoinette. There are many stories about Marie Antoinette, but one tale is especially interesting. It involves her attempted escape from Paris during the French Revolution. According to the legend, Marie Antoinette and Louis XVI dressed in the clothes of simple travelers in order to escape from France. However, although Marie Antoinette's clothing was simple, her fragrance was not. Marie Antoinette and her husband were caught when someone smelled the expensive perfume that she was wearing. They knew that she was not an ordinary person, because only a member of royalty could afford such an expensive scent.

1. What are the three nouns in the paragraph that refer to **smells**?

    _____, _____, _____

2. What are the two nouns in the paragraph that refer to a type of

    story? _____, _____

3. What is the adjective in the paragraph that means "relating to or

    belonging to a king or queen"? _____

4. What is the noun form of the adjective in question 3?

    _____

READING

Read the text once without stopping.

A Nose for Science

1   In 1791, Marie Antoinette[1] escaped Paris with her husband, Louis XVI. Dressed as simple travelers, they left for Austria. But before they arrived, they were caught. How? The **legend** says that when the queen stepped down from her carriage[2] in a cloud of expensive **perfume**, everyone knew she must be **royalty**. No ordinary person could afford to wear anything that smelled so heavenly. The queen eventually paid for the mistake with her life.

_____

[1] *Marie Antoinette* = wife of Louis XVI, the king of France from 1774 to 1792. They were both put in jail and killed during the French Revolution.

[2] a *carriage* = a vehicle with wheels that is pulled by a horse, used in past times

2   This is just one of the many perfume **tales** that scientist Luca Turin enjoys retelling. Turin is a biophysicist[3] with an unusual hobby—collecting perfume. And as unlikely as it might seem, Turin's hobby has led him to develop a scientific theory that could win him a Nobel Prize[4]—or at least make him very rich.

3   Turin has been **obsessed** by smell since he was a boy and he used to **entertain** himself by analyzing the **scents** of wild plants. He has an unusually sensitive nose and is very good at identifying different scents. Turin describes his excellent sense of smell in this way: "Every perfume I've ever smelled has been to me like a movie, sound and vision . . . To me, smell is just as real as they are." When he was a young scientific researcher in Nice, France, Turin frequently visited local perfume shops, collecting rare **fragrances**. He was well known for his ability to smell a perfume and analyze it, immediately identifying the individual scents that it contained.

4   As he added to his perfume collection, Turin was also progressing in his scientific career. Although trained as a biologist, he considered the division of science into separate fields—biology, chemistry, and **physics**—to be artificial. He moved freely from one field to another, following a **path** determined only by his interest and intellect. In that way, he gained a wider range of knowledge than most scientists possess.

5   At the same time, Turin's fascination with perfume grew. One day he and some friends visited a large **discount** perfume store where Turin bought almost everything on the shelves. On the way home, he entertained his friends by describing the fragrances in language that was so **poetic** that they told him he should write a book.

6   He decided to do exactly that. In 1992, Turin's book was published as *Parfums: Le Guide* (*Perfume: The Guide*). In it, Turin skillfully critiques some of the world's most famous fragrances. For example, this is how he describes Rush, by Gucci: "It smells like an infant's breath mixed with his mother's hair spray[5]. . . What Rush can do, as all great art does, is create a yearning,[6] then fill it with false memories of an invented past . . . "

---

[3] a *biophysicist* = a scientist who studies the natural forces that affect living things

[4] a *Nobel Prize* = a prize given in Sweden each year to people from any country for important work in science, literature, economics, or work toward world peace

[5] *hair spray* = a sticky liquid that is forced out of a special container in a stream of very small drops and that you put on your hair to make it stay in place

[6] a *yearning* = a strong desire or feeling of wanting something

(continued)

7   Turin's book caused a sensation among the **secretive** "Big Boys"—the seven large companies that control the world scent market. Turin's talent at translating smell into words won him a rare invitation to visit their laboratories. There, Turin discovered that the widely accepted theory about how we are able to identify particular smells—by the shape of their molecules[7]—did not seem to work. Under this theory, it should be fairly easy for a chemist to "build" new molecules and accurately predict what they will smell like. But in fact, this is not the case. Each new smell the Big Boys create involves an **investment** of millions of dollars. That is because only a very small percentage of the new molecules possess the desired fragrance.

8   Now Turin had a new obsession: solving the mystery of smell. As a scientist with an extremely sensitive nose, an obsession with perfume, **access** to the Big Boys' laboratories, and a wide range of scientific knowledge, he was particularly well suited to the challenge. Within just three years, Turin believed that he had the answer. The key was not the shape of the molecules, but rather their vibrations.[8]

9   Turin sent a paper presenting his theory to the prestigious science journal *Nature*, and waited anxiously for a response. However, a few scientific reviewers recommended that *Nature* turn the paper down. (It was eventually published in the journal *Chemical Senses*.) Scientists who had based their careers on the old theory of smell also reacted negatively, and he was even accused of **fraud**.

10   Turin's explanation? He is sharply critical of the **standards** for publication in science journals. He argues that the reviewers turned his paper down due to their narrow **focus** on just one field of science. Therefore, they couldn't make sense out of a complex theory involving biology, chemistry, and physics.

11   Luca Turin has since started his own company, Flexitral, where he uses his theory to create scent molecules to sell to the Big Boys. And like all scientists with controversial ideas, he waits for the day when his achievements will be properly recognized.

---

[7] a *molecule* = the smallest unit into which any substance can be divided without losing its own chemical nature

[8] a *vibration* = a continuous, small shaking movement

Comprehension Check

Read these sentences. Circle T (true), F (false) or ? (can't determine the answer from the reading). If you circle F, change the sentence to make it true. Check your answers with a classmate. If your answers are different, look back at the reading.

1. Turin's interest in smell led him to become a scientist.   T   F   ?

2. Turin wrote a scientific book about perfume.   T   F   ?

3. Turin came up with a new theory about how we are able to distinguish different scents.   T   F   ?

4. Turin's theory is widely accepted within the scientific community.   T   F   ?

5. Turin thinks that the scientists who reviewed his theory did not treat him or his theory fairly.   T   F   ?

6. Turin will receive a Nobel Prize.   T   F   ?

EXPLORING VOCABULARY

Thinking about the Target Vocabulary

Guessing Strategy

Words that express cause-and-effect relationships can help you guess the meaning of unfamiliar words or phrases. Look at the example.

*He described the fragrances in language that was so **poetic** that they told him he should write a book.*

In this sentence, the cause-and-effect relationship expressed by *so . . . that* indicates that poetic language is good enough to be in a book, so you can infer that it is well written. The exact definition of *poetic* is "graceful, beautiful, and having deep feelings."

Try It!

Read the sentence, and write a definition of the boldfaced target word.

Turin was so **obsessed** with coming up with a theory of smell that he couldn't think of anything else.

Obsessed means _____.

A   Look at the target words. Which words are new to you? Circle them here and in the reading. Then read "A Nose for Science" again. Look at the context of each new word. Can you guess the meaning? Use the Guessing Strategy where possible.

Target Words

legend (1)	entertain (3)	discount (5)	access (8)
perfume (1)	scents (3)	poetic (5)	fraud (9)
royalty (1)	fragrances (3)	secretive (7)	standards (10)
tales (2)	physics (4)	investment (7)	focus (10)
obsessed (3)	path (4)		

B   Complete the word-form chart with the target words as they are used in the reading. Write the base form of verbs and the singular form of nouns.

Nouns	Verbs	Adjectives	Other
legend			

Using the Target Vocabulary

These sentences are **about the reading**. Complete them with the words in the box. Circle the words or phrases in the sentences that help you understand the meanings of the target words.

access	fraud	path	royalty
discount	investment	physics	secretive
entertaining	legends	poetic	standards
focus	obsessed		

1. Scientist Luca Turin enjoys _____ people with interesting stories about perfume.

2. Turin is fascinated by different scents. In fact, you could say that he is _____ with smell.

3. One day, Turin went to a _____ perfume store. The prices were very low, and he bought almost every perfume there.

4. Turin is a scientist, but he is also a very artistic writer. His descriptions of perfume are remarkably _____.

5. The makers of expensive perfume are so _____ that they almost never let anyone visit their labs.

6. Turin was given _____ to the laboratories of the perfume makers because they were impressed by his perfume guide.

7. Turin has used his knowledge of science, particularly biology, chemistry, and _____, to come up with a scientific theory of how we are able to smell.

8. Turin follows a different _____ from others. He doesn't follow the way other people do things. He comes up with his own way.

9. Some scientists do not believe Turin's theory, and one has accused him of deliberately changing or inventing data—in other words, scientific _____.

10. Turin believes his paper was turned down because a small number of powerful scientists have too much of an _____ in the old theory of smell to admit that Turin's theory is correct.

11. According to Turin, the reviewers of his paper couldn't see the big picture because of their _____ on their individual fields of science.

12. Turin hopes that by telling his story, he can help change the _____ that prestigious science journals use when they decide whether or not to publish a paper.

DEVELOPING READING SKILLS

Understanding Purpose

To understand a text, it is important to understand *why* the writer wrote the text, or the writer's **purpose**. When you read, try to answer these questions about the information in a text:

- Why did the writer include this particular information?
- Why did the writer present the information in this particular order or in this particular way?

Complete the sentences. Circle a or b.

1. The writer includes the legend about Marie Antoinette
   a. to teach the reader some French history.
   b. to get the reader interested in the text.

2. The writer includes the quote from Luca Turin in paragraph 3
   a. to help the reader understand why Turin is so interested in smell.
   b. to convince the reader that smell is an important sense.

3. The writer includes information about Turin's perfume guide because
   a. it shows that Turin has a very sensitive sense of smell.
   b. it shows what a talented writer Turin is.

4. The writer of the text believes
   a. that Turin's theory of smell could be correct.
   b. that Turin should not have challenged the scientific community.

Summarizing

 A Put a check (✔) next to the topics that should be included in a summary of the reading.

_____ **a.** the legend about Marie Antoinette's perfume

_____ **b.** Turin's visit to a discount perfume store

_____ **c.** Turin's perfume guide

_____ **d.** Turin's description of the fragrance Rush

_____ **e.** Turin's lifelong fascination with smell

_____ **f.** Turin's scientific background

_____ **g.** the shape theory of smell

_____ **h.** Turin's theory of smell

_____ **i.** *Nature*'s reaction to Turin's theory

_____ **j.** Turin's opinion about why his theory is not accepted by many scientists

B Use both Part A and your answers to Understanding Purpose to write a summary of the reading. Do not copy—paraphrase.

EXPANDING VOCABULARY

Using the Target Vocabulary in New Contexts

Complete the sentences with the target words in the box. Be careful. There are two extra words or phrases.

access	fragrance	path	secretive
discount	fraud	physics	standards
entertain	investment	poetic	tales
focus	obsessed		

1. She is so _____ with detail that she can't see the big picture.

2. Originally, these gloves were priced at $100, but I got them at a 50 percent _____.

3. The academic _____ for entering a prestigious university are very high. Fortunately, I have excellent grades.

4. The reviewer said the movie was wonderful. He said it would _____ the whole family.

5. The former president of my company was accused of _____. The company lost a lot of money while he was president.

6. That business is a good _____. You will make a lot of money from it.

7. My _____ professor is the best scientist at the university.

8. _____ to that room is restricted. Only a few employees can enter.

9. Stay on the walking _____, and you won't get lost. It's easy to follow.

10. Your _____ should be on the main ideas. Don't worry about the details.

11. I don't understand why my son is suddenly so _____. What is he hiding?

12. You have such an original and _____ way of expressing yourself. How did you learn to speak so beautifully?

Word Families

As you have seen in previous chapters, adjectives can have a variety of suffixes, such as -ous, -ful, -ic, -al, -ed, and -ing. Other adjective endings include the suffixes -ive, -ent, and -ary.

Complete the sentences with the adjectives below.

fraudulent   **legendary**   **obsessive**   **secretive**

1. There is no reason to be so _____. Everyone already knows what happened.

2. The _____ movie actor died yesterday at the age of eighty-two.

3. I'm concerned about you. You are becoming _____ about your work. Don't be such a perfectionist!

4. He was arrested for possessing _____ identification papers.

Understanding Word Grammar

A **reflexive pronoun** is an object pronoun that is used when the subject and object of a verb are the same. Never use a reflexive pronoun if the subject and the object of the verb are different. Look at the examples.

Correct: *He used to entertain **himself** by analyzing the scents of wild plants.*	The reflexive pronoun *himself* is used **correctly** in this example because the subject and object of the verb are the same.
Incorrect: ***His mother** entertained himself by telling him Greek legends.*	The reflexive pronoun *himself* is used **incorrectly** in this example because the subject and object of the verb are different.

The reflexive pronouns in English are *myself, yourself, himself, herself, itself, themselves, yourselves, ourselves,* and *oneself.*

Answer these questions. Use the boldfaced verbs in your answers. Be careful. When you answer the questions, the pronouns may change.

1. What do you and your friends do to **entertain yourselves**? When your friends are busy, what do you do to **entertain yourself**?

   _____

   _____

2. Do you think teachers should try to **entertain their students**? Why or why not?

   _____

   _____

3. In which sports is it common for the players to **injure themselves**? Have you ever **injured yourself** when you were playing a sport? Have you ever **injured anyone else** when you were playing a sport? Explain what happened.

   _____

   _____

4. Are you someone who likes to **analyze yourself** and your behavior? Do you like it when other people try to **analyze you** and your behavior?

   _____

   _____

PUTTING IT ALL TOGETHER

Discussion

Share your ideas in a small group. As you talk, try to use the vocabulary below. Each time someone uses a target word, put a check (✔) next to it.

access	invest	physics
focus	legend/legendary	secretive
fraud/fraudulent	obsession/obsessive	standard

1. "A Nose for Science" is about a scientist who has come up with a new theory that is not generally accepted by the scientific community. Look at the list of scientists below. First, match the scientists to their theories or discoveries. Then, circle those whose ideas were not accepted at first by the scientific community but later were proven to be true. Talk about why their ideas weren't accepted at the time. Consider whether there were any powerful people or groups who argued against accepting their ideas. Finally, compare your answers to those of other groups.

   Scientist

   _____ Marie Curie

   _____ Charles Darwin

   _____ Albert Einstein

   _____ Galileo Galilei

   _____ Isaac Newton

   _____ Louis Pasteur

   Theory or Discovery

   a. the theory of relativity

   b. the theory of gravity

   c. the theory of evolution

   d. the discovery of the relationship between bacteria and disease

   e. the discovery of the elements radium and polonium

   f. the discovery that planets orbit (turn around) the sun

2. How do the following things smell to you? Complete the chart on page 265 individually. Then share your answers with your group. Did any of your classmates' answers surprise you?

	Wonderful	Good	Neutral	Bad	Disgusting
Freshly cut grass					
Horses					
Fresh fish					
Frying onions					
Leather					
A new car					
An infant					

Writing

Complete one or both of these writing topics. When you write, use at least five of the target words from the chapter. Underline the target words in your paper.

1. Choose one of the scientists your group discussed. Do some research on him or her in the library or on the Internet, and write a report. Include the following information in your report:

   • Background (nationality, education, family, etc.)

   • How he/she developed the theory or made the discovery

   • Research, experiments, etc., done to back up the theory or discovery

   • Scientific and public reaction to the theory or discovery

   • When and how the theory or discovery was finally accepted

   Write the report in your own words (don't copy—paraphrase). Give your teacher a list of the websites, articles, and books that you used in your research.

2. Think of a smell that you associate with a particular memory of a person, place, or situation. Write a description of the memory. Use specific details to make your description come alive.

REVIEWING READING SKILLS AND VOCABULARY

Read the text. Do not use a dictionary.

1   There is concern among some in the scientific community that fewer and fewer young people are choosing careers in science and technology. Studies of university students confirm that this reduction could soon lead to a shortage of new scientists. At a time when fascinating scientific discoveries seem to be occurring almost every day, how can this lack of interest be explained?

2   Experts who have reviewed the data believe that the key to the problem is in the way that science is taught. They claim that the teaching practices used in introductory science classes are suitable for only a small percentage of learners. For example, while most people are visual learners, most science professors use very few visual images in their teaching. Instead, they present information verbally, either through written words and formulas, or spoken words in lectures. This leaves the visual learners in the class without the means to make sense of the information.

3   But what about laboratory classes? Aren't they perfectly suited to visual learners? Maybe, but there's a problem. In a standard physics lab, for example, students usually focus on detailed procedures, rather than the big picture. They are given an experiment to perform, but have little opportunity to analyze what they are doing and explore how it relates to the larger theory and to their everyday lives.

4   What can be done to make science teaching meaningful to more students? Experts in science education believe that teachers need to focus on the educational well-being of all of the students in their classes. To that end, they should come up with methods and activities that will be effective for a variety of learners.

Comprehension Check

Read these sentences. Circle T (true), F (false), or ? (can't determine the answer from the reading). If you circle F, change the sentence to make it true.

1. Scientists are worried that students who graduate from universities with science degrees are not well trained.   T   F   ?

2. The way that science is taught in schools is not effective for the majority of the students.   T   F   ?

3. Science teachers often use visual images that confuse their students.   T   F   ?

4. In most science lab classes, students have a chance to understand theories and relate them to their individual experiences.   T   F   ?

5. Overall, science teachers are not very interested in the well-being of their students.   T   F   ?

Guessing Meaning from Context

Find a word or phrase in the text that matches each of the definitions below. The numbers in parentheses are the paragraphs where you can find the word or phrase.

Definition	Word or Phrase
1. pictures that describe ideas (2)	_____
2. with words rather than pictures (2)	_____
3. a series of numbers or letters that represent a mathematical or scientific rule (2)	_____
4. for that purpose (4)	_____

Understanding Inference

Use inference to answer these questions.

1. Does the writer of the text imply that visual images are more important in the teaching of science than in other subjects? Explain.

   _____

   _____

   _____

2. Give two or more specific examples of visual images that science teachers could use in class to make science easier for visual learners.

_____

_____

_____

Summarizing

Write a summary of the text. Remember, do not copy—paraphrase.

EXPANDING VOCABULARY

Studying Phrasal Verbs

In Chapter 17 you learned the phrasal verb **turn down**. There are many phrasal verbs that are formed with the verb **turn**.

A **Read the sentences, and write the meaning of the boldfaced phrasal verbs.**

1. On the night the restaurant opened, there were so many customers that they had to **turn** people **away**.

_____

_____

2. Don't worry about him. He's always late. He'll **turn up** eventually.

_____

_____

3. Has anyone **turned in** a set of keys? I think I lost mine somewhere in the building.

_____

_____

4. You should be proud of your son. He's **turned into** a fine young man.

_____

_____

5. I liked my boss at first, but after a few weeks, his negative attitude **turned** me **off**.

_____

_____

B Answer these questions in complete sentences. Use the **boldfaced** phrasal verbs.

1. When was the last time you were **turned away** from a restaurant or other public place?

_____

_____

_____

2. What would you do if you were waiting for a friend and he never **turned up**?

_____

_____

_____

3. If you found $100 in an empty classroom, would you **turn** it **in**? Why or why not?

_____

_____

_____

4. At what temperature does water **turn into** ice?

_____

_____

_____

5. What kinds of movies **turn** you **off**?

_____

_____

_____

Word Families

When you learn a new word, check to see if it contains a word part—a prefix, suffix, or root. Then, use your understanding of the meaning of the word to help you guess the meaning of the word part. The next time you see a word that contains that word part, it will be easier for you to guess its meaning.

The words *physics* and *physician* both contain the root *phys*. The word *unique* contains the prefix *uni-*, and the word *agricultural* contains the prefix *agr-*. Use your understanding of the meanings of the words to write the meanings of the word parts.

1. The root *phys* means _____ .
2. The prefix *uni-* means _____ .
3. The prefix *agr-* means _____ .

 Working with a partner, answer the questions. Make sure you use the **boldfaced** words in your answers.

1. How often do you go to your doctor for a **physical**?
2. What is a **unisex** bathroom? Are there **unisex** bathrooms in public places in your city?
3. Would you like to live in an **agrarian** community? Why or why not?

PLAYING WITH WORDS

Look back at the lists of target vocabulary on pages 233, 245, and 258. In a small group, write as many target words and phrases as you can under each category. Be ready to explain your answers. Some words might fit under more than one category, and some words might not fit under any category.

Success and Failure	Health	Scientific Research	Smell	Money
prestigious confirm		confirm		prestigious

BUILDING DICTIONARY SKILLS

Finding Idioms

An **idiom** is a group of two or more words that has a special meaning that is different from the ordinary meaning of the separate words. For example, the phrase *see the big picture* is an idiom. Most dictionaries do not have separate entries for idioms. Instead, they can be found under the entry for a key verb or noun in the idiom.

Read the dictionary entries, and circle the idioms.

1.

> **pic·ture¹** /'pɪktʃɚ/ *n* **1** IMAGE [C] a painting, drawing, or photograph: *a **picture of** Nelson Mandela* | ***Draw/paint a picture of** your house.* | *a group of tourists **taking pictures** (= taking photographs)* | *Leo's picture (=photograph of him) is in the newspaper.* **2** SITUATION [singular] the general situation in a place, organization, etc.: *The **political picture** has greatly changed since March.* | *You're missing the **big/bigger/wider picture** (=the situation considered as a whole).* **3** DESCRIPTION [C usually singular] a description that gives you an idea of what something is like: *To get a better **picture of** how the company is doing, look at sales.* | *The book **paints a clear picture** of life in Ancient Rome.* **4** BE IN/OUT OF THE PICTURE *informal* to be involved or not be involved in a situation: *With his main rival out of the picture, the mayor has a chance of winning the election.* **5** ON A SCREEN [C] the image that you see on a television or in a movie: *Something's wrong with the picture.* **6** GET THE PICTURE (*spoken*) to understand something: *I don't want you around here anymore, get the picture?* **7** MOVIE [C] (*old-fashioned*) a MOVIE: *Grandma loved going to the pictures.*

2.

> **mean³** *n* **1** MEANS [plural] a method, system, object, etc. that is used as a way of achieving a result: *We'll use any means we can to raise the money.* | *My bicycle is my **main means** of transportation.* | *The oil is transported **by means of** (=using) a pipeline.* **2** MEANS [plural] ECONOMICS the money or income that you have: *They don't have **the means to** buy a car.* | *Try to live **within your means** (=only spending what you can afford).* | *a man **of means** (=who is rich)* **3** BY ALL MEANS (*spoken*) used to mean "of course" when politely allowing someone to do something or agreeing with a suggestion: *"Can I invite Clarence?" "Oh, by all means."* **4** BY NO MEANS (*formal*) not at all: *The results are by no means certain.* **5** A MEANS TO AN END something that you do only to achieve a result, not because you want to do it: *This job is just a means to an end.* **6** THE MEAN MATH the average amount, figure, or value → MEDIAN, MODE: *The mean of 7, 9, and 14 is 10.*

3.

> **free¹** /fri/ *adj* **1** NOT RESTRICTED allowed to live, exist, or happen without being controlled or restricted: *Students are **free to** choose the activities they want to work on.* | *The media is **free from** governmental control.* | *the right to **free speech*** **2** NO COST not costing any money: *I won free tickets to the concert.* | *Admission is free for children.* **3** NOT CONTAINING STH not having any of a particular substance: *sugar-free bubble gum* | *The water is **free from** chemical pollutants.* **4** NOT BUSY not busy doing other things: *Are you **free for** lunch?* | *Hansen does volunteer work in her **free time**.* **5** NOT BEING USED not being used at this time: *Excuse me, is this seat free?* **6** FEEL FREE (*spoken*) used in order to tell someone that s/he is allowed to do something: *Feel free to ask me any questions after the class.* **7** NOT A PRISONER not a prisoner or SLAVE: *Muller will be free in three years.* | *The UN demanded that the three hostages be **set free** (=be given their freedom).* **8** NOT SUFFERING not suffering or not having to deal with something bad: ***free of** danger* | *Patients undergoing the treatment are now **free from** cancer.* | *a happy and trouble-free life.*

B **Complete each sentence with the correct idiom from the dictionary entries above.**

1. If you have any problems, _____ to give me a call. I'll be happy to help you.

2. Now that his former girlfriend is _____, he is free to date someone else.

3. Some students study just because they enjoy it, but for many students, studying is _____.

UNITS 4–6

Vocabulary Self-Test 2

Circle the letter of the word or phrase that best completes each sentence.

Example:

She was seriously _____ in a car accident.

a. ignored   **b.** bitter   **c.** injured   **d.** ashamed

1. She is nine months _____. She will be having her baby any day now.

   a. innate   **b.** out of sight   **c.** obvious   **d.** pregnant

2. When I moved to England, it took me a long time to _____ driving on the left side of the road.

   a. get used to   **b.** back up   **c.** pull in front   **d.** make up

3. How did you _____ your car? Did you have an accident?

   a. eliminate   **b.** fasten   **c.** possess   **d.** damage

4. I have tried to _____ her behavior, but I just can't understand her.

   a. turn down   **b.** recognize   **c.** come up with   **d.** make sense of

5. Put on your _____. It's cold outside.

   a. gloves   **b.** stains   **c.** legends   **d.** perfume

6. I don't believe in _____. I think that with hard work, you can make anything happen.

   a. function   **b.** fate   **c.** controversy   **d.** familiarity

7. You should never touch a _____ animal.

   a. socialized   **b.** puzzled   **c.** wild   **d.** mild

8. If you want to drive, you need to buy car _____ in case you get into an accident.

   a. vehicle   **b.** insurance   **c.** discount   **d.** permission

9. When his wife died, he never thought he would recover from his _____.

   a. grief   **b.** well-being   **c.** version   **d.** honor

272

10. I need to _____ this into English. Can you help me?

    a. calculate   **b.** accuse   **c.** greet   **d.** translate

11. I don't appreciate his jokes. They just aren't _____ to me.

    a. disgusting   **b.** moody   **c.** humorous   **d.** cheerful

12. I need to know the _____ meaning of that word. It's very important.

    a. precise   **b.** suitable   **c.** former   **d.** striking

13. When you go to a job interview, it is important to wear the _____ clothing.

    a. particular   **b.** deliberate   **c.** proper   **d.** artificial

14. I will always _____ the smell of that perfume with my mother.

    a. reveal   **b.** focus   **c.** entertain   **d.** associate

15. That vase looks heavy, but it isn't because it's _____.

    a. domestic   **b.** immature   **c.** hollow   **d.** endless

16. Receiving a Nobel Prize is a great _____ for any scientist.

    a. shame   **b.** observation **c.** honor   **d.** legend

17. Children who are learning how to read usually start by reading _____.

    a. out loud   **b.** in contrast   **c.** eventually   **d.** out of sight

18. The price of a new car _____ from $10,000 to $40,000.

    a. backs up   **b.** ranges   **c.** flashes   **d.** calculates

19. If a police officer comes to arrest you, it is illegal to _____.

    a. possess   **b.** analyze   **c.** focus   **d.** resist

20. Oranges are usually sweet, but this one is very _____.

    a. contagious   **b.** mild   **c.** suitable   **d.** bitter

21. Despite the bad news, the _____ mood of the crowd was positive.

    a. eventual   **b.** overall   **c.** humorous   **d.** harmonious

22. It was a _____ that she died so young.

    a. pile   **b.** fraud   **c.** tragedy   **d.** witness

23. Are you angry with him? You didn't _____ him when he came in.

    a. greet   **b.** confirm   **c.** ignore   **d.** abuse

24. It is a _____ opportunity. You will never have such a good opportunity again.

    a. royal   **b.** unique   **c.** poetic   **d.** mild

25. I tried to talk to him, but he completely _____ me.

    a. ignored   **b.** infected   **c.** invested   **d.** reviewed

26. He is _____ to find her. He won't stop searching until he does.

    a. disgusted   **b.** reserved   **c.** puzzled   **d.** determined

27. Her _____ with money is destroying her life.

    a. discount   **b.** function   **c.** mood   **d.** obsession

28. I can't go on the trip. My mother won't give me _____.

    a. physician   **b.** standard   **c.** permission   **d.** request

29. What _____ are you wearing? It smells heavenly!

    a. stain   **b.** fragrance   **c.** legend   **d.** flash

30. It is a complex _____. Only an expert can explain it to you.

    a. scent   **b.** lid   **c.** infant   **d.** procedure

31. The answer is _____. I don't know why I didn't think of it before.

    a. secretive   **b.** proper   **c.** contagious   **d.** obvious

32. It feels good to _____ when you first wake up in the morning.

    a. entertain   **b.** stretch   **c.** slip   **d.** gesture

33. If your _____ is always on the details, you might not be able to see the big picture.

    a. interference   **b.** investment   **c.** possession   **d.** focus

34. Some people have a special _____ with dogs. They can almost read their minds.

    a. bond   **b.** tale   **c.** drum   **d.** guilt

35. She's a _____ woman. Everyone who meets her remembers her.

    a. well-being   **b.** mild   **c.** innate   **d.** striking

36. Please don't walk on the grass. Stay on the _____.

    a. theme   **b.** journal   **c.** lid   **d.** path

See the Answer Key on page 275.

Vocabulary Self-Tests Answer Key

Below are the answers to the Vocabulary Self-Tests. Check your answers, and then review any words you did not remember. You can look up words in the index on the next two pages. Then go back to the readings and exercises to find the words. Use your dictionary as needed.

Vocabulary Self-Test 1, Units 1–3 (pages 132–134)

1. b	**10.** c	**19.** c	**28.** d
2. a	**11.** b	**20.** c	**29.** c
3. a	**12.** d	**21.** c	**30.** a
4. a	**13.** c	**22.** a	**31.** d
5. d	**14.** d	**23.** a	**32.** b
6. b	**15.** d	**24.** b	**33.** c
7. a	**16.** b	**25.** c	**34.** c
8. b	**17.** d	**26.** c	**35.** b
9. d	**18.** c	**27.** a	**36.** c

Vocabulary Self-Test 2, Units 4–6 (pages 272–274)

1. d	**10.** d	**19.** d	**28.** c
2. a	**11.** c	**20.** d	**29.** b
3. d	**12.** a	**21.** b	**30.** d
4. d	**13.** c	**22.** c	**31.** d
5. a	**14.** d	**23.** a	**32.** b
6. b	**15.** c	**24.** b	**33.** d
7. c	**16.** c	**25.** a	**34.** a
8. b	**17.** a	**26.** d	**35.** d
9. a	**18.** b	**27.** d	**36.** d

Index to Target Words and Phrases

absence, 49
abuse, 241
acceptable, 105
access, 256
accuse, 163
achieve, 60
actually, 105
advantage, 106
aggression, 73
agricultural, 231
analyze, 211
ancient, 184
anger, 137
announcement, 15
anxious, 73
appearance, 105
appreciation, 183
approach, 105
artificial, 150
artistic, 15
associate, 138
athletic, 105
at least, 48
attempt, 139
attitude, 73
auditory, 184
background, 73
back up, 197
beauty, 5
belief, 15
benefit, 118
be used to, 197
biologist, 184
bitterly, 210
bond, 184
brilliant, 15
bring up, 106
burn out, 61
calculate, 163
call for, 28
cell, 93
challenge, 4
championship, 60
characteristic, 27
check out, 198
cheerfulness, 139
chemical, 15
chimpanzee, 197
choosy, 150
clever, 27
combine, 210
come out, 92
come up with, 231

compete, 27
complaint, 48
complex, 4
concentrate on, 60
concern, 48
conduct, 73
confirm, 231
conscious, 150
contact, 74
contagious, 242
contribute, 27
controversy, 210
convinced, 105
courage, 105
critical, 60
cure, 93
damage, 163
data, 73
deliberately, 241
depressed, 49
desirable, 93
despite, 61
determine, 93
determined, 229
diet, 118
discount, 255
disease, 93
disgust, 138
domestication, 198
dropout, 49
drum, 184
due to, 15
economic, 73
effective, 118
eliminate, 197
endless, 184
entertain, 255
equipment, 27
eventually, 210
evidence, 184
evil, 4
evolved, 198
examine, 73
experiment, 49
expert, 48
expression, 26
eyebrow, 150
facial expression, 150
factor, 117
familiarize, 197
fascinated, 4
fasten, 197
fate, 230

feature, 105
flash, 163
focus, 256
former, 230
fortunate, 119
fragrance, 255
fraud, 256
freedom, 73
free of, 243
frown upon, 149
function, 230
gender, 93
gene, 92
generation, 92
gesture, 162
get one's start, 3
get rid of, 93
gifted, 60
glove, 229
greet, 150
grief, 138
grow out of, 26
guilt, 138
harmful, 118
harmonious, 150
heavenly, 15
historically, 106
hollow, 184
honor, 139
humanity, 106
humorous, 150
identify, 105
ignore, 243
illiterate, 15
illness, 93
immature, 198
imply, 210
in charge of, 118
incident, 163
in contrast, 138
indeed, 138
individual, 93
infant, 209
infect, 241
inherit, 92
injured, 162
injustice, 60
innate, 197
in short, 106
instruction, 93
insurance, 163
in tears, 49
intellect, 104

intend, 118
interact, 27
interfere, 230
investment, 256
involved, 4
journal, 184
key, 184
knowledge, 15
laboratory, 14
lack, 48
lead to, 105
legal, 162
legend, 254
lid, 197
likely, 48
literature, 60
live, 26
make sense of, 185
make up, 150
meaningful, 210
means, 242
mild, 242
mood, 150
moral, 4
muscle, 150
mystery, 14
observe, 138
obsessed, 255
obvious, 197
official, 48
on the basis of, 74
operation, 118
original, 4
out loud, 150
out of sight, 210
overall, 197
overweight, 73
particularly, 138
path, 255
pattern, 49
peer, 61
perfectionist, 60
performer, 27
perfume, 254
permission, 242
personality, 28
physically, 73
physician, 243
physics, 255

pick on, 73
pile, 210
poetic, 255
poison, 118
popularity, 4
possess, 210
practice, 241
precise, 184
pregnant, 162
prescribe, 118
pressure, 60
prestigious, 229
prevent, 93
procedure, 242
progress, 117
proof, 16
proper, 149
protest, 210
publish, 61
pull in front of, 162
puzzle, 211
rage, 162
range, 163
rapid, 4
read someone's mind, 196
realize, 92
recognize, 139
recover, 118
reduce, 49
related, 3
remarkable, 14
replace, 93
reportedly, 4
request, 242
reserved, 150
resist, 229
restricted, 105
reveal, 139
review, 243
rhyme, 26
royalty , 254
scale, 184
scent, 255
scratch, 27
secretive, 256
see the big picture, 229
self-esteem, 73
sensational, 163
sensitive, 60

severe, 117
shame, 138
shortage, 106
slam, 162
slip, 231
socialized, 197
species, 184
spin, 27
stain, 231
standard, 256
stand by, 15
stand out, 27
stand up for, 73
stay up, 48
stretch, 211
striking, 198
structure, 184
suffer, 118
suitable, 230
surgery, 242
survey, 73
survive, 61
sweating, 231
system, 184
tale, 255
talented, 4
technique, 27
technology, 4
tend to, 60
the deaf, 185
theme, 184
theory, 15
the wild, 210
threatened, 16
tragedy, 163
trait, 92
translate, 138
turn down, 243
unique, 229
universal, 138
vaccination, 241
vehicle, 163
victim, 73
virtue, 149
visual, 185
well-being, 231
witness, 162

Revkin, A. "Hunting down Huntington's—Nancy Wexler's lifelong research into fatal hereditary disease present in her family." Retrieved on June 19, 2008 from http://findarticles.com/p/articles/mi_m1511/is_n12_v14/ai_14558988.

Seltz, Johanna. "Teen Brains Are Different." *The Boston Sunday Globe*, (May 28, 2000): E1.

Solomon, R. C. "Some Notes on Emotion, 'East and West'." *Philosophy East and West*, 45, (1995): 171–202. [electronic version].

Turin, L. "Flexitral Odorants by Design. Rational Odorant Design. (n.d.)." Retrieved June 24, 2004 from www.flexitral.com/index.html.

Who Named It. (n.d.). "How Listening to a Milkmaid's Story Can Change the World." Retrieved June 24, 2004 from http://www.whonamedit.com/doctor.cfm/1818.html.

ACKNOWLEDGMENTS

I would like to first thank Dr. Jeong-Wha Choi, who graciously agreed to allow me to use her story. I would also like to thank Samuela Eckstut for being so generous with her time, advice, and encouragement.

I would also like to thank the reviewers whose comments on early drafts of the first edition of this book were very helpful: **Christina Cavage**, Atlantic Cape Community College, Atlantic City, NJ; **Leslie Corpuz**, Tidewater Community College, Virginia Beach, VA; **Anthony Halderman**, Cuesta College, San Luis Obispo, CA; **Martha Hall**, The New England School of English; **Steve Horowitz**, Central Washington University, Ellensburg, WA; **Susan Jamieson**, Bellevue Community College, Bellevue, WA; **Kathy Sherak**, San Francisco State University, San Francisco, CA; **Julie Un**, Massasoit Community College, Brockton, MA; **Jo Dee Walters**, formerly affiliated with San Diego State University, San Diego, CA.

I'd also like to extend my gratitude to Linda Butler, whose vision and concept for the series were a constant source of guidance and inspiration as I worked on this project. Her feedback on the manuscript was also invaluable.

A great many people at Longman helped in the making of this book, most of all Pietro Alongi, Editorial Director; Amy McCormack, Acquisitions Editor; Paula Van Ells, Director of Development; Thomas Ormond, Developmental Editor, Susan Tait Porcaro and Wendy Duran, Illustrators; Helen Ambrosio, Project Editor and Photo Researcher; and Wendy Campbell and Carlos Rountree, Assistant Editors.

Finally, I would like to thank Claudia for always being there to remind me of what is important.

TEXT CREDITS

PHOTO CREDITS